THE BUILDIN

FOUNDING EDITOR

ADVISORY EDITC

EDITOR: BRIDGET CHERRY

LONDON:
THE CITY CHURCHES

SIMON BRADLEY AND NIKOLAUS PEVSNER

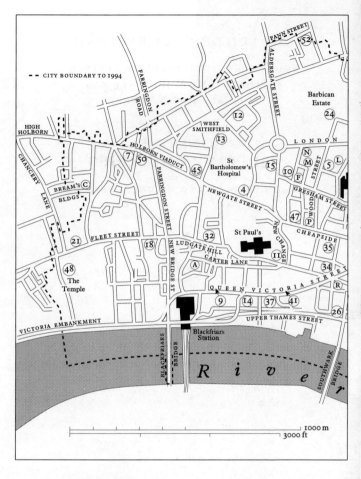

- - - CITY BOUNDARY TO 1994

CITY CHURCHES

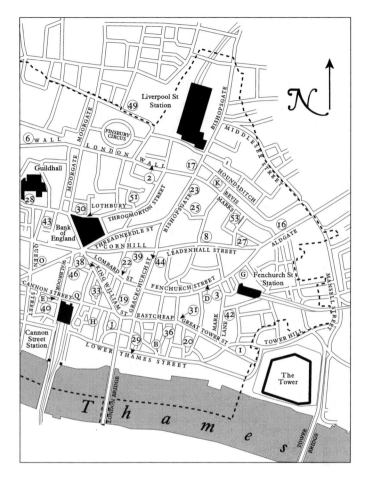

City of London churches. Map

THE BUILDINGS BOOKS TRUST

was established in 1994, registered charity number 1042101.
It promotes the appreciation and understanding
of architecture by supporting and financing
the research needed to sustain new and revised volumes of
The Buildings of England, Ireland, Scotland and Wales

The Trust gratefully acknowledges:

grants to cover the costs of research and writing
London 1: The City of London from
THE CORPORATION OF LONDON

a research grant from
THE BRITISH ACADEMY

assistance with photographs from
THE ROYAL COMMISSION ON HISTORICAL
MONUMENTS OF ENGLAND

a grant to cover the costs of text illustrations from
KINNEY AND GREEN

London
THE CITY CHURCHES

BY

SIMON BRADLEY

AND

NIKOLAUS PEVSNER

THE BUILDINGS OF ENGLAND

PENGUIN BOOKS

PENGUIN BOOKS
Published by the Penguin Group
27 Wrights Lane, London w8 5TZ, England
for
THE BUILDINGS BOOKS TRUST

Penguin Putnam inc., 375 Hudson Street, New York, New York 10014, USA
Penguin Books Australia Ltd, Ringwood, Victoria, Australia
Penguin Books Canada Ltd, 10 Alcorn Avenue, Toronto, Ontario, Canada M4V 3B2
Penguin Books (NZ) Ltd, 182–190 Wairau Road, Auckland 10, New Zealand

Penguin Books Ltd, Registered Offices: Harmondsworth, Middlesex, England

First published 1998

ISBN 0 14 071100 7

Copyright © Simon Bradley and the estate of Nikolaus Pevsner, 1998
All rights reserved

The moral right of the author has been asserted

Typeset at Cambridge Photosetting Services, Cambridge
Made and printed in Great Britain
by Butler & Tanner Ltd, Frome and London
Set in 9/9.75pt Monotype Plantin

CONTENTS

LIST OF TEXT FIGURES AND MAPS

PHOTOGRAPHIC ACKNOWLEDGEMENTS

All photographs are RCHME: Crown copyright with the exception of the following:

A. F. Kersting: 18

FOREWORD

The kernel of this book comes from Sir Nikolaus Pevsner's London 1: the Cities of London and Westminster *(1957) in the* Buildings of England *series, of which revised editions were published in 1962 and 1973. The present text is based on* London 1: The City of London *(1997), an expanded and fully revised volume devoted to the City alone. Numerous, mostly minor textual adjustments have been made to suit the format of a book devoted exclusively to the churches of the present-day City. The term 'churches' covers those of the Church of England, whether still in use or surviving only in part, and the five places of worship of other faiths. St Paul's Cathedral lies outside the scope of the book, as do the archaeological and topographical traces left by the many great monastic churches of the Middle Ages. For a full account of these, and of St Peter ad Vincula in the Tower of London,* London 1: The City of London *must be consulted. However, the Introduction does refer to lost churches where relevant.*

The area covered is that defined by boundary revisions in 1994, which tidied up the ancient, straggling outline between the City and its neighbouring boroughs to suit present-day topography.

The principles of previous Buildings of England *volumes have been followed in terms of the omission of certain church furnishings (bells, hatchments, chests, plate, and most moveable furniture). Where a pair of dates is given for a building, the first is generally that for the acceptance of the design, the second for its completion.*

ACKNOWLEDGEMENTS

A great debt has been inherited from the old London 1 *volume in its three successive incarnations. Above all I was fortunate to have Sir Nikolaus Pevsner's text as a starting point. Much of his writing remains in the present volume. In the new and amended sections I hope to have caught something of his tone. Acknowledgements are also due Bridget Cherry, Sir Nikolaus's collaborator on the 1973 edition. Initial research for the first edition was carried out in 1950–3 by Mrs K. Michaelson. Mr H. S. Goodhart-Rendel made available his notes on Victorian church restorations, and Sir Thomas Kendrick his on Victorian glass. Proofs were read by H. L. Howgego of the Guildhall Library, H. Clifford Smith, the Rev. Canon Atkins, Margaret Whinney and Ian Nairn. George McHardy, R. H. Harrison and Nicholas Taylor, amongst many others, provided much assistance on points of detail. Corrections and additions submitted by readers of the earlier editions proved very useful when the revisions came around.*

For the present volume my first debt is to fellow members of the Buildings of England *staff: to Elizabeth Williamson, whose judicious editing refined and rendered down many long drafts without impairing their flavour; to Stephany Ungless, for her scrupulous attention to the texts in proof; to Alison McKittrick, for her no less scrupulous assistance in locating and preparing illustrations; and to Bridget Cherry, for much expert help and guidance. John Newman, advisory editor, made many helpful suggestions on the C17 and C18 sections. Georgie Widdrington designed the book, Antonio Colaço the cover and Lesley Straw the inset. Susanne Atkin was the indexer. Secretarial assistance was ably supplied by Caroline Reed, Sabrina Needham and Susan Machin. The map and drawn plans are the work of Alan Fagan. The book has benefited enormously from the specialist assistance of John Schofield of the Museum of London Archaeology Service. He revised many of the entries on the medieval churches, and updated the medieval section of the Introduction in line with the latest archaeological knowledge.*

The work of revision would not have been possible without the generous financial support of the Corporation of London under Michael Cassidy, until recently Chairman of the Policy and Resources Committee, supplemented by a half-year grant from the British Academy. Laurie Kinney generously made available the City premises of his firm Kinney & Green, which made a grant towards the cost of illustrations. I am also most grateful to many of the Corporation's own staff for help and guidance over the churches, especially to Ralph Hyde, Jeremy Smith, John Fisher, Lynne MacNab and others at the Guildhall Library, and to all at the Corporation of London Record Office. Most of the plates come from Derek Kendall's magnificent and invaluable photographic survey of the churches undertaken for the RCHME *in 1994–5; Peter Guillery of the Commission also took a close interest in the progress of the book. I am also indebted to the library staff of the Courtauld Institute, Institute of Historical Research,*

Society of Antiquaries, National Monuments Record, Camden Local History Library, and the Council for the Care of Churches.

Others who read and commented on drafts of the churches' text were Paul Jeffery (PJ), Donald Findlay (DF) and Teresa Sladen (TS). To Geoffrey Fisher (GF) and Adam White (AW) thanks are due for much information and help concerning church monuments. The following authors kindly allowed access to proofs of works in progress: Anthony Geraghty (AG), on Wren's City Church Office; Paul Jeffery, on Wren's churches; and Caroline Swash (CS), on post-war stained glass. Thanks are also due for assistance and information to Tye Blackshaw, the Rev. Oswald Clarke, Thomas Cocke, Sir Howard Colvin, Father Richard Hayes, John Robinson, Paul Sutherland and Robert Thorne. I am also grateful for corrections and amendments sent in since 1973 by Geoff Brandwood, Dennis Corble, Peter Cormack, Peter Eyres and Roger White. Finally, special thanks are due to the custodians of the City churches for their help and assistance on my visits to their marvellous buildings.

INTRODUCTION

THE CITY CHURCHES*

Three things make the churches of the City of London unique. The first is their setting, for the City is an area utterly unlike anywhere else in England. Originally the chief port of Roman Britain, it was re-established as the chief Thames-side settlement in the C9, and in the C12 it received from the crown the privilege of self-government. What the City did not do thereafter was extend its boundaries to take in the newly built-up areas around the ancient settlement. Indeed, C19 and C20 municipal reformers more than once threatened to subsume it into this greater London, which was after all where most of the City's working population by then chose to live. Instead, the City Corporation survived as the governing body of what is now the financial centre of Europe. Today most of the buildings lining its well-kept streets are banks and offices, many designed on a grand scale and built in rich materials with much ornamental display. The

Panorama of City of London.
Engraving by Samuel and Nathaniel Buck, 1749

*A † means that the church, or its relevant part, no longer exists.

irregular medieval street network largely remains, however, so that
1 churches and secular buildings alike are juxtaposed in endlessly surprising ways. Nowhere else in England can rival this intermingling of
the very ancient and the very modern.

The second unique feature is the sheer density with which the
churches are crammed together. Within an area of just over one
square mile – only slightly larger than Kensington Gardens and Hyde
Park combined – may be found thirty-nine Anglican churches, some
barely a hundred yards from one another. What is more, all are
nominally still in use for worship, though in a few cases no longer
that of the Church of England. Towers, standing walls or foundations may still be seen of another nine former parish churches, and
the churchyards remain of some fifteen more. In addition there are
four churches or chapels built for other Christian faiths, and one
synagogue. Even so, this plenitude of churches whole or ruined is
barely over half the original number: many were demolished in the
C19 and early C20 and their sites sold, and several more were
destroyed in the Second World War; going further back, thirty-four
were destroyed in the Great Fire of 1666 and not rebuilt.

Mention of the Great Fire brings us belatedly to the third and
most famous singularity of the City churches, namely the rebuilding
of some fifty of them after the Fire by *Sir Christopher Wren* and his
office. The old parish churches were for the most part unambitious,
at least by comparison with the great medieval churches of other English
cities (the most impressive survivor in the City, St Bartholomew-
the-Great, was originally part of a priory church; the most perfect,
the Temple Church, served the London headquarters of that military
order). Thanks to Wren's new buildings, however, the City became
a kind of architectural laboratory for the development of the
Protestant parish church, just as St Paul's attempted to crystallize an
ideal form for a Protestant cathedral. Wren's parish churches have
plans centralized, plans longitudinal, and plans that variously com-
bine the two. They also developed an inexhaustible wealth of new
types of spire. Here, too, are some of the first significant essays in the
Gothic Revival. No less influential were the pulpits, fonts and reredoses
commissioned by the congregations, versions of which may be found
all over England. City parishes outside the burnt area sought throughout the C18 and early C19 to acquire up-to-date churches of their
own, with the result that the City also boasts as good a concentration of Georgian examples as may be found anywhere. But this is
to anticipate, for it is time to tell the story of the City churches in
more detail.

The Middle Ages, c. 600–1500

The early history of the churches of London is still obscure. The first
firm date is 604, when St Paul's Cathedral was founded by Mellitus
at the request of King Ethelbert of Kent. The policy of the Augustinian
mission was to re-establish continuity with the Roman settlement
(cf. Canterbury Cathedral, within the Roman walls); but while C7
coins of Londinium have been found it is unclear to what extent the
present area of the City, that is to say the old Roman town, was still
inhabited. Rather, the archaeological evidence indicates that the
London described in the early C8 by the Venerable Bede (*Lundenwic*,

the capital of the East Saxons) occupied the area immediately to the w, along the Strand around Aldwych. The return to the more defensible walled City left by the Romans came in 886, on the initiative of King Alfred, in response to the ravages of the Danes. In 982 London was again sacked, but London Bridge had been rebuilt by 1000, with landing-points established or re-established on the river at Queenhithe and Billingsgate.

This narrative suggests that we should not expect to find many ANGLO-SAXON CHURCHES earlier than the latest C9; but there is anyway very little surviving from before the Conquest. Standing remains are confined to part of the w end of All Hallows Barking. The foundations point to an aisleless church of *c.* 70 ft by 24 ft (21 metres by 7 metres) with ample use of Roman brick; an arch and portion of a quoin at the NW corner still survive. They are difficult to date, but current opinion (supported by excavated examples at other church sites) is that the fragments are C11, and not C7–C8 as once thought: a date which also suits better what we know of the history of Anglo-Saxon London. The C11 is also the date of fragments of two Saxon crosses at All Hallows. A foundation as early as the C8 has been proposed in the case of St Alban Wood Street, where the outlines of a church of pre-Conquest type were found in 1962. It has been suggested that it originated as the chapel of the palace of the Saxon kings, before Edward the Confessor's move to Westminster in the mid C11, but the theory cannot be proved.

The NORMANS are somewhat better represented, though the greatest surviving Early Norman ecclesiastical monument in London, the Chapel of St John in the White Tower, lies outside the scope of this book (*see London 1: The City of London*). The same is true of the pitifully small remains of Norman Old St Paul's and of the great houses of the religious orders, founded mostly in the C12 and C13. As for Norman parish churches proper, the only firmly datable work is Archbishop Lanfranc's aisled and arcaded crypt at St Mary-le-Bow (*c.* 1077–87). It is probably connected to the Canterbury workshop, and neither in its sophisticated style nor its unusual form is it typical of ordinary parochial work. No less untypical is the one great C12 church which has survived, albeit only in part: it is St Bartholomew-the-Great, founded as an Augustinian priory in 1123, the E part of which was converted to a parish church at the Reformation. The three-storey elevations of its interior, without vertical divisions, have a somewhat eclectic appearance, due in part to protracted construction up to *c.* 1160. Thus the main arcade arches are still unmoulded, but in each arch of the gallery are four lesser arches which probably represent a later insertion.

p. 110

p. 63, 2

The GOTHIC STYLE is foreshadowed at the crossing of St Bartholomew, which has the earliest pointed arches in London (*c.* 1145–60). For the early maturity of the style one must go to the Temple Church, consecrated in 1185. As the church of a military order it is also untypical of an ordinary parish church, for it is round, in deference to the form of the church above the Holy Sepulchre in Jerusalem. The Templars favoured this circular plan, used also by the Hospitallers for their church just outside the City, St John at Clerkenwell (*c.* 1140). But the forms used in the Temple Church are essentially Gothic, a Gothic undoubtedly familiar with France and probably also with Canterbury where rebuilding of the

p. 133, 3

choir had begun in 1175; quatrefoil Purbeck piers with shaft-rings and capitals enriched by stiff-leaf foliage, pointed arches, and slim vaulting shafts standing on the capitals of the piers. Only in its ornament – the blank triforium with interlaced round arches, and the elaborate w door – does the late English Norman style make an appearance.

The next monument of the Gothic style in the City is the choir
4 added to the Temple rotunda (consecrated 1240). It too is a special case, being a hall-choir, that is a room in which the aisles are of the same height as the nave. The piers are extremely slender and a unity of space is thus achieved which is very different from the classic French Gothic separation of streams of space from each other. The retrochoir of Winchester had preceded the Temple in this scheme, and it also occurs in the retrochoirs of Southwark and Salisbury at about the same time. It must be regarded as an English speciality, and at the Temple its linear thinness of forms and its airiness will be found aesthetically entirely successful. The windows of the Temple choir are still all lancet-shaped, the standard form of Early English Gothic.

The next phase of Gothic, with the lights combined with plate
61 tracery in the heads, is represented only by the surviving E bay of St Bartholomew's nave, c. 1230. Of other great enterprises of the C13–C14, the retrochoir of St Paul's and the new churches of the Friars are lost to us. The latter in particular are tantalizingly obscure, although the nave of the Austin Friars' church, rebuilt after 1354, lasted until 1940 (see Dutch Church). There is also the curiosity of the shattered church tower of Elsing Spital, a hospital for the blind founded in 1331 with secular priests but quickly turned over to the Augustinians (see St Alphage).

All Hallows London Wall.
Engraving by R. West and W. H. Toms, 1730

So far very little has been said of the ordinary PARISH CHURCHES of London, Anglo-Saxon and CII remains apart. The churches were naturally less spectacular than the buildings of the religious orders. Very few of the 110 or so known to have existed in the later Middle Ages survived the Great Fire, and of these about half were subsequently rebuilt. The story of their development can however be filled in from archaeology, documentation and topographical views, and the churches that remain give a good idea of their characteristic final forms. [p. 18]

The first churches appear to have begun as the private chapels of manors and larger tenements. Twenty-seven are datable before 1100: a figure that is almost certainly too low, since archaeological investigations have repeatedly demonstrated that most churches antedate the first written record of their existence. In some cases a pre-Conquest origin is suggested by church dedications, though their reliability as a guide has been contested. Examples include the four churches dedicated to the Saxon St Botolph, three of which survive as C18 rebuildings. Only in the CII and CI2 were these churches made parochial, to be joined by new foundations to a number approaching the full late-medieval complement. Some chapels acquired parochial status as late as the CI5 (St Katharine Cree, St Stephen Coleman †).

Gothic parish churches proper begin with the ambiguous (and very exceptional) case of St Helen Bishopsgate, a nunnery church to which a parish nave was added. The two naves and chancels lie side by side. The church has CI2 and CI3 parts, but is to the eye mostly mid CI4 and of about 1475, when Sir John Crosby was its benefactor. St Ethelburga nearby, badly damaged by a terrorist bomb in 1993, is a little older, around 1400; very small, with only one aisle. It is only one-sixth of the area of St Sepulchre outside the City's w wall, of which the tower, vaulted porch and much of the nave are CI5. Also of the CI5 are St Olave Hart Street and the aisles of All Hallows Barking (damaged in the Second World War but remade in CI5 style, replacing arcades of two medieval periods). As elsewhere in England, the Reformation found parish church building in full flood: churches rebuilt on the eve of the Reformation and beyond include St Andrew Undershaft (1520–32), St Giles Cripplegate (c. 1545–50), and also St Katharine Cree (tower, 1504). Masonry of this and older periods has been observed at several churches encased in Wren's external renderings, for instance the N aisle of 1501 at St Mary-at-Hill, surviving to full height (revealed when damaged by fire, 1988). [p. 89, 7] [p. 5, 6] [8]

Like most English parish churches, these buildings were commonly the product of centuries of growth and enlargement. The complexity of this process, aggravated in many cases by cramped sites, is known from excavations. The kernel was generally a single-celled Saxon or Saxo-Norman church or chapel (St Bride, St Benet Sherehog †). The first stage of growth might be represented by an apse (St Bride, St Pancras Soper Lane †). The fabric generally included much reused Roman brick, as at All Hallows Barking, though at least one church, St Andrew Holborn, is described as built of timber (c. 959). [p. 77]

The addition of N and S aisles to the nave began at some churches around 1230. The CI3 also saw chapels added towards the E ends of some churches, especially attached to the chancel. Undercrofts from below such chapels survive at St Bride (*c.* 1300) and All Hallows Barking (C14). Later in the Middle Ages chapels were more commonly formed by parclose screens within the aisles, although the standard late medieval form of nave and two aisles only appears in the City around 1400, and is confined to the larger churches (the relative paucity of large guild chapels is partly explained by the presence of chapels at the halls of the greater City Livery Companies). A clerestory is generally present, and there is usually no structural division between nave and chancel. A tower appears near the w end as a matter of course from the C14 (St Giles Cripplegate, All Hallows Staining). These were intended primarily as belfries, a function served in other cases by turrets (St Ethelburga, C15–C16) or in exceptional

p. cases by detached bell-towers (St Bride, C12). Quite a number of w
77 towers survive, some recased by Wren when he rebuilt the churches after the Fire. Pre-Fire views reveal that the commonest form was a square crenellated top with corner turret, as at All Hallows Staining; the type is familiar from all over the Thames Valley. These crenellations became widespread in the mid C15, both on the tower and the church proper. Grander churches had tall corner pinnacles (St
6 Sepulchre, old St Michael Cornhill †, with angle buttresses) or a spire (St Laurence Pountney †, St Dunstan-in-the-East †). St Mary-le-Bow (†) had exceptionally a C15 stone lantern on flying buttresses, like that surviving at St Nicholas, Newcastle upon Tyne. One peculiarity of many London churches was that the main entry was usually through the tower rather than through a separate porch (St Andrew Undershaft, St Katharine Cree). The grand porches familiar from great town churches elsewhere are represented only by a mid-C15
5 three-storey example at St Sepulchre.

By the C15 ragstone had long overtaken reused Roman work as the preferred material, used sometimes as rubble (St Ethelburga), sometimes in good, large, even courses (St Andrew Undershaft). Reigate stone, being more easily carved, was used for dressings; in the C14 also it was employed with flintwork in alternating bands, as may be seen at St Helen Bishopsgate and St Bartholomew-the-Great. Plain ashlar is rare, though sections of C16 work were preserved in Wren's rebuildings of St Mary Aldermary and St Mary-at-Hill.

Gothic details may briefly be described. Church windows are of little interest; mostly there is no tracery at all, just stepped lancet lights under a depressed arch (All Hallows, St Andrew Undershaft). Where tracery is introduced it has simple panelling motifs. Piers vary in shape, but exhibit no outstanding originality. They may be quatrefoil (St Olave), or of four shafts with four diagonal hollows (St Andrew Undershaft), or of the same section with triple shafts in the four
8 hollows (St Giles), or with the wave-mouldings doubled (St Helen). There are much-restored sedilia in the C14 Lady Chapel of St Bartholomew-the-Great, which also has a very pretty oriel of *c.* 1517 from which the Prior could overlook the choir. Roofs are much renewed and generally of little distinction.

FUNERAL MONUMENTS make a modest show in comparison to the splendours of Westminster Abbey. Many were in Old St Paul's and the friars' churches and were destroyed with them. The pages of Stow's *Survey of London* (1603) give a melancholy idea of their number and magnificence. The earliest surviving monument is the only one of the famous knights which escaped war damage at the

Temple Church. It is of *c.* 1225. About a generation younger is the 9
effigy of a bishop in the same church, his head characteristically 10
framed by a trefoiled gabled arch. In the late Middle Ages the canopied
tomb became a standard type. The early C15 commemorative
monument to Rahere in his foundation of St Bartholomew-the- 12
Great has a canopied tomb-chest with effigy and two attendant
bedesmen. The fullest sequence is at St Helen, notably the late C14
recumbent effigies of John de Oteswich and wife, and the tomb-chest 11
with alabaster effigies of Sir John Crosby (†1476) of Crosby Hall
and his lady. A common, less ambitious late medieval type in and
around London is the wall monument in the form of a tomb-chest
with shallow-headed canopy, where brasses, often placed vertically
at the back, are substituted for effigies. Some of these tombs functioned also as Easter Sepulchres. Many are entirely of Purbeck
marble, the material in which the brasses were set: two unusually fine
examples are the tombs of Alderman Croke (†1477) at All Hallows
Barking, and of Hugh Pemberton (†1500) at St Helen. A variant of
this type is the tomb at St Helen to Johane Alfrey (†1525), which
follows a distinctive London design whose earliest known appearance is at St Mary, Lambeth, 1507. The Alfrey tomb uniquely both
served as an Easter Sepulchre and incorporated a squint below. A
wholly Gothic version of the formula persisted into the later C16
(Ann Packington †1563, St Botolph Aldersgate).

MEDIEVAL CHURCH FURNISHINGS are more scanty still. The best
collections of BRASSES are at All Hallows Barking, notably the Flemish
Evyngar brass (†1533), and at St Olave Hart Street. St Bartholomew-
the-Great has a simple C15 font; St Andrew Undershaft has modest
heraldic stained glass of *c.* 1530. No screens survive, but St Helen
has a few C15 stalls, relics of the nunnery. Painting is represented by
four fine late C15 Flemish panels at All Hallows Barking, from the
vanished Royal Lady Chapel associated with the church.

Dislocation and Destruction: the Reformation and Great Fire

The most drastic change wrought on C16 London was Henry VIII's
DISSOLUTION OF THE MONASTERIES and the confiscation of their
properties. The survival of St Helen Bishopsgate, St Alphage and
part of St Bartholomew-the-Great was due to their being taken over
by existing congregations. The rest of the monastic churches were
demolished or subdivided for various functions. The N aisle of St
Bartholomew-the-Great retains typical makeshift enclosures of this
type from later in the C16, while part of the W front of its C13 nave
survives incorporated in a timber-framed gatehouse made in 1595.
New parishes were established within other ex-monastic precincts at
the old Minoresses' church (Holy Trinity Minories, 1539 †) and at
the Franciscan convent at Blackfriars (St Ann, rebuilt 1598 †). A few
parish churches disappeared or were merged: St Mary Axe was
demolished in 1561, and the parishes of St Audoen and St Nicholas
Shambles united into the new one based on Christ Church, the old
chancel of the Dominicans (Greyfriars). The appearance of many of
the churches in this period is captured on the so-called copperplate
map, a mid-C16 pictorial representation of London on which major
buildings are shown. One later foundation, St James Duke's Place
(1622†) formed part of the wave of repairs and rebuilding in the

1620s–30s, of which more shortly; it was built on the site of the chapter house of Holy Trinity Priory, N of Leadenhall Street.

In the absence of substantial church architecture, the later C16 is best represented by CHURCH MONUMENTS. Most of these adopt the RENAISSANCE STYLE which had first been taken up in court circles in the 1530s. Of the Renaissance there is nothing so early in the City churches, but there are some exceptionally good tombs from the 1560s and 1570s. Most sophisticated is that at St Helen Bishopsgate to Sir Thomas Gresham (†1579), founder of the Royal Exchange and altogether the paramount merchant of mid-C16 London. Fashioned after a Roman sarcophagus, it is of outstandingly fine workmanship, fluted up the sides and with thick strapwork cartouches. The strapwork fashion derives from the Low Countries, with which most of Gresham's trade was carried on. In the 1560s also Netherlandish sculptors themselves moved to London to take advantage of the demand for their work. Their productions were typically much less restrained than Gresham's tomb, as witnessed by the Pickering monument (†1574) also at St Helen. This early example of the free-standing type with the effigy beneath a canopy of columns (which here number six) is attributed by Adam White to the *Cure* workshop. Single recumbent figures are represented by the Throkmorton monument (†1570) at St Katharine Cree, also attributed to the *Cure* workshop, and the Plowden monument (†1584) at the Temple Church. The former has an unusual straight lintel, the latter the more common round-headed niche, with obelisks. Obelisks appear also on the Spenser monument at St Helen (†1609, attributed to *Nicholas Johnson*), which combines recumbent and kneeling figures.

The wall-mounted monuments which appear from the mid C16 generally have small kneeling figures (Sir Andrew Judd †1558, St Helen; Bayninge brothers †1610 and 1616, St Olave Hart Street). Two curious exceptions may be mentioned: the Legh monument at St Dunstan-in-the-West (†1563), which has little caryatids, and the Smalpace monument at St Bartholomew-the-Great (†1558 and 1588, attributed to *Giles de Witt*), which combines small busts with an incised slate panel. Of monuments from the early C17 that of John Stow (†1605) at St Andrew Undershaft, perhaps also by *Johnson*, is a good instance of the frontal seated figure, here represented writing at a desk.

CHURCH ARCHITECTURE underwent a revival in the 1620s and 1630s, under the aegis of William Laud, Bishop of London and later Archbishop of Canterbury. During these decades repairs or partial rebuilding are recorded at more than half of the City churches. Much of this no doubt merely made up for years of neglect; but one near-complete rebuilding has come down to us: it is St Katharine Cree, which apart from the tower was rebuilt in 1628–31. The result is instructive in its mixture of Gothic and classical forms: a much less pure idiom than the contemporary court style of Inigo Jones, whose chief work in the City, the recasing of the nave and W front of Old St Paul's, began in 1633. The arcades of St Katharine are Corinthian, with round coffered arches, but they support flattened rib-vaults of plaster. Externally the church appears approximately Perp, but with curious stepped three-light windows, and an E window derived from the C13 retrochoir of Old St Paul's: a sign that the living, evolving tradition of Gothic was dead. The immediate juxtaposition of Gothic and classical parts is also found at Lincoln's Inn Chapel, *c.* 1619–23, and in much C17 work at Cambridge and (especially) Oxford. The completed tower of St Mary Aldermary in 1626–9 and the rebuilding of St Alban Wood Street in 1633–4 (†) were at least partially Gothic, though the evidence is complicated by further rebuilding after the Great Fire; the brick tower of St Bartholomew-the-Great, 1628, also has simple Gothic motifs.

A more advanced classicism, albeit less refined than that introduced to the court by Inigo Jones, appears at St Helen Bishopsgate in the s doorcase dated 1633. Its banded half-pilasters and eared surround 18 derive from drawings or engravings by Serlio and by such later C16 authors as du Cerceau and Wendel Dietterlin. This native classicism was dubbed 'Artisan Mannerism' by Sir John Summerson; it also appears abundantly in funeral monuments (*see* below). One obscure but tantalizing project, suggestive of the much purer classicism associated with the court, was the rebuilding in 1638–40 of St Michael-le-Querne (†), with *Inigo Jones* as a consultant to the parish. His advice appears to have been less than welcome, though whether questions of taste or of politics lay behind the conflict is unclear, for the church was destroyed without a trace in 1666. Furthermore, when churches were again rebuilt and embellished towards the end of the Interregnum, the results were modest and the few ornamental features (notably the œil-de-bœuf window) wholly in the artisan style: the tower of All Hallows Barking (1658–9), and the little vestry at St Olave Hart Street (1661–2, with a charmingly naïve plaster 21 ceiling).

One speciality of C17 City churchyards was the *memento mori.* There are stone gateways adorned with cadavers or skulls at St Katharine Cree (1631) and St Olave Hart Street (1658), and 19 'Resurrection stones' carved with scenes of the Last Judgement at St Andrew Holborn and St Mary-at-Hill.

CHURCH FURNISHINGS of the earlier C17 are naturally confined to the area that escaped the Great Fire. STAINED GLASS of *c.* 1630 with foliage patterns may be seen at St Katharine Cree. The only remaining PULPIT is at St Helen, a very good example of strapwork decoration. It probably dates from a campaign of embellishment of the early 1630s, although the forms show little advance from the no less fine pulpit of 1613 at All Hallows Barking (destroyed). More advanced in style is the beautiful inner s doorcase at St Helen, probably also of the 1630s. FONTS are represented by three pieces, all of 1630–2. That at St Katharine Cree still has strapwork ornament in the Jacobean manner. At St Helen and St Andrew Undershaft the form of a faceted bowl on a baluster appears, a type multiplied in the churches refurnished after the Great Fire.

The font at St Andrew was made by *Nicholas Stone*, a leading master mason and the single most important carver of FUNERARY MONUMENTS in early Stuart London. These owed much to Dutch fashions, for Stone spent the years 1606–13 working for Hendrik de Keyser, Amsterdam's Master Mason, whose daughter he married. The survival of Stone's notebooks means that we are unusually well informed about his activities, which coincided with a new originality of types and conceits, very different from the relative stability of late C16 compositions. Partly this was due to the greater tolerance of

religious imagery: the Chamberlayne monument (†1617) at St
Bartholomew-the-Great, attributed to *Maximilian Colt*, already has
angels holding back curtains to show the kneeling effigy. *Stone's*
grandest monuments in London are at Westminster Abbey, and his
most famous sculpted portrait, of Dr John Donne, is at St Paul's. Of
his monuments in the City churches the most important is that to
Sir Julius Caesar (†1636) at St Helen Bishopsgate: a black marble
sarcophagus with the conceit of a document carved in parchment-
coloured marble instead of an effigy. Lesser tablets by the artist also
adopt black and white marble instead of alabaster, of which the
Hutton monument at St Dunstan-in-the-West, made 1640, adopts
the increasingly popular formula of pedimented tablet with columns.

Stone's architectural frames tend to be purer than the usual
London masons' work of the early C17 referred to above. Their
favourite coarse, eclectic classical ornament appears at the monument to Elizabeth Freshwater (†1617) at St Bartholomew-the-Great.
A greater restraint appears at the monument to Sir Hugh Hamersley
(†1636) at St Andrew Undershaft, which has columns and pediments
closer to Stone's preferred forms. It has attendant figures of soldiers,
a device that recurs at the atmospheric Bond monument (†1643) at
St Helen. The kneeling effigies seen at the Freshwater and Hamersley
monuments were increasingly supplanted by the device of a bust in
a niche, on which a greater degree of portraiture might be attempted.
Circular niches came first (Cuthbert Fetherstone †1615, St Dunstan-
in-the-West); oval niches supplanted them (Lady Richardson †1639,
St Botolph Aldersgate; James Rivers †1641, St Bartholomew-the-
Great). The bronze bust of Sir Peter le Maire at St Margaret
Lothbury, 1631 (not displayed in 1998), is attributed to *Hubert Le
Sueur*, the favourite sculptor of Charles I's court, though it is uncertain
if this was ever intended to form part of a monument. The only
signed monument of the period, *Henry Boughton's* tablet to Anthony
Abdy (†1640) at St Andrew Undershaft, is not of special interest
otherwise.

Sir Christopher Wren and the City Churches

The Great Fire of 1666 is the watershed in the history of C17
London. It marks the beginning of the AGE OF WREN, for *Sir
Christopher Wren* (1632–1723) was to dominate the architecture of
London into the next century. His multifarious attainments had
already won him the post of Professor of Astronomy at Gresham
College, in 1657. Furthermore, his uncle Matthew Wren was Bishop
of Ely and a leading figure in the Restoration Church. This connection had already secured for Wren the task of rebuilding Pembroke
College chapel, Cambridge, and even before the Great Fire his mind
was busy with further schemes to modernize Old St Paul's. He could
hardly have guessed then at the opportunities lying ahead.

The Fire laid waste 436 acres, including some five-sixths of the
City within the walls. The burnt area went from the Temple and
Fetter Lane in the W, up to Aldersgate and Cripplegate in the N, and
E as far as Leadenhall Market and Tower Hill. Within this area 85 of
the 107 parish churches were gutted or destroyed entirely.

Speculative PLANS for rebuilding in a more modern, more com-
modious, and more dignified way appeared at once, and it is inter-

esting to compare what their authors had in mind by way of churches for the rehoused citizens. In *Wren*'s well-known French-influenced design, dominated by *rond-points* with radiating avenues, only nineteen churches appear. *John Evelyn* also recommended a reduction in the number of churches, to be situated where they might adorn the City. *Richard Newcourt* envisaged a grid of stand-ardized parish blocks, each centred on a church of identical size. But nothing so drastic was carried out, and in the event the new churches – fifty-one of them – were built where their predecessors stood. St Andrew Holborn, outside the burnt area but in a poor struc-tural condition, was also rebuilt. Of these churches, only twenty-four remain, plus six towers.

St Paul's apart, the churches are *Wren*'s principal contribution to the appearance of London. To this day they are the outstanding accents of the City, and some of them individually its highest archi-tectural attainments. How they were built has been the subject of much debate. Funds came from a tax on coal enacted in 1670, that is they were state, not parish funds. A third of the money was allocated to the churches, a third to St Paul's, and the remaining third to pay for street improvements. The tax was renewed in 1686 and 1700 to allow the churches and St Paul's to be completed. The churches were entrusted to a Commission, which swiftly appointed Wren 'to direct and order the dimensions, formes and Modells of the said Churches'. He was joined by *Robert Hooke* and by *Edward Woodroffe*. Woodroffe died in 1675 and was replaced by *John Oliver*, though neither seems to have played a part in the work of design. The case of Hooke is altogether different. He collaborated with Wren at the great columnar Monument on Fish Street Hill, and it is clear from his secular buildings that he was amongst the most capable archi-tects of the day. Drawings in his hand strongly suggest that he and not Wren was the author of several of the churches, notably St Benet 28 Paul's Wharf and St Edmund the King.

Furthermore, several churches were begun by impatient parishes without waiting for directions from the Commissioners, and these cannot be attributed either to Wren or to Hooke. The naves of St Michael Cornhill and St Sepulchre are the surviving examples, both of them churches where a large part of the medieval fabric had sur-vived and could be reused. The continuing shortage of money meant that Wren was himself reluctant to demolish sound medieval fabric, and many of the churches are, in their lower stages at least, structurally medieval: a circumstance usually betrayed by irregular angles in the plan. St Anne and St Agnes and St Andrew Holborn have recased w towers, St Michael Cornhill and St Mary-at-Hill later replacements of medieval towers repaired after the Fire. More-over, attribution of the later spires is complicated by the employment of *Nicholas Hawksmoor* and *William Dickinson*, who worked in Wren's office respectively after 1693 and 1695. It would be unwise to treat a church as an architectural orphan simply because there is no documentary evidence tying it to Wren, for there can be no doubt that he remained in overall control. But it may be better to regard several as collaborative, even somewhat contingent exercises rather than as manifestations of a single architectural genius.

Wren had few guides as to what a Protestant church should look like. Calvinist Holland supplied some recent precedents (*see* below);

but in England the Restoration Church had revived a dignified emphasis on the E end, from which altars had been removed during the Interregnum. In recognition of this, a dozen of the new churches had chancels, though they were mostly very shallow. But it was also expected that due prominence be given to the pulpit and desk, from which the Word was preached and the congregation led through the liturgy. In his very last years Wren set out his own understanding of the problem in a well-known memorandum: the principal requirement is 'that all who are present can both hear and see'; for Romanists it may be enough 'if they hear the Murmur of the Mass, and see the elevation of the Host', but English churches 'are to be fitted for Auditories'. The last requirement, and the need to accommodate the swollen congregations of amalgamated parishes, explains the extensive use of galleries, which were already being installed in the City in the 1620s. It also explains why Wren felt free to experiment with centrally planned churches, which had been the paramount problem of church design in the Italian Renaissance. Modifications of it were still eminently topical in Italy and France in Wren's day. But these considerations in no way explain the unique variety of plans which Wren devised in the course of his work for the City churches. It is this variety that makes their study so rewarding, and we may not be wrong in discovering in it also something of the scientist's delight in experimenting. How many types of useful parish church can be developed? What use can be made of types worked out in other countries and in other ages? Such thoughts must have exercised Wren's mind as he produced design after design, from 1670 to 1686. In some cases a direct derivation from an antique prototype is documented or can be inferred. At the same time this variety can also be looked at as a national, not an individual phenomenon. It is inconceivable that a French architect of the Age of Louis XIV or indeed an Italian or a German Baroque architect would have gone so far in changing from one principle to another in plans as well as elevations. From this point of view also Wren's plans deserve close study. An effort is here made to arrange them systematically, whether they survive or not.

The smallest and most common type is represented by a single unaisled interior without distinctive spatial features. The walls were often markedly irregular, due to the retention of the medieval plan. The tower was placed usually in the NW or SW corner (St Michael Paternoster Royal, St Nicholas Cole Abbey); sometimes it projected in whole or part (St Mary Somerset †). This asymmetry seems to have been due as much to Wren's preferences as to the medieval arrangement. St Olave Jewry (†) was exceptional in the regularity of its plan, for Wren gave it a central W tower and unique tapering coffin-shaped sides: the latter a clever response to a site that was curtailed on one side. St Edmund the King, probably by *Hooke*, also had a tower placed centrally on the entrance front. The ceilings were commonly coved, with penetrations from the windows. A more complex variant of this type has a single aisle, often on the same side as the tower (St Margaret Lothbury, St Clement Eastcheap). The main space in such churches represents the former nave and other aisle combined. The walls invariably have ranges of pilasters, turning to columns in the aisle, where a gallery was accommodated (St Margaret Pattens, St Benet). St Lawrence Jewry is also of this type,

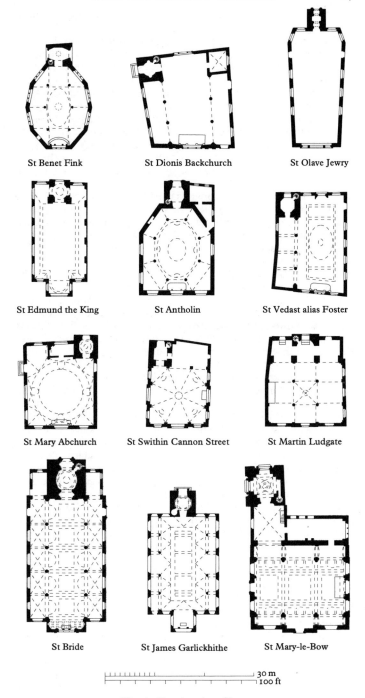

St Benet Fink   St Dionis Backchurch   St Olave Jewry

St Edmund the King   St Antholin   St Vedast alias Foster

St Mary Abchurch   St Swithin Cannon Street   St Martin Ludgate

St Bride   St James Garlickhithe   St Mary-le-Bow

30 m
100 ft

Wren's City churches. Plans

as is St Vedast, where the church patched up by the parish had to be
rebuilt again in 1695–1701.

The remaining churches fall into two categories, longitudinal and
central, with many transitions between them. The longitudinal is
the most usual plan, with nave and aisles in the Gothic tradition.
Columns replace piers, and groined vaults or tunnel-vaults of plaster
the open roofs and load-bearing vaults of English Gothic, with kingpost trusses concealed above. In part this represents the further
development of the type seen at St Katharine Cree, stripped of residual
Gothicisms. It is indeed striking that the parochial rebuildings at St
Michael Cornhill, St Sepulchre and St Dunstan-in-the-East (†) all
adopted simple Tuscan or Doric arcades. Many of Wren's churches
represent a similar perpetuation of the medieval plan type (St
Augustine †, St Mary Aldermanbury †, St Peter upon Cornhill).
36 The Gothic churches of St Alban (†) and St Mary Aldermary belong
in the same category. In other cases he worked without the con-
straint of reusing so much old fabric, and a tighter, more regular
design was the usual result. The earliest, St Bride Fleet Street, has
five bays and a clerestory: features associated with the basilica
described by Vitruvius. Later churches adopted the formula Wren
first used at St James Piccadilly, Westminster, in which the aisles
are of two storeys and the columns rise from square piers that also
support the galleries (St Andrew Holborn). St Andrew-by-the-
34 Wardrobe is similar but has square piers above the galleries too.
Naves were usually barrel-vaulted (St Peter upon Cornhill, St George
Botolph Lane †), occasionally groin-vaulted (Christ Church †). For
the aisles groin-vaults were more common, though transverse barrel-
vaults were sometimes preferred (St Peter upon Cornhill), and flat
ceilings not unknown (St Dionis Backchurch †).

Centrally planned City churches are far fewer, being confined
strictly to five examples. Two of these had domes spanning a square
space contrived within a rectangular plan. At St Mary Abchurch the
33 dome is a hemisphere springing from low down the walls. St Swithin
(†) had an octagonal domical vault. The other three follow the
venerable type of the inscribed cross or cross-in-square. The type
goes back to the Early Christian centuries (e.g. Tarrasa in Catalonia,
c6), appears in Italy in the c9 (S. Satiro, Milan), became popular in
Milan and Venice with the Renaissance (S. Giovanni Crisostomo,
Venice), and then went to Holland. It appeared in London first
at the Broadway Chapel in Westminster, built 1635–42, and was imitated at St Matthias Poplar not long afterwards. Wren may have
taken the pattern from these buildings or from knowledge of its
recent Dutch exemplars, notably the Nieuwe Kerk at Haarlem. His
versions have a square vaulted centre on four free-standing columns,
four equal cross-arms, and lower vaulted or flat bays in the four
corners. At St Martin Ludgate (1677–86) the detail is exactly as at
31 Haarlem: groin-vaulted centre, tunnel-vaulted arms, flat-ceilinged
corner bays. At St Anne and St Agnes (1677–87) the corner bays
35 are also flat. St Mary-at-Hill (1670–4) had a central lantern, since
rebuilt. But from the European point of view the most characteristic
problem of church design in the c17 is neither the longitudinal nor
the central plan, but the combination of the two. In Italy and
France, and later in Germany, the symbol of this typically Baroque
tendency is the oval. Wren in his most interesting plans is a

European in this sense. He does not often make use of the oval, but combinations of longitudinal with central elements fascinated him as much as they did Bernini or Le Vau or Balthasar Neumann. Examples can again be divided into two groups: central plans elongated, and longitudinal plans centralized.

First, central plans elongated. St Mildred Bread Street (†) was a plain parallelogram and had a saucer-dome above the centre and short barrel-vaulted bays to the E and W. St Antholin (†) had an elongated octagon of columns and an oval dome set within an irregular space that tapered towards the W. St Benet Fink (†) was an elongated decagon with an elongated hexagonal centre on columns and an oval dome with a lantern. Then, longitudinal plans centralized. These are usually associated with lesser entrances in the N or S walls of the church, which in most cases appear to have passed out of use at an early date. St James Garlickhithe is of five bays with a coved ceiling. The aisles are narrow, the arcade has giant columns and a straight entablature. But for the wider middle bay the entablature turns to the outer walls, thus forming a central transept rising to the height of the nave ceiling. Similarly at St Mary Aldermanbury (†) the nave had five bays and a barrel-vault, but the middle bay was groined where it was intersected by a barrel-vaulted transept. St Magnus appears to have been similar originally. The type is a descendant, but not a copy, of de Keyser's Westerkerk in Amsterdam. A different line of descent can be traced for St Mary-le-Bow, which has the exceptional feature of three wide bays of different widths and piers with applied half-columns: features the *Parentalia* tells us were derived from the Basilica of Maxentius in Rome.

St Stephen Walbrook, begun in 1672, is the most complex case and one which can be regarded as a trying-out of some elements for St Paul's. It is longitudinal but has a large dome with lantern lighting. The dome is intersected by the nave and chancel axis as well as a transeptal cross-axis. But the dome is much wider than the width of the arms and stands within a square of twelve columns. To gain the bottom circle of the dome eight arches are built up, four over nave, chancel and transept ends, and four at the diagonals. The outer corner bays moreover are treated as at St Mary-at-Hill. But for a full analysis of this truly Baroque conception, pp. 127–8 must be consulted. p. 127, 30

The EXTERIOR ARCHITECTURE of the churches was also highly varied. In most cases the churches were partly hidden by the surrounding houses, or faced narrow alleys where architectural display would have been inappropriate. But even the smallest and plainest churches had at least one show front. At St Lawrence Jewry, St Dionis (†) and St Michael Wood Street (†) the E front was developed into a grand pedimented composition with pilasters or half-columns. The exposed E end of St Matthew Friday Street (†) was given a row of five identical round-headed windows. The E end of St Olave Jewry (†) had a big Venetian window. At St Peter upon Cornhill it is elaborated into two storeys. In other cases the sides were developed into symmetrical compositions with even windows and doorcases at each end (St Andrew Holborn, St Bride). St Anne and St Agnes has the rare feature of a strong central emphasis on each side, made by the gable over the central window. Round-headed windows were the most common type, though segment-headed windows were also used (St Martin, St Andrew Holborn). Larger windows have mullions

30 and transoms, especially those at the E and W (St Stephen, St
23 Vedast). Surrounds ranged from simple frames to ornate hoods on
26 brackets (St Nicholas Cole Abbey, St Magnus). Circular windows
were used for clerestories or set over doors. St Michael Queenhithe
(†) had a continuous sequence of them above the round-arched
windows of the three main fronts. Oval windows also appear (St
Stephen Walbrook, St Antholin †). Doorcases are usually fairly plain,
rising to pedimented surrounds of rusticated stone (St Antholin †)
1 or columns (St Margaret Lothbury), and at St Mary-le-Bow to an
27 elaborate composition with columns and cherubs in a niche, closely
derived from a work by J. Hardouin Mansart. Other typical features
include quoins and the adornment of the parapet with urns and
pineapples (Christ Church †, St Edmund). Wren appears to have
taken much of his vocabulary from Jones's refacing of Old St Paul's,
particularly from the windows of the nave aisles and clerestory, and
from the simple treatment of the towers. He also followed Jones in
the extensive use of the hard white limestone known as Portland
stone, which was transported by sea from Dorset.

Brick was used sometimes in default of stone for lesser elevations
(St Mary-le-Bow), sometimes for a whole church (St Clement
Eastcheap, St Andrew-by-the-Wardrobe). The brick was often rendered then or later, and St Andrew-by-the-Wardrobe was so noted
by Edward Hatton in 1708. Only rarely was brick used for effects
28 unobtainable from stone, notably at St Benet Paul's Wharf, attributed to *Hooke*, which has chequerworked brick, alternating evenly
with stone on the striped quoins. These walls were not of solid brick
but of brick facing to a rubble core, which allowed the economical
reuse of the old stone.

Some of the grandest effects were obtained when the tower was
united with the nave by scrolls or curved screen walls to make a
29 formal composition, as at St Martin and St Edmund; and this brings
us to the TOWERS and SPIRES generally. Jones's St Paul Covent
Garden (1631–8) had only an apologetic belfry, but the City parishes
were proud of their steeples and of the bells they housed, and in the
event every new church had a proper tower. They are more varied
and unpredictable even than the church plans, and it has been
remarked more than once how carefully they were distributed so
that similar designs nowhere stood too close together. Just to describe
the different types of balustrade used would take a long paragraph.
p. The steeples were certainly the feature most admired by the visitor
25 to London. 'Londra è il paese dei bei campanili', wrote Count

Wren's City church towers and spires, drawn by G. Cobb.
Top row: St Clement Eastcheap; St Andrew Holborn;
St Mary Somerset; All Hallows Bread Street; St Mary Aldermary;
St Michael Cornhill
Second row: St Mary Aldermanbury; St Lawrence Jewry; St Benet Fink;
St Mary Magdalen; St Peter upon Cornhill; St Mary Abchurch
Third row: St Augustine Watling Street; St Nicholas Cole Abbey;
St Edmund the King; St Margaret Pattens;
St Antholin Watling Street; St Michael Paternoster Royal
Bottom row: St Stephen Walbrook; St Mary-le-Bow;
St Bride; St Michael Crooked Lane; Christ Church Newgate Street;
St Magnus the Martyr

Algarotti in 1753. He knew only one steeple in Italy worthy of comparison. Yet it appears that Wren may have come to the idea of a
forest of tall steeples only by stages. Of the great steeples only St
Mary-le-Bow was conceived and executed in the first wave of church
building, up to 1680. St Bride and St Magnus have similarly broad,
pilastered towers, which suggests that stone spires were intended for
them from the start. At other churches a steeple was erected as an
afterthought, and at St Edmund a small cupola of the 1670s was
actually removed in the early C18 to make way for the present leaded
spire. It may be that Wren did not expect money from the Coal Tax
to continue to roll in for so long. Whatever the reason, the business
of adding spires to existing towers kept his office occupied well into
the 1710s, and there is no reason to suppose that the plainer towers
would not have been given steeples too if the Coal Tax had not
expired in 1717.

The simplest type is therefore the plain square tower with parapet
or balustrade (St Clement Eastcheap, St Andrew-by-the-Wardrobe).
The next stage was the addition of pinnacles or obelisks at the
24 corners (St Andrew Holborn, St Olave Jewry, also the eight-pinnacled
St Mary Somerset). Four of the five Gothic towers, St Alban Wood
Street, St Christopher-le-Stocks (†), St Michael Cornhill and St Mary
Aldermary, were also of this type. In other cases a modest leaded
turret was provided (St Anne and St Agnes, St Mary Aldermanbury †).
The turrets of Jones's w towers at Old St Paul's were doubtless an
influential precedent for this type. At St Lawrence, the cupola was
elaborated with architectural elements into something more like a
true spire. Another more elaborate treatment was to set the lantern
28 on a dome or broad base: at St Benet Paul's Wharf and St Benet
Fink (†) the lantern was of lead, at St Mary Magdalen Old Fish
Street (†) of stone. Greater height was achieved when a spirelet or
leaded obelisk replaced the lantern. St Peter upon Cornhill has a
spirelet on a rounded dome, St Mary Abchurch and St Margaret
1 Lothbury an obelisk on a square ogival dome. At St Martin the
dome is a bell-shaped octagon. St Augustine Watling Street has a
broadly similar profile, but a much more complicated vocabulary of
small superimposed stages. Greater height might also be achieved by
26 drawing the cupola upwards into a trumpet shape (St Nicholas Cole
Abbey, St Edmund); still greater height by following the Gothic
precedent of an elongated octagonal spire (St Margaret Pattens, St
Swithin †, St Antholin †).

The largest and most complex spires were generally of stone.
Three closely related designs at St Michael Paternoster Royal, St
22 James Garlickhithe and St Stephen Walbrook have recessed two-
stage structures with playful detail and small columns. The first has
an octagonal core, the others a square one. Each of the rest is *sui
generis*. St Mary-le-Bow modulates from a circular colonnaded stage
through a ring of unique stone arches or bows to a modified
becolumned octagon and terminal obelisk. Christ Church made
similar use of columns, but applied them to a square core. St Michael
Crooked Lane (†) had a circular leaded core, garnished with volutes
rather than columns. At St Bride the spire is developed entirely from
one octagonal motif, repeated in four diminishing stages below the
usual obelisk, with much piercing of the lower three. The most
23 Baroque of all is St Vedast, with its Borrominesque contrast between

a first concave-sided stage and a second convex-sided stage of the spire. St Magnus has a tall octagonal cupola of stone, modelled on the tower of St Charles Borromeo church at Antwerp (1614–24): one of the few instances where a direct Continental source may be suggested for a Wren spire.

The one Gothic spire in this category is St Dunstan-in-the-East, 25 where a needle-spire is carried on four steep flying buttresses thrown up diagonally from the corner pinnacles, much as in the Gothic steeple of old St Mary-le-Bow and St Nicholas Newcastle. The use of the GOTHIC STYLE for several of the churches is indeed the most convincing proof of Wren's belief in variety rather than uniformity. In a memorandum of 1713 on Westminster Abbey he does admit that the classical is the 'better style', but he suggests that the Gothic examples amongst his 'Parochial Churches of London ... appear not ungraceful but ornamental'. It is the very opposite of the attitude to architecture and decoration at the Court of Louis XIV. The boldest of Wren's other efforts in the Gothic style is the interior of St Mary Aldermary. This is a problematic building in terms of patron- 36 age (it was paid for by a private benefaction) and the survival of pre-Fire work in the walls and tower, but there can be no doubt that the delightful fan-vaults and Gothic saucer-domes are by Wren or his office.

The towers themselves are usually square in plan and straight-sided. Exceptions are the oblong tower of St Augustine and the tower of St Olave Jewry, with its battered lower stages. Lower stages have round-headed or circular windows similar to those that light the church, but for the bell-stage straight-headed openings are some-times preferred (St Margaret Pattens, St Augustine). At St Benet Fink (†) the opening was oval, while St Peter upon Cornhill has triple openings on each side instead. All Hallows Bread Street (†) had similar triple openings, but they were a later addition, set above the bell-chamber and open to the air. Sometimes the bell-stage is tied to the cornice by a pediment (St Nicholas Cole Abbey, St Benet 26 Gracechurch †) or by ornamented keystones (St Mary Somerset, St Martin Ludgate). The three great towers of St Bride, St Mary-le-Bow and St Magnus in addition have paired pilasters flanking the bell-stage.

Questions of authorship for the spires are different again from those of the church proper, especially where the later designs are concerned. Wren was so busy at St Paul's, Greenwich and Hampton Court that delegation must have been almost irresistible. The increasingly Baroque flavour of many of the steeples is not in itself enough to dismiss them from the Wren canon, for his towers at Greenwich and on the w end of St Paul's show a similar development. But many of the spires make inventive use of certain motifs familiar from the later work of *Hawksmoor*, notably masks instead of cherubs' heads, Baroque volutes, and obelisks of more classical profile, and it may be that several of the designs are wholly or partly from his pen. He worked in the office only between 1695 and 1701, but a drawing exists in his hand for the steeple of St Edmund, built 1706–7. The explanation may be that he continued informally to work for the office, or that drawings were used some years after they were made. The latter may be likelier, particularly as the office more than once erected on one tower a steeple originally designed for another. There

is evidence for this in an album of drawings in the Guildhall collection, datable c. 1700, one of which shows the tower of St Michael Paternoster Royal with the steeple eventually built at St James
22 Garlickhithe.* These steeples may be associated with Hawksmoor, as may that at St Stephen Walbrook, the third of the trio of inset stone steeples. He may also have had a hand in the spires of St
23, Vedast and St Augustine and the tower of St Andrew Holborn, with
24 its strange openings and finials. At St Michael Cornhill there is documentary evidence for his involvement, though only for the uppermost stage of 1718–22. The rest of the tower, in a less vigorous Neo-Gothic, was probably by *William Dickinson*, who remained in the City church office; he has also been associated with the completion of the tower of St Mary Aldermary in 1701–4.

The only task of rebuilding comparable in scale and duration to the City churches was that of St Paul's, declared complete only in 1711. The finished building and the progress of its design are described in *London 1*. Only the symbiosis between the building of the cathdral and its daughter churches need be remarked here, for many craftsmen worked on both enterprises. Amongst the masons or carvers, *Edward Pierce* and *Jonathan Maine* stand out (Pierce incidentally also gave us the best likeness of Wren, the bust at the Ashmolean, Oxford). Another name that recurs more often than average is that of the plasterer *Henry Doogood*, usually in collaboration with *John Grove*.

Furnishing the Wren Churches

The importance of the furnishings of Wren's churches greatly transcends the capital, for they influenced at first or second hand the whole Restoration church throughout England and its nascent Empire. Only at two parishes, St Andrew-by-the-Wardrobe and St Mary Somerset, did the Coal Tax pay for the furnishings as well as the fabric of the new churches. Elsewhere they were the responsibility of the parishes. Even so, the results have a remarkable consistency of style and quality, due in part to the employment of many of the carvers who worked for Wren on the buildings proper. In many cases also vestries commissioned furnishings modelled on those in other, completed churches which they had seen and admired. A few post-Fire furnishings are older than the churches housing them, having been ordered for the temporary 'tabernacles' that did duty for many parishes awaiting their new building. Churches which had survived the Fire frequently procured similar fittings. The best complete ensemble was at St Mary-at-Hill, where the high pews and galleries were supplemented by good work of 1848–9. Badly damaged by fire in 1988, it awaits restoration in 1998. Much of the woodwork in other churches was lost in the Second World War, although it has been augmented by pieces saved from churches demolished in the C19 and before.

The greatest ornament is reserved for the REREDOSES. All have panels with the Decalogue, Creed and Lord's Prayer, usually framed by columns or pilasters and surmounted by a pediment or pediments and urns in various combinations and proportions. They are

* *See* Paul Jeffery, *Architectural History* 35 (1992).

often larger than Wren anticipated, sometimes so much so that they
block the E window. Evidence from St Mary-at-Hill and St Magnus
(a two-storey reredos) suggests that they may have been enlarged
and extended into the C18 in some cases. At churches with projecting chancels, such as St James Garlickhithe and St Margaret Pattens,
the reredos tends to be more modest. Besides the architectural
elements there is usually rich carving of foliage, garlands and cherubs'
heads. Only at St Mary Abchurch can the carving be attributed to 38
Gibbons, who is associated by an indestructible popular myth with
any good late C17 wood-carving in England, but whose surviving
work in the City is mostly concentrated at St Paul's. *Wren* himself
designed a new reredos for the Temple Church (1682–3), which
nicely illustrates how congregations in older churches tried to keep
up with the new fashions. Sculpture was occasionally incorporated:
St Michael Paternoster Royal preserves two excellent sculpted stone
figures of Moses and Aaron, from the former All Hallows the Great, 50
while fine Baroque angels of gilt wood perch on the reredos of St
Magnus.

Against the reredos stood the COMMUNION TABLE, the legs or
supports of which were sometimes elaborated: as standing angels at
St Benet Paul's Wharf, with cherubs at St Clement Eastcheap, perch- 44
ing doves at St James Garlickhithe. St Stephen Walbrook has an
elliptical table, following the outline of the COMMUNION RAILS. At
St Stephen these have balusters of the usual spiral form, with foliage
carving on the posts and rail. Variant baluster types include the open
double-helix (St Margaret Lothbury), shafts tapering from a central
ring (St Edmund), and miniature Doric piers (St Peter upon Cornhill).
At St Olave Hart Street the base rests on little carved lions. In the
early C18 wrought iron was preferred: at St Andrew Undershaft (by
Tijou, 1704), St Magnus and St Sepulchre. St Edmund, St Martin
and St Mary Abchurch have in addition C17 or early C18 railed
enclosures around their fonts.

PULPITS are all of one hexagonal type with fielded panels on each
face, but are given variety through the different shapes employed
(square, oval, round-headed) and through different patterns of carved
foliage and cherubs' heads. That at All Hallows Barking has pedimented sides. Where the stairs survive, the balustrade generally
matches the communion rails (St Clement, St Edmund). The great
testers or sounding-boards survive less well, but there are excellent
examples with standing cherubs and other adornments at St Clement, 39
St Margaret Lothbury and St Stephen Walbrook. At St Mary 30
Abchurch the pulpit retains both its tester and its lofty original staircase, for pulpits of this period originally comprised only the highest
part of a 'three-decker' ensemble. DOORCASES are often very fine
indeed. The series at St Martin and St Mary Abchurch are amongst
the best. All the churches were wainscotted, though this was plain by
comparison.

FONTS were an opportunity for the masons to display their skills,
and the names of their makers are often recorded. The usual pattern
is an octagonal shaft and bowl ornamented with foliage and cherubs' 42
heads. That at St Margaret Lothbury has four reliefs of Biblical 45
scenes on the bowl. Wooden FONT COVERS were made to match,
although these are not always displayed. Most have a low decorated 42
base and an ogee top. At St Stephen Walbrook and St Edmund the

base is unusually tall and the top is adorned with little figures. St
Mary Abchurch has a four-sided top with figures that is raised and
lowered on a spiral shaft. St Nicholas Cole Abbey, St Clement
Eastcheap and St Peter upon Cornhill have covers with eight open
ribs, the latter two enclosing a carved dove. The cover at All Hallows
Barking has an extraordinary wooden sculpture of cherubs, flowers
and ears of wheat, surmounted by a dove. It is attributed to *Gibbons*.
Also in the Gibbons style, though not original to the City, is the
excellent carving of King David at St Botolph Aldgate.

In exceptional cases a SCREEN was provided, airy examples of
which remain at St Peter and St Margaret Lothbury. Such a prominent feature was too 'High' or too archaizing for most parishes.
Instead, the nominal boundary of the chancel was sometimes marked
by little carved figures of the lion and unicorn on the pew ends (St
Anne and St Agnes, St Mary Abchurch). The lion and unicorn
are of course the supporters of the ROYAL ARMS, which were displayed in all the new churches, as had been the practice since the
Reformation. Those at St Benet Paul's Wharf and St Margaret
Pattens are amongst the finest. Sometimes they were modelled in
plaster, although none of these remains. SEATS were mostly cut
down and reordered in the C19, but some high pews remain at St
Mary Abchurch, and several churches keep the tall churchwardens'
pews at the far W. At St Margaret Pattens they have canopies.
GALLERIES remain at St Benet Paul's Wharf and St Margaret Pattens,
with WEST GALLERIES at many more churches. Many of the latter
supported organs, which in the late C17 were mostly supplied by
Renatus Harris or *Bernard Smith* ('*Father Smith*'). Though the instruments have generally been much rebuilt, the remaining cases
abound in fine wood carving. Those at St Katharine Cree, St Mary
Woolnoth and St Peter upon Cornhill are by *Smith*, those at St
Andrew Undershaft, St Clement and St Sepulchre by *Harris*.

A peculiarity of the City churches is the SWORD REST, which was
used by the Lord Mayor on his state visits. The earliest example, of
wood, is at St Helen (1665). St Mary Aldermary also has a wooden
example, dated 1682. But the usual material was wrought iron, used
either in attachments to a single shaft (pole type) or as an upright
symmetrical frame (frame type). The earliest dated example is at St
Magnus (1708), though there are references from at least 1680. The
design did not much alter throughout the C18, from which particularly good sequences may be seen at All Hallows Barking and St
Olave Hart Street. Another use of metalwork was for the delightfully
varied weathervanes of the steeples: a key for St Peter upon Cornhill,
a gridiron for St Lawrence, a dragon of copper for St Mary-le-Bow,
and so on. Other church metalwork includes railings, of which there
are good early C18 examples at St Dunstan-in-the-East.

PAINTING was used sparingly in most churches, though there is
evidence that painted curtains etc. were once common at the E end.
Panels with figures of Moses and Aaron were sometimes incorporated
in the reredos, of which examples remain *in situ* at St Stephen Walbrook
and St Magnus, *ex situ* at St Anne and St Agnes, St Margaret
Lothbury and St Michael Cornhill. The most spectacular decoration
is at St Mary Abchurch, where *William Snow* painted the dome in
c. 1708 with seated Virtues and a heavenly choir. STAINED GLASS was
not unknown, but the only large window, in St Andrew Undershaft,

was destroyed by a terrorist bomb in 1992. It had five upright figures of monarchs, of *c.* 1690–1700. A good deal of heraldic glass was lost from the churches in the Second World War, though a panel (*ex situ*) remains at St Magnus.

CHURCH MONUMENTS of the later C17 and early C18 survive in large numbers, though many perished in the Blitz. Large compositions are rare, however. The reason is not hard to see. The wealthy preferred to be regarded as belonging to their country (or suburban) estates, where they were often Lords of the Manor. So they wanted to be buried away from London. Hence the great wealth of sumptuous monuments in the home counties. Whole types of monument of great importance from the national point of view cannot be seen in the City, notably that with life-size figures in contemporary costume standing in niches, common from the last decades of the C17. There is only one each of the standing effigy type (Sir Andrew Riccard †1672, St Olave Hart Street) and the semi-reclining effigy type (Sir John Hiccocks †1726, Temple churchyard), neither in good condition.

Wall monuments of relatively modest dimensions make up the remainder. There are busts at St Olave Hart Street (Mrs Pepys †1669, by *Bushnell,* and one other), St Sepulchre (Edward Arris †1676 and wife), and St Stephen Walbrook (Sir Percival Gilbourne †1694). The Tillotson monument (†1694) at St Lawrence Jewry, attributed to *Gibbons,* has a portrait relief and attendant cherubs. The pedimented and columned tablet remained popular, though black and white marble fell out of fashion. The columns sometimes took spiral form (Sherwood monument †1690–1703, St Mary Abchurch). Larger tablets were adorned with urns and with cherubs, cherubs' heads and drapery (Rachel Chambrelan †1687, St Helen; Thomas Davall †1700, St Mary-at-Hill). Other architectural forms include the standing column (All Hallows Barking, †1696 and †1699 or later) and the obelisk (Cottle monument, St Benet, probably early C18). The most enjoyable are often of the cartouche type, which dispense with architectural forms in favour of shields, scrolls and drapery, with cherubs' heads and skulls the usual ornament. All Hallows London Wall (†1684) and St Bartholomew-the-Great 48 (†1685 and 1704 and later) have good examples. The type remained popular well into the C18: *see* the Gale monument, St Peter upon Cornhill (†1739 and †1741). Signed or documented pieces are uncommon, but include works by *Thomas Cartwright Sen.* (St Andrew Undershaft), *William Kidwell* (St Mary-at-Hill), *John Settle* and *Thomas Stayner* (all at St Dunstan-in-the-West), and *William Stanton* (St Andrew Holborn and Temple Church). Many of these artists also worked as master masons.

The City Churches in the Georgian Era

Religious architecture remained a matter of active endeavour for the City's crowded congregations. Work continued into the 1710s on the spires of Wren's churches, as we have seen. The later C17 also saw the beginning of buildings for non-Anglican congregations. The first of these to concern us, and the only survivor in the City from before Victorian times, is the exceptionally important synagogue in Bevis 32 Marks (1699–1701). It is plain outside in the manner of a large Nonconformist chapel, but of great dignity and beauty inside and in

its fittings. The other surviving religious buildings of the period are all rebuildings of parish churches that had escaped the Great Fire, or were inadequately repaired after it. The little Holy Trinity Minories, built in 1706 by an unknown architect and destroyed in 1940, belonged to the same tradition of vernacular City classicism as the synagogue. Next in sequence is *Hawksmoor*'s St Mary Woolnoth,
51 1716–27, the only church in the City paid for under the Fifty Churches Act of 1711, after the rules were bent to allow rebuilding of existing structures. Even amongst Hawksmoor's churches, the ingenuity of its centralizing plan and the dramatic and capricious exterior are outstanding. This was far too personal a style to find
53 ready imitators. The next rebuildings, of St Botolph Bishopsgate (1725–8, by *James Gould*) and St Botolph Aldgate (1741–4, by *George*
p. *Dance the Elder*), reverted instead to the Wren tradition as carried on
73 in Westminster in the 1710s and 1720s by James Gibbs, the most influential church architect of the early C18. They are of brick with quoins and stone spires or steeples. In plan St Botolph Bishopsgate is a simple barrel-vaulted basilica, while the flanks of St Botolph Aldgate show traces of an imperfectly developed cross-axis. St Katharine Coleman (†), Fenchurch Street, of 1739–40 by *James Horne*, was also Gibbsian in detail, though very impoverished.

The finest church of the later C18 is All Hallows London Wall
52 (1765–7), *Dance the Younger*'s first building. In its exquisite and exceptionally thoughtful interior the twin Neoclassical concerns with antique sources and logical simplification are harmonized. The contrast with its characteristically humble medieval predecessor, recorded in West and Toms' engraving of 1730, could hardly be greater. Dance's vault, apse and lunettes served the builder-architect *Nathaniel Wright* as the model for his reconstruction of St Botolph Aldersgate in 1789–91, though with the addition of aisles; the E end was again
55 rebuilt in 1829–30. *William Hillyer*'s earlier rebuilding of the nave of St Alphage (1775–7,†) was a more conservative pedimented box, the medieval tower being retained. The next rebuildings were *Jesse Gibson*'s St Peter-le-Poer, Old Broad Street (1788–92, dem. 1874), one of a sprinkling of circular classical churches in late C18 England, and *S. P. Cockerell*'s St Martin Outwich (1796–8, dem. 1908), with a markedly French front of grooved stone. None of these churches had much in the way of a steeple.

Gothic arrived with *Dance the Younger*'s rebuilding of the octagonal vaulted nave of St Bartholomew-the-Less in 1789–91. This was a very stark affair, made more archaeologically correct in *Thomas*
58 *Hardwick*'s rebuilding in the 1820s. Archaeological ambition also marked *David Laing*'s rebuilding of the nave of St Dunstan-in-the-East in 1817–21, which had an aisled plaster-vaulted interior, the details reasonably correct Perp; only the shell survives, however. The
p. last flourish of the centralized plan was *John Shaw Sen.*'s St Dunstan-
81, in-the-West (1830–3), an inventive design with an octagonal nave
57 with iron-framed roof and an octagonal lantern steeple.

St Dunstan was the last medieval City church to be replaced by a new building, though short-lived new churches were provided in three poor districts in the first half of the C19: NW of Bishopsgate (All Saints Skinner Street, by *Michael Meredith*, 1828–30, Gothic); N of Fleet Street (Holy Trinity Gough Square, by *John Shaw Jun.*, 1837, Neo-Norman); and W of Moorfields (St Bartholomew Moor

Lane, a classical church by *C. R. Cockerell*, 1849–50). There was also the Neo-Norman St Thomas in the Liberty of the Rolls, by *C. Davy* and *J. Johnson*, 1842 (dem. 1886), on the site of Bream's Buildings, off Chancery Lane. Some mention is also needed of the grand non-Anglican buildings put up during the early c19, none of which remains. The best examples were all built as part of the Moorfields development, laid out N of London Wall to plans by *Dance the Younger*. *Williams Jay*'s Albion Chapel in Moorfields (1815–16) and *William Brooks*'s Unitarian Chapel in South Place (1824) were assertive pedimented classical structures. Nearby was *John Newman*'s Roman Catholic church of St Mary Moorfields (1817–20), also Grecian, but still more ambitious in scale. Parts of the spectacularly lit interior survive in its late Victorian successor and namesake in Eldon Street.

FUNERAL MONUMENTS are generally of less interest than those of the c17. The leading sculptors of the mid c18 were of Continental origin, of whom *Michael Rysbrack* left minor Palladian monuments at St Margaret Pattens (1740) and St Michael Paternoster Royal (†1750, with bust), *Louis François Roubiliac* a small monument at St Botolph Aldersgate (†1750, with portrait relief). The architect-designed church monuments that are such a feature of the c18 elsewhere are as far as is known not represented, though the architectural motif of an obelisk was increasingly popular. The anonymous monument to Sir Richard Hoare (†1754) at St Dunstan-in-the-West is the largest example. For the later c18, there are portrait busts at St Margaret Lothbury by *Nollekens* (Anne Simpson, 1795), at St Giles Cripplegate by the elder *Bacon* (1793). Both the elder and younger *Bacon* also carved monuments with allegorical female figures in relief; that at St Stephen Walbrook to Thomas Stonestreet, 1803, is 56 particularly attractive.

PAINTING, that is wall and ceiling painting, is reasonably well represented. At St Andrew Undershaft there survives part of a scriptural scheme by *Robert Brown*, probably of 1725–6. Painted altarpieces of scriptural subjects were occasionally introduced to churches: at old St Mary Magdalen, *c.* 1720, also by *Brown*, now at St Martin Ludgate; at St James Garlickhithe, by *Andrew Geddes*, 1815. The E end of All Hallows London Wall was designed to accommodate a 52 painting by *Nathaniel Dance-Holland*, after Pietro da Cortona.

A variation on painted altarpieces for churches was STAINED GLASS. One outstanding window, a night-piece of the Agony in the Garden by *James Pearson* (1788), remains at St Botolph Aldersgate. St Andrew-by-the-Wardrobe has a window of *c.* 1712–16 by *Joshua* 46 *Price*, introduced in the post-war restoration.

CHURCH FURNISHINGS of the c18 and early c19 are naturally much less numerous than those of the late c17. New churches such as St Mary Woolnoth and the three St Botolphs retain most of their original fittings. Highlights include the magnificent baldacchino and bulging pulpit at St Mary Woolnoth and the fanciful pulpit at St Botolph Aldersgate, which is supported on a dwarf palm tree. Many churches acquired organs only in the c18 or early c19, and most of the great organ-builders are represented: the *Jordans* (St Magnus 40 the Martyr, 1712), *Thomas Griffin* (St Helen, 1742–4, St Margaret Pattens, 1749), *John Byfield* (St Botolph Aldgate, 1744), *G. P. England* (St Stephen Walbrook, 1765), *Samuel Green* (St Botolph Aldersgate,

1791). Though the instruments often do not survive, the superb cases almost always do. Exceptional individual fittings include the finest of all the carved pelicans that adorn the City churches, carved as late as 1775 by *Joseph Glazeley* for St Michael Cornhill.

Victorian Losses and Transformations

The population of the City declined dramatically after *c.* 1840. More and more of its workers moved outside the bounds, and more and more City premises were rebuilt or turned over to commerce and trade. The process was accelerated by the coming of the railways and their termini (Fenchurch Street opened 1839, Blackfriars, Cannon Street, Holborn Viaduct, Broad Street and Liverpool Street in the 1860s–70s), and by the new roads that criss-crossed the old street fabric (Cannon Street, Queen Victoria Street, Holborn Viaduct etc.). A population of 123,000 in 1841 had shrunk to 107,000 in 1861, to 51,000 in 1881, and 27,000 in 1901.

The consequences for the City churches were drastic. The late C18 and early C19 had already seen sporadic demolitions for specific City improvements: St Christopher-le-Stocks in 1782–4, for the Bank of England; St Michael Crooked Lane in 1831, for the new London Bridge approaches; St Bartholomew Exchange and St Benet Fink in 1840–4 for the new Royal Exchange. Under the Union of Benefices Act (1860), however, the Church was empowered to demolish redundant churches and sell the sites to finance church extension in the suburbs. From the late 1860s the demolition of City churches became routine, many of Wren's masterpieces being amongst them. Those in the financial centre around the Bank and Royal Exchange were especially vulnerable, having at once the smallest congregations and the most valuable sites. Protests saved individual churches (St Stephen Walbrook was threatened more than once, incredible to relate), but could not halt the process. Their site values calibrate the demand for City land as the Victorian economy boomed: an estimated average of £2,000 in 1833; £24,000 for St Benet Gracechurch in 1868; £47,000 for St Dionis Backchurch in 1878. Here and there the tower alone was kept: at St Mary Somerset (dem. 1869) and All Hallows Staining (dem. 1870) as landmarks, at St Olave Jewry (dem. 1892) as part of a rectory. Only after *c.* 1905 did the process slacken, by which time twenty churches had gone. It is incidentally to these demolitions that we owe the fittings in many remaining churches, some transferred on demolition, others brought back in restoration after the Second World War. Further fittings remain in the late C19 and C20 suburban churches built with the proceeds of the land sales; the greatest collection is at All Hallows Twickenham, the tower of which is that of Wren's All Hallows Lombard Street, re-erected in 1939–40.

The other side of the Victorian coin is CHURCH RESTORATION, which necessarily followed a distinctive course in the City, due to its concentration of classical church buildings. The medieval churches were naturally re-medievalized in the approved manner, most notably the literal-minded but scholarly campaign of 1841–3 at the Temple Church by *James Savage*, *Sydney Smirke* and *Decimus Burton*. Time's injuries to St Bartholomew-the-Great were made good later in the C19 mostly by *Aston Webb*, with the new parts in a much more

St Michael Cornhill.
Interior as restored by Sir George Gilbert Scott, 1857–60

personal style (1886–98). Classical churches presented different problems to restorers. Until the early 1850s they were treated with remarkable respect: at St Mary-at-Hill (*James Savage*, 1848–9) and St Stephen Walbrook (*John Turner*, 1849–50), the carver *W. Gibbs Rogers* was employed on woodwork very close in spirit to the age of Wren. The City's ecclesiastical heritage is also deliberately evoked in *John Davies*'s rectory in Martin Lane (1851–3), with its steeple-like bell-tower and clock projecting in the c17 manner.

Sir George Gilbert Scott broke this consensus with his transformation of St Michael Cornhill, 1857–60. His new porch is rich Italo-French Gothic, his interior Lombardic, with inserted tracery, polychrome decoration (mostly removed), and a new marble reredos, and carving by *W. Gibbs Rogers*. The church also has the best Victorian

59 stained glass in the City, a powerful sequence by *Clayton & Bell*. Other drastic schemes followed, all at churches destroyed or burnt out in the Second World War: by *Scott* at St Alban Wood Street, 1858–9; by *Woodthorpe* at St Mary Aldermanbury, 1863, and St Swithin, 1869; by *Teulon* at St Andrew Holborn, 1869–72 (though Teulon's Gothic rectory and court house remain there). From *c.* 1870 a gentler approach prevailed, and even so fierce a spirit as *Butterfield* kept most of the fittings in his campaigns at St Clement Eastcheap (1872) and St Mary Woolnoth (1875–6). *Pearson* is represented only by a porch at All Hallows Barking, from work of 1884–95, and by a few fittings surviving from his work at St Helen Bishopsgate (1892–3).

Other architects busy on City church restorations included *Sir Arthur Blomfield* and (especially) *Ewan Christian*, the architect to the Ecclesiastical Commissioners. They and their late Victorian con-temporaries routinely removed all galleries but that at the w, cut 31 down pews, and formed a raised chancel with stalls, but tended not to replace C17–C18 fittings with new ones. St Stephen Walbrook suffered more than most, its pews being replaced with benches by *Alexander Peebles* in 1886–7. Generally new work was confined to stained glass (much of it in itself unusually good) and stencilled or painted decoration, the latter since removed without exception. The most appealing scheme is *Bentley*'s embellishment of St Botolph 54 Aldgate (1888–95), which he transformed with white-painted balus-traded galleries and a graceful plaster angel frieze.

NEW RELIGIOUS ARCHITECTURE was mostly the preserve of non-Anglican faiths. The French Protestants had a Gothic church in St Martin's le Grand, 1842–3, the Greek Orthodox a Neo-Byzantine church in London Wall, 1850, both by *T. O. Owen*, both demolished in the 1880s. The Great Synagogue in Duke's Place, rebuilt in 1852 by *James Wallen*, was destroyed in the Second World War. The largest 62 Nonconformist chapel is *Lockwood & Mawson*'s City Temple in Holborn Viaduct (1873–4, much rebuilt 1955–8), Italian Renaissance, with a tower to one side rather in the Wren manner. Hardly less assertive was *Tarring*'s Congregational Memorial Hall in Farringdon Street, a Gothic pile of 1872–5, demolished *c.* 1970. *George Sherrin*'s Roman Catholic St Mary Moorfields, 1899–1903, is modest by com-parison, the front with the character of street architecture.

The Twentieth Century

The central event of the C20 for the City churches was the Second World War, in which twenty-three of the forty-nine remaining Anglican churches were badly damaged or destroyed. Up to 1940 the process of demolition had continued, mostly at the expense of C18 and C19 build-ings; Wren's All Hallows Lombard Street was demolished for its site value as late as 1938–9, on the condition that its tower be re-erected elsewhere (*see* above). But the Blitz turned the churches into emblems of threatened English civilization, and they were valued more highly thereafter. Only five were wholly written off: the Wren churches of St Stephen Coleman, St Mildred Bread Street, St Swithin Cannon Street and St Mary Aldermanbury (the latter re-erected in the USA), and the little Holy Trinity Minories. Of St Alban and St Augustine only the towers were kept, the latter incorporated into the new St Paul's Cathedral Choir School. The burnt-out shells of Christ

Church Newgate Street and St Dunstan-in-the-East were more fortunate, the steeples being restored and the nave walls used to enclose new public gardens. That at St Dunstan, made 1967–71, is particularly well-planned and attractive. At Christ Church, however, the scandalous demolition of the E wall for road widening in 1974 spoils the effect. The site of St Mary Aldermanbury also became a public garden in which the remaining foundations are displayed.

Two NEW CHURCHES were built for non-Anglican congregations, to replace lost buildings. The destroyed Dutch Church was rebuilt by *Arthur Bailey* (1950–4) as a pleasant, somewhat tame stone-faced structure, uninfluenced by the revolution in planning associated with the Liturgical Movement. It was raised up above a lower hall for secular uses: a plan also followed at the modest Jewin Welsh Church, Fann Street (1956–61 by *Caröe & Partners*).

The most ambitious CHURCH RESTORATION project was the Temple Church, the destroyed aisles and vaults of which *Walter H.* 3, *Godfrey* re-created with scrupulous care in 1947–57. Eleven more 4 severely damaged Anglican parish churches were fully restored. Some benefited from the system of Guild Churches, which aimed to promote or explore particular aspects of the mission of the Church. Even so there is nothing to parallel the innovative reconstructions of bomb-damaged churches in contemporary Germany, a difference which says much about differing national attitudes to the recent past. Only at the medieval All Hallows Barking, restored by *Lord Mottistone* of *Seely & Paget* (completed 1958), was anything drastically new attempted; and even here the concrete-vaulted nave is traditionally detailed, though in a quirky, independent-minded way. Of the Wren churches, the most altered was St Michael Paternoster Royal (by *Elidir Davies*, 1966–8), where the nave was shortened to allow offices to be inserted. *Marshall Sisson*'s reconstruction of St Andrew-by-the-Wardrobe in 1959–61 adopted another solution, putting offices 34 in closed-off aisles beneath the re-created galleries.

The rest are generally faithful to the pre-war architectural details, with the odd exception of St Giles Cripplegate, restored as the parish church of the Barbican Estate by *Godfrey Allen* (completed 1960). Its curious late C18 E end was replaced with one to a medieval pattern, 8 on the strength of evidence located in the wall: an echo of the usual techniques of Victorian church restoration. The other medieval casualty, St Olave Hart Street, responded well to straightforward restoration (by *E. B. Glanfield*, 1951–4). Of the Wren period churches, *Cecil Brown*'s restoration of St Lawrence Jewry as the Corporation's church (1954–7) and *Stephen Dykes Bower*'s collegiate replanning of St Vedast (1953–63) deserve the palm. At the former, new carved fittings in a traditional idiom were provided; at the latter, the architect incorporated Wren-period church fittings saved from C19 demolitions. Dykes Bower's characterful rectory alongside is also worth seeking out. A less successful essay in the collegiate fashion is *Godfrey Allen*'s restoration of St Bride (1955–7), where the galleries were omitted and the aisles screened off to create a space that is too long and narrow. *Seely & Paget*'s restoration of St Andrew Holborn, completed 1961, reinstated the galleries and thereby also the old proportions. Wren's shell was re-created at St Mary-le-Bow and St Nicholas Cole Abbey (respectively by *Laurence King*, 1956–64, and *Arthur*

Bailey, 1961–2), but furnished in each case in a manner wavering indecisively between period imitation and something more decidedly contemporary.

The post-war period also saw enormous advances made in church archaeology, both at sites of churches destroyed in the bombing or in the Great Fire, and in buildings under restoration. The displays in
p. the crypts of All Hallows Barking and (especially) St Bride add
77 immeasurably to the visitor's understanding of the evolution of the parish church plan in London.

CHURCH FURNISHINGS of the period are for the most part tactfully traditional, even when, as at St Lawrence, they do not replicate their predecessors. Otherwise the most inventive work was done in STAINED GLASS, both in restored churches and in others which had lost windows to the bombs. Nowhere else in England can one see such a concentration of good work of the period. *Brian Thomas* supplied dignified, warmly coloured windows for St Vedast and St Andrew Holborn. Comparably strong, intricate designs are achieved
4 at *Carl Edwards*'s E windows at the Temple Church, though their inspiration is early medieval rather than Renaissance. *Max Nauta*'s excellent window at the Dutch Church also stands out. Less powerful colours, clearer, thinner lines, and a preference for areas of clear glass characterize the work of the artists who carried on the pictorial
64 pre-war style: *Christopher Webb* (St Lawrence Jewry), *Lawrence Lee* (St Magnus, 1949–53, and St Mary Aldermary, 1952), *Gerald Smith* (St Sepulchre, 1946 etc.), *M. C. Farrar Bell* (St Botolph Aldersgate,
63 1955–8) and *Hugh Easton* (St Peter upon Cornhill, 1951–60). A more avant-garde school combined strong colours with much bolder leading: an approach vastly more compelling artistically, though undeniably at odds with architecture of the Wren period in particular. Highlights are *John Hayward*'s sequences at St Mary-le-Bow
66 and St Michael Paternoster Royal (1964 and 1968), and *Keith New*'s
65 work at St Nicholas Cole Abbey and All Hallows Barking (1962 and 1964).

Little work of note has been installed since the post-war restoration schemes were completed, so the story can swiftly be brought up to the present. The favourite addition has been figurative sculpture, notably by *Josephina de Vasconcellos* (St Bartholomew-the-Great, *c.* 1990), and *John Robinson* (All Hallows Barking, 1970). The Clayton monument in the same church (†1972), by *Cecil Thomas*, is a very late example of the naturalistic recumbent effigy formula. Abstract and semi-abstract sculpture is represented by a late work in Travertine by *Henry Moore*, the circular altar at St Stephen Walbrook: the
30 centrepiece of a drastic and fiercely contested re-ordering of that church (1978–87, by *Robert Potter*). *Quinlan Terry*'s no less controversial re-ordering of St Helen Bishopsgate (1993–5, after damage from terrorist bombs) has introduced a Neo-Georgian w gallery, but the other new fittings there are not noteworthy. St Ethelburga was partly destroyed in the second of these explosions (1993); it is pleasing to close with the announcement in 1997 of its imminent restoration by *Purcell Miller Tritton*, for use as a Centre for Reconciliation and Peace.

FURTHER READING

The literature concerned with London is vast, and of the works concerned with the City a high proportion have something to say about
the churches. There is space here to do no more than point out the
highlights. For more detailed research, *The Bibliography of Printed
Works on London History to 1939*, edited by Heather Creaton (1994),
lists hundreds of items relevant to individual parishes. The fullest
collection of material relating to the City churches is at the Guildhall
Library, including very strong holdings of prints, drawings and
historic photographs.

   Gerald Cobb, *City of London Churches* (3rd ed. 1989), remains the
best overall survey of the churches and their fittings, including the
medieval period. It also contains a more detailed bibliography than
can be supplied here. The standard history of Saxon and early
medieval London is C.N.L. Brooke and G. Keir, *London 800–1216*
(1975), which also takes account of post-war archaeological dis-
coveries. Many of these are described in more detail by their exca-
vator W.F. Grimes, in his *The Excavation of Roman and Medieval
London* (1968). The early period is also covered by Alan Vince,
Saxon London (1990) and by Martin Biddle in the introduction to
M.D. Lobel (ed.), *The British Atlas of Historic Towns*, vol. 3, *The City
of London* (1989). John Schofield, *The Building of London* (1984, 2nd
ed. 1993) is a succinct account of sacred and secular buildings
between the Conquest and Great Fire, while his article in *Transactions of the London and Middlesex Archaeological Society* 47 (1996)
summarizes what is known of the medieval parish churches. The
British Archaeological Association Conference Transactions for 1984
(1990) contains several important articles, notably those on late
medieval church monuments (Bridget Cherry) and the Temple
Church (C.M.L. Gardam). John Stow's *Survey of London* (1603) is
available in several editions, the best that by C.L. Kingsford (1908,
reprinted 1971). The chief journals for the medieval period are the
Transactions of the London and Middlesex Archaeological Society and
the *London Archaeologist*.

   An unrivalled account of the design and construction of the C17
City churches is Paul Jeffery, *The Parish Churches of Sir Christopher
Wren* (1996), in which will be found a very useful bibliography. The
literature on Wren begins with the *Parentalia* by Stephen Wren
(1750). The *Wren Society*'s volumes (1924–43) include the building
accounts of several churches, many drawings from Wren's office,
and a near-complete sequence of measured drawings made by John
Clayton in the 1840s. Further drawings were published by Sir John
Summerson in *Architectural History* 13 (1970). Books on Wren
include works by Margaret Whinney (1971), Geoffrey Beard (1982),
and Kerry Downes (1982). On Hooke there is a survey by Margaret
Espinasse (1956), on Hawksmoor a monograph by Kerry Downes
(2nd ed. 1979), although neither addresses in detail the intricacies of
their work for Wren's City churches office. For individual architects
H.M. Colvin, *Biographical Dictionary of English Architects 1600–1840*
(3rd ed. 1995), and the *Directory of British Architects 1834–1900* (British
Architectural Library, 1993) should be consulted. For sculptors there

is Rupert Gunnis, *Dictionary of British Sculptors 1660–1851* (3rd ed. forthcoming); for the C16 and early C17 a dictionary is in preparation by Adam White.

Contemporary topographical accounts include Edward Hatton, *A New View of London* (1708) and Strype's revision of Stow's *Survey* (1720). James Elmes's *London in the Nineteenth Century* (1829), available in modern facsimile, illustrates all the City churches, as does G. Godwin and J. Britton, *The Churches of London* (2 vols., 1838), which has in addition more detailed written descriptions. There is also Charles Clarke, *Architectura Ecclesiastica Londini* (1819). John Britton et al., *Illustrations of the Public Buildings of London* (3 vols., 1825–38) contains some good measured drawings. Later books are by A.H. Mackmurdo (1883), G.H. Birch (1896) and T.F. Bumpus (1908). Other general surveys of the churches include the RCHME's volume (1929), the fourth of five volumes covering London, although this excludes anything later than 1714. Colin Amery, *Wren's London* (1988) is a useful collection of historic photographs. Dispersed church fittings are surveyed by R.H. Harrison, in *Transactions of the Ancient Monuments Society*, New Series 8 (1960).

There is no single account of the Victorian period. M.J. Peel, *Bishop Tait and the City Churches 1856–1868* (Ecclesiological Society, 1992) describes the struggles of the hierarchy to speed up the rate of demolition. C. Welch, *A Modern History of the City of London* (1896), is a yearly chronicle with much detail of restorations etc. Andrew Derrick, 'The post-war reconstruction of Wren's City churches', *A.A. Files* 26 (1993), describes and assesses that process.

Studies of particular churches are numerous, many of them excellent. Two are covered by *Survey of London* volumes on their respective parishes: All Hallows Barking (vol. 9, 1924) and St Helen Bishopsgate (vols. 12 and 15, 1929 and 1934). The *Survey* has also produced a monograph on St Bride Fleet Street in its pre-war state (1944). In addition most City churches have detailed published histories. Two notable recent examples are by Paul Jeffery, *The Parish Church of St Vedast-alias-Foster* (2nd ed. 1994), and *The Parish Church of St Mary-at-Hill* (1996), both for the Ecclesiological Society.

Finally one should list guides and surveys suitable for immediate reference: Sir John Betjeman, *The City of London Churches* (2nd ed., 1993); Elizabeth and Wayland Young, *London's Churches* (1986); Melvin Blatch, *A Guide to London's Churches* (2nd ed., 1995); and B.F.L. Clarke, *Parish Churches Of London* (1966). For lost churches there is Gordon Huelin, *Vanished Churches of the City of London* (1996).

VISITING THE CITY CHURCHES

Not every church in the City is in regular use for worship, but most are open to visitors during weekday working hours, and many are used for lunchtime services, talks and concerts. The usual closing time is 4 p.m. Far fewer are open at weekends, although Sunday services are held at churches which retain parochial status. The best days to look at churches from the outside only are Saturday and Sunday, when the streets are largely empty of traffic and crowds. Weekday evenings in high summer are likewise surprisingly peaceful.

Even the most inaccessible interiors are generally visitable through the excellent City Churches Walks organized by the Friends of the City Churches (formed 1994). These usually take place twice a year, on two consecutive weekdays, during which time all the churches open their doors. Concerts, recitals and talks are arranged in conjunction. There is a small registration fee for participants. Most churches also are also kept open during the 'Open House' weekend, held usually in mid-September. Up-to-date information on opening times and services may be obtained from the Friends of the City Churches, at 77 Cowcross Street, London EC1 6BP (tel. 0171 253 3500).

The five following WALKING TOURS cover all the City churches in this book. None should take more than an afternoon, though more time will be needed if all the interiors are to be inspected. The first four tours all begin at the City's hub, by the Bank and Mansion House. They cover the four quarterings lying NE, SE, SW and NW, in that order. In each case the route is out and back, so that any one tour can be followed by any other. The fifth tour covers the area west of the line made by New Bridge Street and Farringdon Street. A double asterisk (**) in the list of churches means that only the tower or tower and shell survive; the number in square brackets after a church is that which represents it on the map pp. 2–3.

FIRST TOUR, NE from the Bank. Most of this area escaped the Great Fire. Only the inner part therefore has churches by Wren (St Michael Cornhill, St Peter, St Margaret Lothbury). The remainder are mostly medieval or C18, apart from the three non-Anglican buildings: the Bevis Marks synagogue, the Dutch Church, and the Roman Catholic church of St Mary Moorfields. The last of these may be omitted to shorten the walk.

St Michael Cornhill [39] – St Peter upon Cornhill [44] – St Andrew Undershaft [8] – St Katharine Cree [27] – St Botolph Aldgate [16] – Bevis Marks Synagogue [53] – St Helen Bishopsgate [25] – St Ethelburga [23] – St Botolph Bishopsgate [17] – All Hallows London Wall [2] – St Mary Moorfields [49] – Dutch Church [51] – St Margaret Lothbury [30].

SECOND TOUR, SE from the Bank. Mostly Wren churches, apart from Hawksmoor's St Mary Woolnoth. The easternmost leg takes in two medieval churches, neither surviving entire: the restored All Hallows Barking, and All Hallows Staining.

St Mary Woolnoth [38] – St Mary Abchurch [33] – St Clement
Eastcheap [19] – St Magnus the Martyr [29] – St Mary-at-Hill
[36] – St Dunstan-in-the-East** [20] – All Hallows Barking [1] –
All Hallows Staining** [3] – St Margaret Pattens [31] – St
Edmund the King [22].

THIRD TOUR, SW from the Bank. All by Wren or his office, the
entire area having been burnt in the Great Fire. The late spires of
the first three churches make an interesting study. The penulti-
mate leg skirts the S flank of St Paul's.

St Stephen Walbrook [46] – St Michael Paternoster Royal [40] –
St James Garlickhithe [26] – St Mary Somerset** [37] – St Benet
Paul's Wharf [14] – St Andrew-by-the-Wardrobe [9] – St Martin
Ludgate [32] – St Nicholas Cole Abbey [41] – St Mary Aldermary
[34].

FOURTH TOUR, NW from the Bank. The longest and necessarily
most circuitous tour, taking in several Wren churches as well as
the medieval churches NW and N of the reach of the Great Fire. A
full six churches do not survive intact. The tour may be shortened
considerably by omitting the Jewin Welsh Church, which is anyway of minor interest.

St Mary-le-Bow [35] – St Augustine Watling Street** [11] – St
Vedast alias Foster [47] – Christ Church Newgate Street** [4] –
St Sepulchre [45] – St Bartholomew-the-Less [13] – St
Bartholomew-the-Great [12] – St Botolph Aldersgate [15] – St
Anne and St Agnes [10] – St Giles Cripplegate [24] – Jewin Welsh
Church [52] – St Alphage London Wall** [6] – St Alban Wood
Street** [5] – St Lawrence Jewry [28] – St Olave Jewry**[43].

FIFTH TOUR, W of Farringdon Street and New Bridge Street. Here
there are fewer churches, standing further apart. City Thameslink
station is a good starting-point and can be reached easily again at
the end of the tour via its northern exit in Holborn Viaduct.

St Bride [18] – St Dunstan-in-the-West [21] – Temple Church
[48] – St Andrew Holborn [7] – City Temple [50].

THE CITY CHURCHES

ALL HALLOWS BARKING
Great Tower Street

First mentioned 1086 as a daughter church of Barking Abbey, Essex. All Hallows is the only London church with standing fabric of Anglo-Saxon vintage (*see* below and Introduction p. 17), revealed by the same severe bomb damage that made necessary the drastic post-war reconstruction by *Lord Mottistone* of *Seely & Paget* (N aisle opened 1949; re-dedication 1957). Other survivals are apparent from outside: C15 aisle walls and NW wall, mid-C17 W tower, and NW porch from *Pearson*'s late C19 restoration.

The C15 aisles have three-light windows with pointed lights under depressed arches. Above rises a new Perp clerestory and E wall of brick. The latter's gable and lacy parapet are based on the Great Hall at Hampton Court. On the gable a relief carved by *Cecil Thomas* of the lamp of the Toc H organization, founded by All Hallows' former rector 'Tubby' Clayton. W tower, also of brick and at an angle to the rest of the church, of 1658–9: a rare period (*Samuel Twine*, bricklayer). Very humble and plain, with the simplest string-courses and round-headed openings. Over the W door the typical artisan's device of a little *œil-de-bœuf* window in a rectangular panel. The stone cornice and spiritedly Baroque copper-clad spire, added in 1958, give the tower a posthumous late-Wren flavour, and make it an important landmark in views from E and W. A square ogee-topped cupola crowned the tower until 1940. Early C18 views suggest the C17 parapet was crenellated. *Aitchison* made unexecuted designs in 1863 for a new French Gothic W end with a sturdy SW tower and spire (drawings in City of London Record Office). Two-storey Perp NW porch and vestry of stone, hard-edged, added by *Pearson* during restoration of 1884–95 to face the newly-made Byward Street (carver *Nathaniel Hitch*). Together with the W wall of the C15 N aisle, the steeple, and the plain post-war SW vestry, it gives the church a very picturesque W aspect. A new parish centre by *John Phillips*, partly underground, is planned for the SE corner of the churchyard (1996).

The nave INTERIOR was courageously reconstructed by *Lord Mottistone* to a new design, with a cross-ribbed free Perp vault of fine grey concrete. Odd Carolean–Baroque-detailed beams like gallery fronts span the intervals between the limestone-faced piers, saving it from starkness. The church had received aisles *c.* 1230–40. Until 1940 two W bays survived, with circular piers and double-chamfered arches. Some fragments remain, assembled in the undercroft. The clerestory and E parts of the former arcades were C15, the date also of the rood stair and loft doors in the surviving N wall. Part of the tiled medieval floor is exposed nearby. In the C14 the chancel was rebuilt and possibly extended, and a SE chapel added; its CRYPT survived the rebuilding of the S aisle and may be inspected (now the Chapel of St Francis). Stone tunnel-vault with single-chamfered transverse arches, an unusual motif. Blocked windows in the S wall. Here is displayed a Byzantine RELIEF of two peacocks with a foliage border, of high quality. NW of the crypt, two C17 or C18 burial vaults.

REMAINS OF THE SAXON CHURCH. Destruction by bombing of most of All Hallows' nave in the Second World War exposed standing Anglo-Saxon fabric at the W end. Initially this was dated to the C7–C8, i.e. not long after All Hallows' mother house at Barking Abbey, Essex (founded *c.* 660–70); but an C11 date is now preferred, from comparisons with several other excavated City churches. The remains consist of a NW quoin of Roman bricks, visible from a first-floor vestry, and a section of wall at the SW, pierced by an arch. By the C16 this opened into a SW tower, as shown in Wyngaerde's view of *c.* 1540 (could this have been heightened from a two-storey *porticus* or side chamber?) Its voussoirs are also of Roman brick, used here in a single order (cf. Brixworth, Northants). More Roman brick in the jambs, mixed with squared rubble. In the crypt remains have also been found of an E wall of early date, which suggests a length of some 70 ft (21 metres) for the Saxon church. Remains of a second wall some 30 ft (9 metres) further E probably date from a C13 extension.

The lengthy main UNDERCROFT, excavated by Mottistone, is entered beneath the tower. In it are displayed the remains of two TESSELLATED PAVEMENTS from a C3 or early C4 Roman house. One remains *in situ* between the tower's Saxon foundations. The other has been relaid in modern times as part of the crypt floor. – Also displayed here, fragments of three SAXON CROSSES found after the bombing. The first is the head with a cross in a circle and an inscription. Experts date it *c.* 1000. The name 'Werhenworth' appears on the second, sculptured cross, which is the most important Saxon survival of its date in London (*c.* 1030–60). Remains of figures indicate a standing Christ (as at Ruthwell in Dumfries and Galloway and Bewcastle, Cumberland), a man with tied legs, and two men side by side. There are also addorsed beasts and interlacings. The third fragment is in the early C11 Ringerike style, but almost certainly carved locally. On the back is part of a stylized lion (cf. the St Paul's grave slab in the Museum of London). – At the E end, a medieval ALTAR TABLE of stone from Chastiau Pelerin, the Crusaders' castle at Atlit below Mount Carmel, in Israel.

OTHER FITTINGS are a mixture of original, new and second-hand pieces. – PULPIT from St Swithin Cannon Street, *c.* 1682. Panels with thick garlands and heavy segmental pediments. Enormous tester like a flat bracket fungus, by *Lord Mottistone*. – FONT COVER. 41 1682, attributed uncontestedly to *Grinling Gibbons*; one of the finest of the period, exquisitely carved in the round with cherubs, leaves, flowers, wheat-ears, fir-cones etc., wholly unlike the usual late C17 architectural formulae. It stands with its plain post-war FONT in a baptistery made in the SW vestry. – ORGAN. By *Harrison & Harrison*, 1957. The white-painted case copies that of Renatus Harris's instrument, destroyed in 1940. – ROYAL ARMS. Late C17; larger than usual. – Carved COMMUNION TABLE and brass COMMUNION RAILS, after late C17 and C18 fittings destroyed in the war. – C16

COMMUNION TABLE (N chapel). – Wrought-iron SWORD RESTS of 1727, 1755 and 1760. All larger and richer than average, that of 1755 extraordinarily so. – The post-war LECTERN incorporates wrought-iron rails of *c.* 1705 and a carved panel from the former Jacobean pulpit. – PAINTINGS. Main altarpiece, Last Supper by *Brian Thomas*, *c.* 1957. – N chapel altarpiece with four late C15 Flemish panels of good quality. From the Royal Lady Chapel N of the church, founded by Richard I and made collegiate in the C15. It may have been a separate building, or else have been subsumed into the present church in the C15 rebuilding. – ALMS BOX of brass on a fluted pedestal, dated 1787. From Christ's Hospital. – SCULPTURE. Small wooden figures of St James of Compostela (C15, nave), St Roche (*c.* 1520, nave), and St Anthony of Egypt (C16, rood stair door). Two works by *John Robinson*, 1970: a bronze group called Mother Love, SW corner; bust of Christ, baptistery. – STAINED GLASS. Heraldic glass by *Farrar Bell & Sons*, 1948–58. – Baptistery windows by *Keith New*, excellent work of 1964. – CURIOSA. Several large model ships suspended in the S aisle.

MONUMENTS. Alderman John Croke †1477, an important piece. Tomb-chest below canopy with two straight-sided depressed arches towards the front and a straight cresting. Fan-vault with pendants beneath. The Purbeck carving is less standardized than average for the date. Two brasses of kneeling groups remain on the back. The tomb serves as a receptacle for the TOC H LAMP, a delicate Arts-and-Crafts gilt piece by *Alec Smithers*, 1923. – Jerome Benali †1583–4, kneeling figure in pilastered frame. – Francis Covell †1621 and wife †1643–4. Figures only, reset. – Giles Lytcott †1696, wife, son and son's wife. Monument in the form of a column, flanked by putti. – Also in the form of a column, and also with a few putti, the Winder Monument (†1699 and †1717). – Toc H Memorials: two tomb-chests with recumbent bronze figures by *Cecil Thomas*, of the Hon. Alfred Forster, 1926, and the Rev. Clayton, 1972. – BRASSES in the chancel and N chapel, the fullest series in the City. In 1643 some had 'superstitious' texts defaced. William Tonge †1389, shield and circular inscription only. – John Bacon †1437 and wife, 2 ft figures with interlaced scrolls (N chapel). – Alderman John Croke, *see* above. – Thomas Gilbert †1483, tablet only. – Resurrection with soldiers, arched late C15 panel, from a late C15 canopied altar tomb destroyed in 1940, probably used as an Easter Sepulchre. – John Rusche †1498, 3 ft figure. – Christopher Rawson †1518 and two wives, 19 in. figures. – Andrew Evyngar †1533. An important Flemish panel, 33 in. long, with husband and wife, children behind and Pietà above (a similar brass formerly at St Mary at the Quay, Ipswich, is in the museum collections of Ipswich Borough Council). – William Thynne †1546 and wife, 30 in. figures – William Armar †1560, brass plate with kneeling figures. – Roger James †1591, 3 ft figure.

ALL HALLOWS LONDON WALL

1765–7, *George Dance the Younger*'s first building. It replaced a medieval church first recorded *c.* 1130 on the same site up against the City wall. The N wall of Dance's church indeed rests on the

p. 18

wall's Roman foundations, the semicircular vestry on those of one of the bastions.* Simple exterior but exquisite interior, an important inspiration to Dance's pupil, Soane. Brick, narrow, made more imposing by being raised up on a crypt. Placed so that the s side, with three semicircular windows high up, flanks London Wall, the projecting apse remains visible, and the w front faces a small church-yard. The ashlar-faced w tower projects beyond the body of the church. Steps up to a Tuscan doorway with frieze and pediment. Plain round-arched bell-stage with corner piers. Circular domed cupola above, more delicate, with the entablature broken out over a ring of Corinthian columns. The St Paul's-pattern cross and ball were added by *Blomfield*, 1898.

52   The interior shows a restraint in number and thickness of motifs unprecedented in England and doubly remarkable if one considers that Dance was twenty-four when he designed the church. No aisles, just the nave and a diagonally coffered apse. Fluted Ionic columns placed against the outer walls carry the semicircular tunnel-vault of the nave. Minimal entablature, no more than an enriched Antique frieze. The vault itself has no projecting transverse arches, just even, shallow coffering, so that the display of carrying is further reduced. The only lighting is from the three semicircular windows piercing the tunnel-vault between the columns. The decoration of the apse derives from the Temple of Venus and Rome (DF). While Dance's later buildings were sparing in their use of Antique motifs, we can recognize here the Neoclassical desire to follow the Ancients more faithfully. But it is the restraint of the detail, the emphasis on purity of spatial expression, and such features as the radical elision of the architrave that most clearly point forward to Soane. Sir John Summerson's theory that this elision betrays the influence of Laugier's Rationalist theories has been challenged by Giles Worsley, who points out that Soane's lectures identify the source in Dance's direct observation of Roman buildings.

The FURNISHINGS were altered in 1890–1, first by *Carpenter & Ingelow*, then by *Blomfield*, and again in 1960–2 by *David Nye*, who restored the church after war damage. Until 1994 the church served as the headquarters and library of the Council for the Care of Churches. – REREDOS. Large oil painting of Acts IX by *Sir Nathaniel Dance-Holland*, after Pietro da Cortona; presented by the younger Dance, the artist's brother. Fine original frame. – W GALLERY on Tuscan columns. – Simple PULPIT, reached from the vestry via a pedimented doorway in the N wall. The pulpit stands mid-way between apse and gallery. – FONT. Late C17 bowl from St Mary Magdalen Old Fish Street, on a baluster of 1902. – FONT COVER by *David Nye*; also the ALTAR, SCREENS etc. – STALLS by *Nye*, reusing *Blomfield*'s, in turn cut down from *Dance*'s pews which rose to dado level. – ROYAL ARMS probably c. 1700, repainted. – RAILINGS of iron, reusing *Goodall*'s communion rails of 1766. – ORGAN by *Noel Mander*, 1962, in a case of c. 1880 by *Hill*, from the Manor House, Highbury. – CHANDELIER by *Lukyn Betts*, 1766 (its counterpart made 1995–6: DF). – SWORD REST of iron, 1753. From All Hallows Staining. – MONUMENTS. Edmond Hammond

---

*Curious late C18 Gothick trimmings, added to make the vestry an ornamental feature to gardens formerly lying N, were demolished in 1905.

†1642, with strapwork. Attributed to *John & Matthias Christmas* (GF).– Joan Bence †1684, cartouche attributed to *Jasper Latham* 48 (GF). – Joseph Patience, architect, †1797. By *Thomas Patience*. Bust on a plinth with circular relief, set on a sarcophagus.

At the E, PARISH HALL of brick (altered), by *H. I. Newton*, 1902, on the site of Dance's rectory. It sheltered poorer workers who arrived on cheap early morning 'Parliamentary' trains, as they waited for their workplaces to open. To the W of the W end, a stretch of the medieval CITY WALL is incorporated in the churchyard wall, over-shadowed by trees.

ALL HALLOWS STAINING
Mark Lane

Pulled down in 1870 except for the humble and much-restored medieval W tower, now standing between the Clothworkers' Hall, W, and the N wall of the offices called Minster Court. The church is recorded by the late C12. The tower's lowest stage may be of this date, though the earliest firmly datable feature is the early C14 cinquefoiled two-light W window. Of the same period the blocked E and S arches, best seen from inside. The NW stair turret, late C14 or C15, seems formerly to have extended to a vanished top stage (shown on the C16 copperplate map. *See* Introduction p. 21). The church was a nondescript mixture of medieval work and repairs of 1674–5. The tower was saved on the initiative of the Clothworkers' Company and restored in 1873.

In 1872–3 two bays of a C12 CRYPT, from the former Lambe's Chapel in Monkwell Street near Cripplegate, were added below the ground to the E. That chapel was established in the late C16 by William Lambe of the Clothworkers' Company in the buildings of a former hermitage called St James-in-the-Wall. This was first recorded in 1189, but the crypt's details suggest a date *c.* 1140: low column-responds with lobed volute capitals, moulded ribs with zigzag or spiral ornament.

CHRIST CHURCH NEWGATE STREET

The tower and part of the bombed shell of *Wren*'s church remain, on the site of the chancel of the Franciscan (Greyfriars) church, established 1225 and rebuilt from 1306. It was the second largest church of medieval London at 300 ft (91 metres) by 89 ft (27 metres). The former nave is marked by an avenue of trees to the W. The old chancel was made parochial in 1547, superseding the nearby churches of St Nicholas Shambles and St Audoen or Ewin, in connection with the foundation of Christ's Hospital to the N. This moved away in 1902. *Wren* rebuilt the church in 1677–87, shortening it at the W (masons *John Shorthose* and *Richard Crooke*).

The tower stands forward of the W wall. It is one of the most splendid in London. Above the first cornice, the bell-stage has louvres divided by pilasters, crowned by segmental pediments and a balustrade.

Everything above was added 1703–4 (mason *Edward Strong Jun.*). Recessed next stage, also square, ending in an even free-standing colonnade. Twelve big urns on top, from *Lord Mottistone*'s restoration of the shell in 1960, replacing (albeit in concrete) those removed in 1814. Rising out of them a dainty square pierced spire with vase and ball finial. The solution can be called a square version of St Mary-le-Bow. Neo-Georgian brick offices attached at the sw, by *Seely & Paget Partnership*, 1981, imitate a vestry of 1760 formerly on this site.

In front lie fragments of stone pineapples etc. from the old walls, partly demolished for road widening at the E end in 1974. Wren's reuse of the lower stages of the medieval walls and the foundations of the pier bases was revealed here in 1976. His w and E walls had the unusual feature of buttresses in line with the aisle colonnades, as if he did not fully trust these old foundations. The N wall and part of the s remain, with quoins and round-headed windows. Nave and aisles, the former groin-vaulted on Composite columns, the latter flat-ceilinged, disappeared in the Second World War. The magnificent plasterwork (by *Doogood*) went with them. The interior was notable otherwise for its exceptional breadth and for its steeply-raked galleries to accommodate the boys of Christ's Hospital. A GARDEN made in 1989 fills the truncated shell. Pergolas mark the positions of the piers.

ST ALBAN WOOD STREET

Wren's correct Perpendicular Gothic tower stands in the middle of the roadway. Restored 1964; in 1984–5 converted into a house by *Frederick Burn, Smith & Partners*. It stood within the NW corner of the church, built 1682–5, the bomb-damaged shell demolished 1955. The tower dates from 1682–7 (first two stages) and 1687–8 (remainder). The mason of both phases was *Samuel Fulkes*. It has flat angle buttresses and another buttress in the centre of each side. They die back into the tower above the level of the belfry aperture imposts. On the N and W sides the central buttresses rise from grotesque mask-corbels. They mark the height of the lost church. Two windows on each side on each tier, bell-openings of two lights, and small cusped circular apertures. The weak pinnacles were renewed in 1878, in a different stone.

St Alban's is documented as early as *c.* 1085, but excavation in 1962 revealed remains probably of an even earlier church. This had a w tower, rectangular nave and square-ended chancel, the latter parts butt-jointed but of similar construction and probably conceived as a whole. While not inconsistent with an C11 date, they may have been the remains of the late C8 chapel of King Offa, identified as the ancestor of St Alban by the chronicler Matthew Paris. To this were added N and s chapels, later extended into aisles. Later still a NE chapel was built. The outer walls were reconstructed in the C17, but attribution of their forms is difficult, for the burnt-out medieval shell which Wren restored had itself been rebuilt in 1633–4 (master mason *Edmund Kinsman*, carpenter *Matthew Banckes Sen.*). According to Strype, Inigo Jones was one of a party which surveyed the old church; but no connection with the rebuilding is proven, though Kinsman did much work for Jones elsewhere. The aisle windows had the odd tracery of the C17, but the piers inside were of the accepted four-shafts-four-hollows variety. Wren gave the church star-shaped plaster lierne-vaults. Apse added by *Scott*, who restored the church in 1858–9.

ST ALPHAGE LONDON WALL

The shells of the C14 crossing tower and N transept, gutted by bombing, are visible from the pedestrian walk on the N side of London Wall. They are the remains of the priory church of Elsing Spital, founded 1331 as a hospital for the blind staffed by secular priests, and taken over by Augustinian Canons in 1340. Walls mostly of flint with some rubble. Two tall plain arches to W and N. Similar but lower arch in the N transept W wall. The E crossing arch is also lower, of three orders with quarter-round mouldings, framing a segment-headed doorway with a cusped niche on the inside. This may have screened the canons' chapel to its E from the hospital space, which was possibly in the 'nave' itself. The rest, demolished in 1923, comprised work of 1775–7 by *William Hillyer*, with a pedimented E front to the old line of Aldermanbury, and a lesser front on to London Wall, N (Gothicized by *Henry Ling*, 1914).

The old parish church proper, abandoned at the Reformation in favour of the vacated priory, was built on the line of the CITY WALL to the N (cf. All Hallows London Wall). Chequerwork masonry from this church, probably C14, remains on the surviving section, N face.

ST ANDREW HOLBORN
Holborn Viaduct

King Edgar's renewal of the Charter of Westminster Abbey, *c.* 959, mentions a St Andrew's Church of timber here. The mid-C15 fabric of its successor stood outside the area burned by the Great Fire, but became ruinous and was rebuilt 1684–6 by *Wren*, the largest of his City churches (*Edward Pierce* and *William Stanton*, masons, *John Longland*, carpenter, *Robert Dyer*, plasterer). Accounts published in *Wren Soc.* Vol. X contain references confirming Wren's authorship. Gutted in 1941 and restored by *Seely & Paget* (reopened 1961).

Wren preserved the C15 tower, but refaced it in 1703–4, retaining the angle buttresses and pointed lower windows. Hollow-chamfered pointed arches survive within it, on W, N and S. At the same time the top stage with its bulbous pinnacles with vases was added, each 24 crowned until the Second World War with a weathervane. The large upper windows are remarkable. A shallow open segmental pediment on pilasters with fluted capitals is placed within a round-headed frame: a deliberate discord. In the tympanum is an oval opening. The cornice above has pairs of deep brackets at each end, instead of Wren's usual even modillions or dentils. In all this the hand of *Hawksmoor* may be suspected. On the W front, facing a garden made

in 1970, STATUES of schoolchildren from the former Parish School
in Hatton Garden, built 1696.

The church itself is evenly treated to suit its island site. Stone-
faced, aisled and balustraded, of seven bays. Round-headed windows,
set over segmental ones in the central five bays, over pedimented
doorways in the end bays. Low NW and SW vestibules, like those at
St Clement Danes, Westminster (1680–2), where Wren also kept the
medieval tower. The NE and SE bays house vestries. The C20 restorers faithfully re-created the lofty barrel-vaulted interior, with
its groin-vaults over the aisles on Corinthian columns rising from
the gallery fronts. Two-storeyed Venetian window in the shallow
chancel. All these features appear at Wren's St James Piccadilly
(1676–82), save only that St James's aisles have transverse barrel-
vaults. The circular skylight over the chancel was probably first
made in alterations by *J. H. Good*, 1818. The excessive gilding dates
from 1975. St Andrew is now the headquarters church of the Royal
College of Organists.

FURNISHINGS. Nothing remains from *Teulon's* restoration of
1869–72. The replacement font, pulpit and organ come from the
Foundling Hospital (*see London 4: North*). – FONT. Presented to the
Hospital in 1804. Slender stone baluster with small basin. – PULPIT.
Mid C19, on an absurdly short Corinthian column. The body is
characteristically Victorian in that it reverts to an earlier type of
arched panels. – ORGAN by *Noel Mander*, 1990, within the modest
Kentian CASE given by Handel in 1750, perhaps designed by the
Hospital's architect *Theodore Jacobsen* (lower parts re-created to the
C18 design by *Julian Harrap*, 1990). – REREDOS, after the pre-war
piece, and other fittings by *Seely & Paget*. – CHANDELIERS of 1977.
– STAINED GLASS. E window, Last Supper and Ascension, by *Brian
Thomas*, 1961, red and green to match the painting of the plasterwork. – More glass by *Thomas* in the NW CHAPEL, reached from
beneath the tower. Here, ALTAR RAILS and part of the REREDOS
from St Luke Old Street (*see London 4*), *c*. 1733. – MONUMENTS.
Captain Thomas Coram, the founder of the Foundling Hospital,
†1751. A mere plain chest. Above it a standing weeping putto and
wall-mounted heads, from the former Manningham monument
(†1722). – William Mellish †1690 and wife †1702, NW chapel. Black
and white marble tablet carved with stiff swags of fruit and cherubs'
heads, by *William Stanton*. Brought in 1993 from the redundant St
Leonard, Ragnall, Notts. – SCULPTURE. Stone slab of the Last
Judgement, C17, on the N wall facing the former churchyard. Said to
come from the former burying ground of the workhouse in Shoe
Lane. Small figures; innumerable bodies climbing out of their
graves. Christ above as in an Ascension. – GATE PIERS. Made
c. 1870, with steps down from Holborn Viaduct. Good wrought-iron
GATES, which were apparently made post-war.

RECTORY, COURT HOUSE and VESTRY CLERK'S OFFICE to the
S, built around a courtyard in 1868–71 by *Teulon*. They replaced
buildings lost to the new St Andrew Street. Plain stock brick Gothic
with stone dressings, all on a modest scale and looking singularly
humble against Wren's church. The circular stair-tower with its
conical spire marks the staircase to the Court House, distinguished
by its big three-light traceried windows. Interiors with typical tough

Teulon forms: Gothic fireplaces, Rectory staircase (E) with timber screen, etc. (Court Room with hammerbeam roof with affinities to Teulon's church designs. Restored by *David Gazeley*, 1994, in poly-chromatic High Victorian Gothic style. Here a grandiose early C17 fireplace and overmantel from the previous Court House. Stuart arms in the centre, carved figures of Saints in flanking niches, with, below them, small reliefs from scripture. Terms flank the fireplace proper.) Also by *Teulon* the endearing little LODGE, with a big central chimneystack, at the courtyard entrance.

ST ANDREW UNDERSHAFT
Leadenhall Street and St Mary Axe

A regular aisled Perp building with a shallow chancel, entered through a tower set to one side at the SW: all features typical of the medieval City church in its final development. The name comes from the shaft of the maypole, set up opposite every year until 1517 and destroyed as an 'Idoll' in 1547 (Stow). The church is first mentioned in the early C12. C15 SW tower with NW stair turret. Upper stage of 1695, altered 1883 by *T. Chatfeild Clarke* who added the spiky pinnacles and turret. Restored S doorway, square-headed, of two orders with wave mouldings and panelling above, C15 or C16 (original panelled DOOR, with ironwork). All the rest was rebuilt 1520–32, at the expense first of Lord Mayor Sir Stephen Jennings (†1524), then of William Fitzwilliams. This part is of good, even squared ragstone with a plinth, best seen on the N side. Rendered E parts and S wall, the latter hidden by buildings on Leadenhall Street. Grander and loftier inside than the exterior suggests, though plain and somewhat dry in the details. Nave and aisles of six bays, the chancel unmarked by any structural division. Arcades with depressed arches on slim piers of the familiar four-shaft-four-hollow section, with capitals only to the shafts. Four-light aisle windows and three-light clerestory windows. Tracery only in the large, restored E and W windows, of five lights, mullioned and transomed. The S arcade stands free of the tower, so that the interior is wholly regular and the clerestory uninterrupted. A blocked light in the tower's E face, towards the S aisle, indicates that this was an external wall before the aisle was added. Blocked doorway in the N aisle wall to the former rood stair, which is housed in an external turret. Nave roof with main ribs on small curved braces and little corbels; faithfully renewed 1949–50 reusing C16 bosses. N aisle roof, C16. Moulded ribs form squares, each subdivided into four further squares. Square bosses of angels with shields. NE VESTRIES: late C17, E, with stone-built W addition by *Clarke*, 1883.

FITTINGS are of a mixture of periods (restorations 1704; 1875–6 by *E. Christian* and *A. Blomfield*, who made the low-walled chancel; Blomfield's brother was rector here). (In store in 1997: two SWORD RESTS, C18, one from All Hallows Staining, Mark Lane, dated 1722; BENCHES, late C18, with painted figures of St Andrew.) – FONT. By *Nicholas Stone*, 1631. Simple octagonal bowl of white marble on a black marble baluster stem. The derivation of the post-Fire type from such designs is clear. FONT COVER, C17, but later than the font. – FONT RAILS with twisted balusters, perhaps made from 1630s communion rails. – PULPIT. Late C17, above average, with unusual circular marquetry panels. On it brass CANDLESTICKS with figures of St Andrew. – DOORCASES to N and S, pedimented with engaged columns, probably of 1704. On the N one a domestic-looking late C18 CLOCK by *E. Pistor*, from the former W gallery. – Carved Gothic REREDOS of 1830. – Wrought-iron COMMUNION RAIL by *Tijou*, 1704. – ORGAN. By *Renatus Harris*, 1695–6 (altered 1749–50, 1858, etc.). Excellent CASE with two seated angels on the convex-curved top. Blomfield crammed it into the S arcade, lopping off the finials (two carved mitres reset on the side). – PAINTINGS. In the spandrels of the arcade, scenes in grisaille from the Life of Christ. By *Robert Brown*, probably of 1725–6. Brown's figures of the Apostles between the clerestory windows have gone. – STAINED GLASS. The important C17 W window was alas largely destroyed by the terrorist bomb of 1992. In its five lights were figures of monarchs between Edward VI and William III; the latter suggesting a date *c.* 1690–1700. According to Dennis Corble, however, it was given by Sir Christopher Clitherow (†1642) and the last figure was a later addition. The tracery lights survive in the restored window (1996), which has shields instead of figures. – E window. Noble Crucifixion and Ascension by *Heaton, Butler & Bayne*, 1875–6. – Aisles. Heraldic glass in the heads of *c.* 1530 commemorates donors to the rebuilding. It is the City's oldest intact group of stained glass. – MONUMENTS. In the N aisle older monuments, including several Lord Mayors. Brass to Nicholas Leveson †1539, wife and children. Groups of kneeling figures. – Sir Thomas Offley †1582 (chancel). Kneeling figures facing one another across a prayer desk, in an enriched frame with columns. Attributed to *Cornelius Cure* (GF). – Simon Burton †1593. Brass plate in stone frame. – John Stow †1605, author of the *Survey of London*. An early example of a full-length upright figure, but shown stiffly seated at a table and writing in the Elizabethan scholarly tradition. Flanked by square pillars with ribbonwork etc. Perhaps by *Nicholas Johnson*. – Alice Byng †1616, with little kneeling figure. – Sir Hugh Hamersley †1636. Large and impressive wall-monument with kneeling figures under curtains. Two soldiers representing the Honourable Artillery Company stand outside the flanking columns. Female figures recline on half-pediments above. Said to be by *Thomas Madden* (AW). – Anthony Abdy †1640, signed *Henry Boughton* (W end). – Sir Christopher Clitherow and family †1642–62, with rustic cornucopia. – W. Innes †1795, with portrait relief. – S aisle. Margery Turner †1607. – Edward Warner †1628, with columns, attributed to *Stone* (AW). – Many good cartouches. The best are: J. Jeffreys †1688, attributed to *Thomas Cartwright Sen.* (GF). – Charles Thorold †1691, convex, signed by *T. Cartwright Sen.* – Peter Vansittart †1705, big and wonderfully rich, with well-carved skulls, garlands and cherubs' heads, high up. Attributed to *Thomas Cartwright Jun.* (GF). – Others apparently also by the *Cartwrights* (e.g. H. Sykes †1710). – Two more C17 monuments are hidden by the organ.

ST ANDREW-BY-THE-WARDROBE
Queen Victoria Street

Known from *c.* 1170. The Wardrobe was the stores department of the Crown (including arms and clothing), transferred from the Tower to a site nearby in the mid C14, and destroyed in 1666. The church was rebuilt in 1685–94 by *Wren*, gutted in 1940, and restored by *Marshall Sisson* in 1959–61. Wren's craftsmen were *Nicholas Young*, mason, *Thomas Horn*, bricklayer, *John Longland*, carpenter, and *Henry Doogood*, plasterer.

The church presides dramatically over the street behind a terraced churchyard. Very plain red brick, much patched, with quoins (but Hatton (1708) found it 'finished or rendered over in imitation of stone'). Round-headed windows above, segmental-headed below. The SW tower projects beyond the body of the church. It is square, of four stages, with a straight top. On the uppermost angles plain piers instead of quoins; weathervane from St Michael Bassishaw, 1712. Removed in 1959–61 were embellishments to bell-stage and parapet by *Thomas Garner*, *c.* 1875, and all but the pediment of an ornamental s portal of 1902. This entrance was moved *c.* 1824 from the adjacent bay to the E. Garner's balustrade on the tower survives, replacing Wren's parapet, which had circular piercings. The churchyard wall with urns and wrought-iron gates was made in 1901 as a memorial to Professor Banister Fletcher, probably by his son *Sir Banister*. Crucifix by *Walter Tapper*.

The interior is aisled, with five regular arcaded bays on piers 34 instead of the usual columns. Tunnel-vaulted nave divided into bays with circular plaster wreaths, groin-vaulted aisles. In the restoration the plasterwork, piers and gallery fronts were re-created, but the aisles have been divided off on the ground floor by solid panelling, and are used as chapel, vestries and offices. The Redundant Churches Fund and Ancient Monuments Society had offices within the church until 1991.

FURNISHINGS. The parish was a poor one, and, exceptionally, the C17 fittings were financed by the Coal Dues. All were destroyed in 1940 except a sword rest and two monuments. The replacements have been steadily assembled from various sources. – PULPIT (with stem and stairs of 1966), FONT and FONT COVER all by *Edward Pierce*, made for St Matthew Friday Street. – New REREDOS designed by *Arthur Ayres*, different from its predecessor but incorporating some old work. – ROYAL ARMS of *c.* 1685, over the tower doorway, from St Olave Jewry. – CHAMBER ORGAN in w gallery, made by *Snetzler* for Teddesley Hall, Shropshire, 1769. – SANCTUARY CHAIR of 1687. – SCULPTURE. Two small wooden figures: St Anne, North Italian of *c.* 1500, holding a small group of Virgin and Child; St Andrew, *c.* 1600. – In the w gallery, memorial RELIEFS to Shakespeare and Dowland, designed by *Peter Foster*, carved by *Paul A. Cooper*, *c.* 1990. – SWORD REST, early C18. – Brass CHANDELIERS, early C18. – STAINED GLASS. w window: Conversion of St Paul, an early work by *Joshua Price*, *c.* 1712–16, after a painting 46 by *Sebastiano Ricci*; made for Bulstrode Park, Buckinghamshire. Painted in enamel stains, the style with strange reminiscences of Giulio Romano. – s aisle windows by *Carl Edwards*, 1968. – MONU-

MENT. Rev. Saunders †1836, by *Samuel Manning* (w gallery). Obelisk with relief of angels bearing him upwards.

ST ANNE AND ST AGNES
Gresham Street

Known by the early C12, as St Agnes. In medieval times both names were used, though at first not together, and the present dedication is unique. Rebuilt after the fire in brick by *Wren* who is named in the accounts as supplying the design, though *Hooke* has also been suggested as designer and certainly made several visits to the site. Built 1677–87, the bulk of work done by 1681. The bricklayer was *John Fitch*; other craftsmen *Robert Walters* and *William Hammond*, masons, *John Hayward*, carpenter, *John Sherwood*, plasterer, and *Thomas Dobbins*, plumber. The parish employed the joiners *Cheltenham* (a parishioner), *Fuller* and *Page* for the fittings. Restored by *Braddock & Martin Smith* in 1963–8 after war damage, and now used by the Lutherans. Before the war it was visible only through a narrow gap in the buildings of Gresham Street, but land s and E of its churchyard has been cleared and a garden made with low serpentine walls (1971–2).

Not a big church, so its attraction is of a homely sort. The centralized plan is immediately apparent from the E, s and N elevations with their central shaped and pedimented gables, each with a big round-headed window rising above the cornice of the bays to each side. Rusticated brick surrounds to these windows and the similar, smaller flanking ones, and brick quoins also at the angles. The warm red Berkshire brick of the E and s fronts dates from the restoration, when the walls were rebuilt from sill level. The church had been stuccoed in 1820–1 by *Charles Tyrell*, and the N side is stuccoed still. (Other restorations in 1763–4, 1781–2 by *James Peacock*, 1800, 1838–9 by *W. M. Brookes*, 1849–50 by *John Wallen*, and 1887–8 by *Ewan Christian*.) The tower, also stuccoed, is plain and small, placed centrally at the w. It looks too small for the church, the consequence of reusing the lower stages and NW stair-turret of the C14 tower (see the door with two-centred arch facing the internal lobby N of the tower). Simple square lantern on a truncated weatherboarded pyramid (contracted for in 1680). It looks more like an artisan's design than something from the Wren office. Contemporary weathervane made by *Robert Bird*, in the shape of an A, for Anne and Agnes. The SW vestibule, rebuilt since the war, originally housed the staircase to a vanished w gallery. The NW vestry is probably that built by *John Bird*, 1706 (Colvin).

The wainscotted interior is of the cross-in-square plan type, like St Martin Ludgate and St Mary-at-Hill, and raises the same problems of derivation as those churches (*see* Introduction p. 28). Here it has a groin-vaulted central square on four Corinthian columns of wood, four vaulted Greek-cross arms, and small lower corner cells with circular panels. The walls are not quite parallel, but the divergence is not obvious. In the corners of each cell winged cherubs' heads. The architraves of these cells rest on corbel-capitals of free design. In the post-war restoration the slim plaster ribs of Wren's central cross-vault were omitted, and Ewan Christian's decorative scheme entirely erased. This plainness is becoming to its present Lutheran use.

FITTINGS were mostly salvaged from elsewhere. Chief original survival is the REREDOS. By *Cheltenham*, a refined tripartite design with fluted Corinthian pilasters and a scrolly broken pediment. The garlanded urn on top replaced the C17 royal arms some time in the C18. Flanking it, large PAINTINGS of Moses and Aaron, *c*.1700, from St Michael Wood Street. – COMMUNION RAILS. Post-war. – PULPIT. Incorporating panels salvaged from that at St Augustine Watling Street, by *Maine*, 1687. – FONT. Post-war, marble, of C17 baluster design. The original is at St Vedast. Bell-shaped COVER from St Mildred Bread Street (by *Cleere*, 1682). – S DOORCASE. With engaged Corinthian columns and broken segmental pediment of Wren period, from Dunster Castle, Somerset. Splendid carved gilt angel on top, from the organ case of St Mildred Bread Street (1744). – ORGAN. 1991, by *R.J. Winn*, using older parts; in an ugly CASE from Southery Methodist church, Norfolk. – SCULPTURE. From St Mildred the tiny carved figure of Time dated 1682–3 over the vestry door, and the Lion and Unicorn on the E columns. – ROYAL ARMS. Carved, Stuart, from St Mary Whitechapel. – SANCTUARY CHAIRS. Late C17 style, but probably Victorian. – LECTERN in the form of a standing angel, *c*.1900. From All Saints, Bermondsey. – CROWN and two MITRES in the middle of the N wall, from an early C19 organ case. – Two restored BUSTS below the central S window, moved here in 1844 from a monument to Sir James Drax †1662 and his son Henry †1682, erected at the site of St John Zachary, Gresham Street. Attributed to *Pierce* (GF).

ST AUGUSTINE WATLING STREET
(ST PAUL'S CATHEDRAL CHOIR SCHOOL)
St Paul's Churchyard and New Change

Immediately SE of St Paul's, the restored tower and spire of *Wren*'s church of St Augustine Watling Street (also known as St Augustine Old Change or Budge Row), sensitively incorporated into the choir school of 1962–7, designed by *Leo de Syllas* of the *Architects' Co-Partnership*.

The church was first mentioned *c*. 1148. Excavations in 1965 indicated a building 61 ft (18½ metres) long, with remains of a N aisle documented in the 1250s. As rebuilt in 1680–4 it was plain and modest, with a barrel-vault on Ionic columns and groin-vaulted aisles (mason *Edward Strong Sen.*). In 1695–6 the tower was completed and a graceful leaded steeple added. Its finial was altered to a heavier pointed spire in repairs of 1830 by *J.H. Taylor* and *Alfred Ainger*. Church body (restored by *Blomfield*, 1878) and spire were destroyed in 1941, but the latter was reconstructed according to its more slender original state by *Paul Paget* of *Seely & Paget*, 1966.

The tower is markedly oblong in plan and modest in scale, perfectly proportioned in relation to both school and cathedral. Simple rectangular belfry apertures, then Baroque obelisk pinnacles and a lacy Baroque pierced parapet. Behind the parapet brackets rise from the corners to an open stage topped by urns, surmounted by a finial like an elongated onion. Surviving drawings in the hand of *Hawksmoor* suggest he was responsible for the design. They show the finial evolving from a giant pine cone like that of Wren's pre-Fire design for St Paul's.

ST BARTHOLOMEW-THE-GREAT
West Smithfield

The most important C12 monument in London, though only a fragment remains of the church founded in 1123. Rahere, a prebendary
of St Paul's and later an Augustinian canon, established St
Bartholomew as an Augustinian priory with a hospital adjoining (cf.
the Augustinian St Thomas's Hospital, Southwark, founded *c*. 1106
in connection with the rebuilt St Mary Overie). The hospital
survived the dissolution of the Priory. The canons' church was about
280 ft (85 metres) long to E wall of the choir; but, except for a fragment of the W front, the C13 nave from the easternmost bay to the W
was pulled down *c*. 1543 when the parish took over the C12 choir and
crossing from the new owner, Sir Richard Rich. As well as the choir,
crossing and W front fragment, the Lady Chapel, added E of the
choir *c*. 1330, also survives. In 1404–9 a Papal indulgence records
work including the rebuilding of the cloister (partly surviving); other
Perp features probably come from the same campaign.

The present exterior, however, is largely post-Reformation, both
C16–C17 and by *Aston Webb* in 1886–98. Earlier restoration by
Hayter Lewis and *William Slater*, 1864, largely internal, is less
apparent. Little trace of previous restorations, by T. *Hardwick*,
1790–1 and 1808, and *John Blyth*, 1830s. The C16 and C17 changes
began in earnest after the brief monastic revival under Mary I, when
St Bartholomew became a Dominican house (1555–8): the parish
rebuilt the N gallery as a schoolhouse in the later C16 and added the
SW tower in 1628. Much of the rest of the fabric fell into decay or
was converted to other uses as the surroundings were more densely
developed: a plan in Wilkinson's *Londinia Illustrata* (1821) shows the
church hemmed in by buildings along Cloth Fair (N) and around
Bartholomew Close (S), the S transept in ruins, and houses made
within the Lady Chapel and N transept. All this explains the dearth
of medieval fabric. C16 and C17 work was retained by Aston Webb,
who owed his employment to the fact that his brother, E.A. Webb,
was churchwarden.* Though not an architect one associates with
church restoration, he responded thoughtfully to the task: his own
sharp, wiry free Gothic in flint and Portland stone for the W front and
new transepts; more archaeological insertions in the medieval context
(Lady Chapel and interiors). The latter are carefully distinguished,
perhaps in response to pressure from the Society for the Protection
of Ancient Buildings. It is an intelligent, honest solution, but not always
an immediately appealing one. Progress was slow, since much adjacent
property had to be bought up and cleared. The finishing touches
kept Webb busy here until 1928. Only slight restorations since.

The GATEWAY opens into the forecourt or churchyard from West
Smithfield. The two half-timbered upper storeys with braces were
built as a house for Sir Philip Scudamore, 1595, and much restored
in 1916 by *Webb* with picturesque gable and shallow oriels. The gateway proper incorporates the restored C13 W doorway to the S nave
aisle. Of four orders, with dogtooth but always without shafts, as the
plinth reveals. Probably of *c*. 1230, like the rest of the nave. To its

---

* E.A. Webb's *Records of St Bartholomew Smithfield* (1921) is the best account of the
church and precinct.

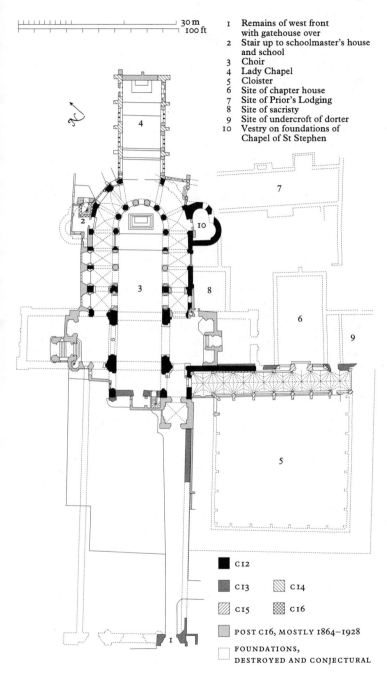

30 m
100 ft

1 Remains of west front with gatehouse over
2 Stair up to schoolmaster's house and school
3 Choir
4 Lady Chapel
5 Cloister
6 Site of chapter house
7 Site of Prior's Lodging
8 Site of sacristy
9 Site of undercroft of dorter
10 Vestry on foundations of Chapel of St Stephen

■ C12

■ C13   ▨ C14

▨ C15   ▨ C16

POST C16, MOSTLY 1864–1928

FOUNDATIONS, DESTROYED AND CONJECTURAL

St Bartholomew-the-Great. Plan

r. a blank arch, suggesting the whole lower front was arcaded. Iron gates by *Blyth*, 1856 (lower part); carvings of St Bartholomew (above) and a Crucifixion, by *W. S. Frith*, 1917, the latter a war memorial to Webb's son. To the r. a red brick house, a reconstruction of 1950–2 by *Seely & Paget* and *L. B. Smith* of the pre-war gatehouse extension of *c*. 1700 (earlier restoration 1932).

Exterior

The footpath to the church follows the line of the demolished nave along the s aisle. On its r., part of the C13 s aisle wall. The w FRONT is really *Webb*'s attempt to make the best of a bad job (1893). He added the two-storeyed s PORCH at the sw angle of the remaining fabric, and refaced with shallow, weak arcading the patched-up brick wall thrown across the e end of the nave in the 1540s. All is in flint and Portland stone with much chequerwork. On the porch triangular-headed panelling and a sinuous niche canopy, rising through the gable merlon to end as a foliate cross. Immediately behind appears the embattled brick TOWER of 1628, built over the far e bay of the s nave aisle. It replaced a parochial steeple of uncertain date on the n side. Its plan is rectangular, broader (N–s) than it is deep. Debased three-light tracery under rounded heads in the lower openings. Pretty little square timber lantern on top.

61   The rest of the exterior must be seen from Cloth Fair, N, accessible across the raised churchyard. First the easternmost and only surviving bay of the NAVE, exposed by demolitions in 1914. The clerestory has a renewed two-light plate-traceried window of *c*. 1230, with a plain circle above two lights. The aisle has gone, so one sees below only the outlines of the C13 aisle vault, superimposed on the C12 arcade and gallery. From this it is clear that the first bay of the nave belonged with the C12 crossing, but was modified to match the C13 work. Next to this bay Webb's N TRANSEPT, with a porch and a big octagonal turret set asymmetrically. Three tall lancets, much pattern-making in stone and flint. Beyond this lies the choir. The ground floor is from the restoration of 1864. The N GALLERY preserves a rare and instructive example of the *ad hoc* adaptation of great monastic churches after the Reformation. Brick facing of *c*. 1600 shows where the schoolroom was made within. Two- and three-light Tudor windows, square-headed, with four-centred arches. Small hipped roof to each bay, partly concealed by the parapet. The early C17 schoolmaster's house, E, is two storeys higher, with a brick stair-turret and half-hipped roof. The school moved out only in 1889. The C14 Perp clerestory appears above, beneath a brick parapet. Two-light tracery, restored in 1864.

At the e end, Webb's apse clerestory, with twin panelled octagonal turrets, and below and beyond it the low four-bay LADY CHAPEL. A will of 1336 calls this 'newly constructed'. Excavations in 1988 revealed two phases of construction, perhaps closely following each other, which suggest that the chapel was already under way before the C12 e end was demolished. Rich inserted a floor in 1544 to make the chapel into a house. Of this date probably the tiny single w light on the N side. When *Webb* restored the chapel in 1895–8 it had been heightened in brick and had latterly functioned as a fringe factory. A good deal of C14 banded flintwork remains. Webb's are the blind e wall, the s wall apart from sections around the lower buttresses,

1. St Margaret Lothbury, by Sir Christopher Wren, 1683–92,
from the south-west

2. St Bartholomew-the-Great, founded 1123, choir, from the east
3. Temple Church, the round nave, consecrated 1185
4. Temple Church, chancel, consecrated 1240

2 | 3
4

5. St Sepulchre, south porch, mid-fifteenth century
6. St Sepulchre, tower, mid-fifteenth century, upper parts 1873–5
7. St Helen Bishopsgate, thirteenth to fifteenth centuries, west front
8. St Giles Cripplegate, nave, *c.* 1545–50

+ hic jacet Raherus Primus Canonicus et Primus Prior hujus Ecclesie

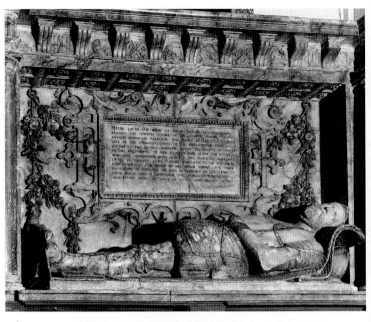

13. St Katharine Cree, Throkmorton monument †1570, attributed to the Cure workshop

14. St Olave Hart Street, monument to the Bayninge brothers †1610 and †1616, attributed to Christopher Kingsfield

15. St Bartholomew-the-Great, monument to Elizabeth Freshwater †1617

16. St Helen Bishopsgate, monument to Sir Thomas Gresham †1579

17. St Bartholomew-the-Great, monument to Sir Robert Chamberlayne †1615, style of Colt

<table>
<tr><td rowspan="2">13</td><td>15</td></tr>
<tr><td>16</td></tr>
<tr><td>14</td><td>17</td></tr>
</table>

18. St Helen
    Bishopsgate,
    south doorcase,
    1633 (photo
    1940)
19. St Olave Hart
    Street, gateway
    to churchyard,
    1658
20. St Katharine
    Cree, interior,
    1628–31
21. St Olave Hart
    Street, vestry,
    ceiling, 1661–2

22. St James Garlickhithe, by Sir Christopher Wren, detail of the tower, 1676–85, spire 1713–17
23. St Vedast alias Foster, by Sir Christopher Wren, 1695–1701, spire 1709–12
24. St Andrew Holborn, tower, refaced by Wren, 1703–4
25. St Dunstan-in-the-East, steeple, by Sir Christopher Wren, 1695–1701, from the south-east

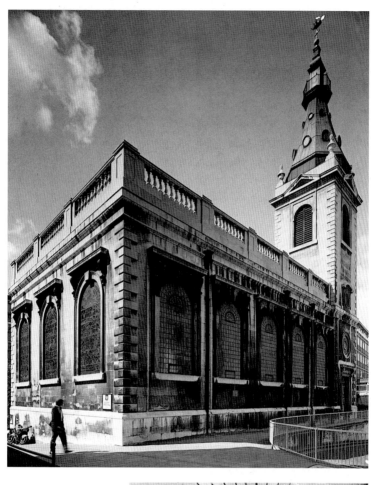

26. St Nicholas Cole Abbey, by Sir Christopher Wren, 1672–8, from the north-east
27. St Mary-le-Bow, by Sir Christopher Wren, 1670–80, west door to the tower
28. St Benet Paul's Wharf, attributed to Robert Hooke, 1678–84
29. St Martin Ludgate, by Sir Christopher Wren, 1677–86, south elevation

33. St Mary Abchurch, interior of the dome, painted by William Snow, *c.* 1708
34. St Andrew-by-the-Wardrobe, by Sir Christopher Wren, 1685–94, interior as restored by Marshall Sisson, 1959–61
35. St Anne and St Agnes, by Sir Christopher Wren, 1677–87, detail of vault
36. St Mary Aldermary, by the Wren office, 1679–82, south aisle, ceiling

37. St Margaret Lothbury, wooden screen, by Woodruffe and Thornton, 1683–4
38. St Mary Abchurch, reredos, by Grinling Gibbons, 1686
39. St Clement Eastcheap, pulpit and tester, by Jonathan Maine, c. 1687
40. St Magnus the Martyr, west gallery, and organ by Abraham Jordan Sen. and Jun., c. 1712

41. All Hallows Barking, font cover, by Grinling Gibbons, 1682
42. St Vedast alias Foster, font, by Thomas Hill, 1680s
43. St Margaret Pattens, royal arms, late seventeenth century
44. St Benet Paul's Wharf, communion table, c. 1686
45. St Margaret Lothbury, detail of font, c. 1680

41 42 | 44
43 | 45

46. St Andrew-by-the-Wardrobe, west window, by Joshua Price after Sebastiano Ricci, *c.* 1712–16
47. St Magnus the Martyr, iron sword rest, 1708
48. All Hallows, London Wall, monument to Joan Bence †1684, attributed to Jasper Latham
49. St Michael Cornhill, wooden sculpture of pelican, by Joseph Glazeley, 1775
50. St Michael Paternoster Royal, statue of Moses, late seventeenth century

51. St Mary Woolnoth, by Nicholas Hawksmoor, 1716–27, from the north-east
52. All Hallows London Wall, by George Dance the Younger, 1765–7, interior (photo 1937)
53. St Botolph Bishopsgate, by James Gould, 1725–8, from the north-east
54. St Botolph Aldgate, by George Dance the Elder, 1741–4, south aisle, detail of ceiling, as altered by J.F. Bentley, 1888–95

51 | 53
52 | 54

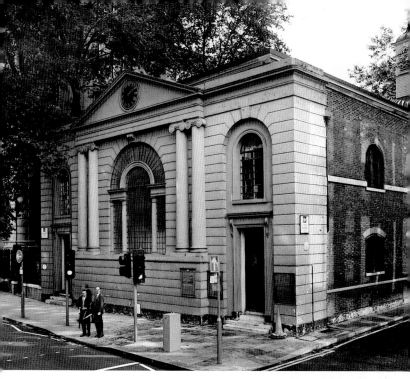

55. St Botolph
    Aldersgate, 1754 and
    1789–91, east front
    rebuilt 1829–30,
    attributed to J.W.
    Griffith

56. St Stephen Walbrook,
    monument to
    Thomas Stonestreet,
    by the younger
    Bacon, 1803

57. St Dunstan-in-the-
    West, by John Shaw
    Sen., 1830–3, from
    the south-east

58. St Bartholomew-the-
    Less, by Thomas
    Hardwick, 1823–5,
    altered by
    P.C. Hardwick,
    1862–3, interior

59. St Michael
    Cornhill, east
    window, by
    Clayton & Bell,
    1858
60. St Michael
    Cornhill, by Sir
    George Gilbert
    Scott, 1857–60,
    north porch
61. St Bartholomew-
    the-Great, north
    transept, by Aston
    Webb, 1886–98
62. City Temple, west
    front by
    Lockwood &
    Mawson, 1873–4,
    rebuilt behind by
    Lord Mottistone
    of Seely & Paget,
    1955–8, from the
    north-west

63. St Peter upon Cornhill, north aisle window, by Hugh Easton, 1951–60
64. St Lawrence Jewry, west window, by Christopher Webb, 1959–60
65. St Nicholas Cole Abbey, east window, by Keith New, 1962
66. St Michael Paternoster Royal, east window, by John Hayward, 1968

63 64
65 66

and most of the even three-light windows. His tracery is firmly Perp, not flowing. A stone and flint-faced extension to the church offices by *Anthony New*, 1989, fills part of the sunken court around the chapel (N side). The S side is visible from Bartholomew Close, reached by an alley E of the E wall. Immediately W of the Lady Chapel here lie C16 brick foundations, from the demolished lodging of Prior Bolton. Projecting from the next bay to the W, the lower walls of the C12 Chapel of St Stephen, otherwise demolished in 1849. Curiously shaped, with apses on the S and E, and *Webb*'s VESTRY of 1914 on top.

Interior

The church represents the four-bay choir of the priory church with the gloomy crossing, transepts, and the first bay of the nave. The choir of 1123 etc., not long, has an apsed E end with an ambulatory (restored), originally with three radiating chapels, the outer pair double-apsed (cf. Norwich, begun 1096). The remains of the SE chapel have already been described; the NE chapel is destroyed; the E chapel replaced by the C14 Lady Chapel. Excavations beneath the last in 1911 revealed a section of straight walling indicating that the C12 chapel was longer than those to either side.

The CHOIR, four bays long, has massive cylindrical piers with 2 many-scalloped capitals and unmoulded arches with a finely moulded running extrados with billet decoration. Four slender sub-arches in the gallery openings, with one relieving arch also with billet decoration. The clerestory, C14, retains the C12 wall passage. The C12 internal elevation may derive from Reading Abbey (founded 1121), which likewise lacked any vertical division of the bays, though the two lower storeys of near-equal height and the rather old-fashioned groin-vaulted ambulatory with plain cross-ribs recall the late C11 Chapel of St John in the White Tower.[*] The first campaign ended probably *c.* 1133, when disruption to the priory's government is recorded. A set-back on the broad compound pier immediately E of the crossing may mark the position of a temporary party wall. This would give a date of *c.* 1145–60 for the following campaign under Prior Thomas, which built the longer W choir bay, crossing, transepts and E bay of the nave. It is likely that the lesser arches were inserted into the gallery at the same time, perhaps to strengthen it, since the main imposts make no provision for any such arcade.

The E end, much altered in the C14 and later, was restored to the Norman plan in 1864 (the stilted arches and two central columns) and 1886 (gallery and clerestory). In the gallery, *Webb* carried on the blank arches of the first bay from the W, but with two sub-arches instead of three. Hatched tympana and the use of Bath stone further distinguish the new work. The C12 E end had been altered in two stages: first in the early C14, when the two central piers were removed and the ambulatory modified for the new Lady Chapel; then *c.* 1405, when a new square E end was made further W, curtailing the first bay of the apse slightly. Its alignment is marked by the truncated E sub-arch of the gallery bay. Here a restored Perp shaft, perhaps from the jamb of an E clerestory window, has been incorporated into *Webb*'s

[*] *See* Lawrence Hoey, *Journal of the Society of Architectural Historians* 48 (1989).

graceful chancel arch. Of 1864 the two central piers, and the piers and half-piers of the two w bays.

The abrupt end of the extrados moulding on the crossing piers probably corresponds to the E end of the canons' stalls, which would have extended under the crossing. The C12 appearance may be reconstructed further from remains of red, black, and yellow paint of that date discovered in the C19 on the arcade voussoirs, and from the corbel-courses across E and W crossing arches, which indicate a flat wooden roof some 47 ft (14 metres) high: lower than *Webb*'s present kingpost roof of 1885–6, incorporating medieval tie-beams.

A very pretty addition is the oriel window on the s side of the gallery. The date is probably shortly before 1517, when recent expenditure by Prior Bolton is mentioned. It served as a kind of ORATORY accessible from his lodgings to the s. It has a three-light opening in the front and single-light canted sides, all glazed. Bolton's rebus appears in the central quatrefoiled panel below. A doorway also with Bolton's rebus in the spandrels survives in the SE corner of the AMBULATORY (the present Chapel of the Knights Bachelor), in a section of plastered early C16 brick walling. The ambulatory and aisles mostly retain the plain C12 responds. On the s side, a blocked two-centred C14 doorway in the first bay from the W gave access to a sacristy, destroyed by fire in 1830. The aisle and ambulatory vault is largely concrete of 1893, apart from two C12 bays in the NE corner, just N of two pointed C14 arches by the Lady Chapel entrance. In the second of these bays a restored late C14 three-light window. The plain C12 arch in the next bay was the entrance to the demolished NE chapel, foundations of which were uncovered in 1988 (corresponding arch on the s). Further W on this side, three deep recesses with late C14 moulded arches, mostly renewed in 1864. They formerly opened into the parochial Chapel of All Saints, built *c.* 1395 as an E extension of the N transept and demolished *c.* 1542.

The CROSSING has full shafts on the N and s arches, corbels on the E and w, and arches of two orders. These parts were probably built in the mid C12, so the stilted N and s arches here may well be the earliest major pointed arches in London. In the spandrels round-headed blind arches and sunk lozenges. W and N arches rebuilt probably *c.* 1405 to correct settlement, hence the polygonal caps to the shafts. If there was a crossing tower, as is likely, it may have been taken down at this time, since a new bell-tower (perhaps an isolated structure) is mentioned as part of the C15 work. Early C15 strainer screen of two depressed pointed arches on the N side, much damaged in the C18–C19 when a smithy occupied the transept. C12 foundations of a s screen were uncovered in 1864.

The TRANSEPTS are *Webb*'s, to an uncomfortably truncated plan. The N transept has a blind gallery and a screen of tracery behind the lancets, the s transept (the present baptistery) twin lancets carried further down. The medieval transepts were some 40 ft (12 metres) deep. The arches into the chancel aisles and into the s nave aisle remain, incorporated into Webb's fabric. On the s side also a C12 gallery arch over the nave aisle arch, with three restored sub-arches.

The NAVE was originally ten bays long. The surviving bay lay immediately E of the pulpitum, part of which probably remains within the w wall. As is clear also from the exterior, the surviving bay is C12, the design similar to the straight parts of the chancel, but modified *c.* 1230 when Gothic aisles were carried up to the crossing. Of this date the wall-shafts in the s aisle bay under the tower, with foliage and bell-shaped capitals, and on each side the plate-traceried clerestory window of *c.* 1230, blocked on the s side by the tower. Excavated fragments show that the Gothic nave had Purbeck-shafted piers. There is no evidence of vaulting of its central vessel. Each of the blocked gallery openings is pierced with a C15 doorway, the N one containing steps up to the level of the crown of the lost C13 aisle vault.

Finally the LADY CHAPEL. Webb's E wall has blind niches of C13 pattern. Of the C14 the N and s windows close to the E wall, the s window being SEDILIA as well. Detached shafts to the inside to form the seats, and a similar arrangement on the N. Webb's window jambs are distinguishable by their octagonal shafts. His open wooden roof is arcaded above the trusses. CRYPT underneath the E part, reached through the new church offices via the NE ambulatory. Entry is through a four-centred doorway, early C16, with carved vines and grapes in the spandrels. The segmental barrel-vault and chamfered transverse ribs were largely reconstructed in 1895.

Furnishings

Except for monuments the church is poor in furnishings. Fine wrought-iron SCREEN to the Lady Chapel, 1897, designed by *Webb* and made by *Starkie Gardner & Co.*, with foliage cresting and candlesticks on top. By the same the screens in the N crossing arches, 1893. – HIGH ALTAR by *Seely & Paget*, 1950, with openwork Tudor-Gothic uprights, weird and effective. A vast early C17 painted reredos on canvas, representing in false perspective an elaborate classical structure crowned by obelisks, was destroyed in 1828. – PULPIT by *Webb*, of stone, with two flights of stairs. – LECTERN also by *Webb*, four-sided with little figures, made from old roof timbers. – STALLS, SCREEN, ORGAN CASE and W GALLERY, 1886–93, of oak, Gothic and unexceptional. Grouped under the crossing. On the lower organ case sickly paintings of monks by *F. E. Beresford*. – FONT of *c.* 1405, the only medieval one in the City proper. Plain, massive octagonal basin and pedestal. – BENCHES. Two pieces of *c.* 1700 with ornate open backs, apparently of foreign workmanship. – DOOR into the cloister, *c.* 1600. – SCULPTURE. The Risen Christ, by *Josephina de Vasconcellos*, *c.* 1990, strikingly juxtaposed with a C13 stone COFFIN (N aisle). – ALTAR PIECE in the Lady Chapel, after Murillo. MONUMENTS. Choir. Rahere †1144. In the NE position preferred for founders' monuments. Made when the E end was remodelled *c.* 1405. The design is very similar to Sir Bernard de Brocas's tomb in Westminster Abbey (†1395) and Gower's monument in Southwark Cathedral (†1408). Tomb-chest under canopy with recumbent effigy of Reigate stone in Augustinian habit. At the feet two small kneeling bedesmen and a larger angel holding a shield. Canopy with three cusped arches crowned by tall concave-sided crocketed gables set against blank panelling. Cresting at the top. Some *Coade* stone repairs of 1815 (by *William Croggan*). The back wall is pierced in three little arches to the ambulatory. Arcading up to the C15 E wall line was destroyed in 1864. – Percival Smalpace †1558 and wife †1588, an odd composition with pilasters and two frontal busts like passport photographs separated by a mullion.

Slate panel below with incised figures of the pair's naked corpses. Attributed to *Giles de Witt* (GF). – Sir Robert Chamberlayne †1615. Kneeling figure under a convex architectural canopy with two well-carved standing angels holding two curtains open. Style of *Colt* (GF). Other versions at Jesus College, Oxford, and elsewhere. – Two grand cartouches with cherubs' heads: John Kellond †1685, attributed to *Edward Pierce* (GF); Jonathan Whiting †1704 and wife †1727, by *Theophilus Allen.*– N aisle. Francis Anthony †1623, with charmingly naïve incised columns with rose-garlands. – S aisle. Sir Walter Mildmay †1589, Chancellor of the Exchequer and Founder of Emmanuel College, Cambridge, and wife. Big standing wall-monument of rich alabaster and coloured marble, with flanking columns but no effigy. – Anthony Lowe †1641, tablet with ornamented frame. – James Rivers †1641, '. . . Who when ambytyon, Tyrany & Pride/Conquer'd the Age, conquer'd hymself & Dy'd'. Frontal bust, book in hand. Attributed to *William Wright* (AW). – Edward Cooke †1652. Similar. Attributed to *Thomas Burman* (GF). – John Millett † 1660, still with ribbon-work. – S transept. Elizabeth Freshwater † 1617, a remarkable piece, though small. Kneeling figure under a pedimented arch. The scrolly volutes and half-pilasters resemble the style which appears on a larger scale at St Helen Bishopsgate in 1633. – N transept. Thomas Roycroft, printer, †1677, with columns, the apron carved in the form of spines of books. – City of London Yeomanry War Memorial, 1926 by *Webb*, with carved angels. – Lady Chapel. Rev. Sir Borradaile Savory †1906. Mid-C17 style with Edwardian Baroque touches. Surely *Webb*'s design.

Monastic Remains

From the SW porch, the main entrance leads via the tower into the tile-roofed CLOISTER. The E side remains, in origin *c.* 1160 (see the N doorway facing into the cloister), but rebuilt *c.* 1405. Of this date the three N bays, restored in 1905 after use as a stable, with some stonework reused in the tierceron vault. The remainder is mostly by *Webb*, 1923–8, replacing vaulting which collapsed in 1834. Flowing reticulated tracery distinguishes these bays. C15 entrance arches into the former CHAPTER HOUSE (sixth bay). It was rectangular, measuring some 53 ft (16 metres) by 28 ft (8½ metres). Surviving fragments suggest a date also *c.* 1160. The W wall, uncovered in 1912, had three arched C15 openings fitted into the older fabric. Further S, behind the C15 fabric and partly obscured by it, remains of an early C13 round-arched doorway, with trefoiled cusping in the tympanum and a segment-arched doorway below. The dorter to the S, with a fine vaulted undercroft, lasted until 1870. The S and W sides of the cloister garth are enclosed by 1950s ward blocks of St Bartholomew's Hospital.

ST BARTHOLOMEW-THE-LESS
St Bartholomew's Hospital, off West Smithfield

The church of St Bartholomew's Hospital stands just inside the main gate on West Smithfield. Its C15 SW tower and W vestry survive from one of the several former hospital chapels, here made parochial in 1546–7 as part of the re-foundation. The rest is an interesting octagonal brick church of 1823–5 by *Thomas Hardwick*, perpetuating work by *George Dance the Younger*, 1789–91 (altered in 1862–3 by *P. C. Hardwick*).

Very plain and humble tower with sw stair-turret and parapet of brick. Renewed w doorway, with two-light window above, also renewed. Could its odd plain tracery be c17? Inside the tower, heavy moulded arches with hollows and thick triple shafts. At half-height unusual banding, the mouldings continued around the walls. w and N walls of the vestry rebuilt in brick, with a restored Perp w window over a doorway blocked by *T. Hardwick*, indicated by surviving sections of rubble walling. Buttresses on the N side of the church were added possibly *c.* 1842, when *Philip Hardwick* rebuilt the hospital's screen wall just beyond.

The raised floor of the interior is the first surprise. It may date from *Dance*'s work. *Thomas Hardwick*'s rebuilding owed much to Dance, 58 who introduced an octagonal Gothic vault fitted into a square by triangular chapels open to the centre. Pointed lunette windows high up pierce a swooping star-shaped plaster rib-vault. Its construction is of iron, after Dance's timbers rotted. Dance put windows only in the lunettes, a device consistent with his fondness for dramatic lighting effects (cf. his similarly polygonal Gothic church at Micheldever, Hants, 1808). To *P. C. Hardwick* are due the projecting sanctuary with half-octagonal end and the geometrical tracery of the lunettes. The effect of the ensemble remains pre-archaeological (see especially the intersecting tracery), and has its modest charm. Restored by *Lord Mottistone* of *Seely & Paget* after war damage, 1950–1.

FITTINGS. PULPIT of alabaster, designed by *P. C. Hardwick*, 1864. – Gothic PEWS with linenfold carving. They look *c.* 1825. – STAINED GLASS. E window by *Hugh Easton*, 1950. – CARVINGS. On the vestry wall, four c15 carvings of angels with shields, apparently reset. The best-preserved pair hold the royal arms. – PAINTINGS. In the vestry: Crucifixion by *Cigoli*, *c.* 1600. – St Bartholomew, c17, Spanish or Italian. – MONUMENTS. Brass in the vestry to William Markeby †1439 and wife, with small figures. – Canopied tomb, *c.* 1500, with shallow arch and quatrefoil frieze, not rich. Mid-c18 alterations. – Serjeant Balthrope †1591. Kneeling figure in niche. – Tablet to Mary Darker †1773, with little relief, and more ambitious tablet with putti by an urn to John Darker †1784; both by *J. Bingley*.

ST BENET PAUL'S WHARF
(ST BENET WELSH CHURCH)
Queen Victoria Street

First mentioned in 1111. The present building of 1678–84, almost 28 certainly *Hooke*'s design, since he made drawings both of the executed design and of a preliminary version (AG). His craftsmen were *Thomas* and *Edward Strong Sen.*, masons; *Israel Knowles*, carpenter; *William Cleere*, joiner; *Doogood & Grove*, plasterers; *Matthew Roberts*, plumber. One of the most lovable of the post-Fire church exteriors, delightfully Dutch. Small, of red and blue brick chequerwork, with stone quoins of even size alternating with brick. Modillion cornice. Hipped roof, with, over the N aisle, three equal projections, also hipped. To the N and s round-headed windows with stone-carved garlands above. In the preliminary design a low attic stage is shown above these garlands. To the E a group of three, the middle one blank because blocked by the reredos inside, and then one more blank window representing the N aisle. Stone-carved garlands here too.

The tower is at the NW end of the nave but set back S of the N aisle, a picturesque arrangement due to the reuse of the medieval tower foundations and lower core. Stubby lead spire on an octagonal lantern above a lead dome with lucarnes. The 1970s Blackfriars Underpass scheme left St Benet isolated and battered by noise from the raised flyover called White Lion Hill (W). In its original setting, at the SW corner of Benet's Hill and the old alignment of Upper Thames Street, the S and E sides were most exposed, not the N and W ones as at present. A churchyard on the N was truncated *c.* 1870 for Queen Victoria Street, and a little NW vestry of 1692 demolished and replaced by one made in the SW entrance lobby, with a new entrance made under the tower. St Benet became the Welsh church in 1879.

The interior is of homely and intimate irregularity, unusual in its full entablature and flat, not coved, ceiling. Corinthian columns to the N aisle, which retains its gallery. Smaller gallery on the W, S of the tower. By means of the columns and pilasters the square shape of the main space is stressed. The N GALLERY was formerly used by members of Doctors' Commons in Queen Victoria Street, and is still used by the College of Arms there. Modest restorations in 1891 by *Herbert Knight* and *c.* 1950 by *Godfrey Allen*, who removed a tiled Victorian floor. Fire damage to the NE corner, 1971, was made good by *J. R. Stammers*.

The C17 FURNISHINGS are largely intact. Magnificent COM-
44 MUNION TABLE, possibly Flemish, with sumptuous figures as legs, a little seated figure of Charity on the stretcher, garlands etc. Among several fittings given by Sir Leoline (Llywelyn) Jenkins in 1686. – COMMUNION RAIL with twisted balusters. – STALLS and PEWS with original parts. – LECTERN attached to the stalls. – Simple REREDOS without columns or pilasters but with a big segmental pediment flanked by pairs of urns. – PULPIT rather simple, with later stairs and stem. Its TESTER hangs under the tower. – Fine DOORCASE to the tower lobby. In its broken pediment magnificently carved ROYAL ARMS. – Carved and painted armorial CARTOUCHES on the N gallery front. – ORGAN, W gallery. By *Hill, Norman & Beard*, 1973, based on a predecessor by *J. C. Bishop*, 1832. – WALL PANELLING. – Two SANCTUARY CHAIRS. – Modest iron SWORD REST. – Octagonal FONT. The stem ends in a capital. The bowl also octagonal, with four cherubs' heads. Contemporary COVER. – POOR BOX on four twisted balusters matching the communion rails. – MONUMENTS. Sir Robert Wyseman †1684 with good portrait bust in medallion. Attributed to *Gibbons* and (the bust) to *Arnold Quellin* (GF). – Mark Cottle †1681 and wife. Black and white marble obelisk with draped canopy, sphere and shield. Probably early C18. – Dr Bryce †1688 and Gregory King (Rouge Dragon Pursuivant) †1712, cartouches. – A C19 inscription records the burial here of Inigo Jones. His monument, designed by *John Webb*, perished in the Great Fire.

ST BOTOLPH ALDERSGATE

First mentioned in the early C12. A view of 1739 shows an aisled building of C15 character, the N wall altered after fire damage in

1666. The present church is C18 and C19, though when the vaults were emptied in 1892–4, the N and S walls were found to stand on medieval foundations. The medieval pier bases indicated that the old nave was 7 ft (2 metres) narrower. N and E walls were rebuilt in 1754, then the rest of the church in 1789–91 by *Nathaniel Wright*. The E end was rebuilt further back to widen Aldersgate Street, possibly by the Parish Surveyor *J. W. Griffith* (Colvin), under a faculty of 1829 (DF).

The E wall is of channelled stucco (painted dark green), with a 55 Venetian window between coupled Ionic columns on a plinth, and pediment above. Flanked by two-storey entrance recesses. Wright's front was of brick, without columns but otherwise similar. The rest is very modest externally. Stock brick with arched windows and a small W tower, also on medieval foundations and out of alignment with the nave. On it a square dome and starved wooden bellcote. A spindly chimney sticks up to its NE. Buildings abutting the N and W fronts were demolished in the C19.

The interior is a surprise: well-preserved late C18, of extreme elegance. Coffered E and W apses, concealed outside behind flat fronts, with galleries, vestries etc. in the angles. Square pillars to N and S carry a fine Greek frieze that continues round the E apse and across the W gallery. Corinthian columns supporting a full entablature (also continuing around the apses) are set above these piers, with the gallery fronts between them. All is painted, with much marbling and woodgraining in dark colours. Coved ceiling with very big plaster rosettes (still with C19 gas sunburners), lit by four interpenetrating lunettes on each side. Apses, lunettes, the reduction of the lower entablature to its frieze and the tight conception of the whole design are all reminiscent of Dance's All Hallows London Wall. Convex-fronted W gallery on Ionic columns. From a top-lit W lobby curved twin staircases rise to the galleries. Those on either side of the organ were for schoolchildren, who were taught in the adjoining upper rooms.

FITTINGS are a mixture of C18 pieces and good replacements from the restoration by *J. Blyth*, 1873–4 (later work by *Ewan Christian*, 1892–4). – Fine simple PULPIT of *c.* 1788, smoothly inlaid, set on a palm tree. Its tester (also on a palm tree) was removed by Blyth. – Mahogany COMMUNION TABLE of 1787. (In the E vestibule another table, dated 1639.) – COMMUNION RAILS of mahogany and gilded iron, *c.* 1788. – Iron MACE REST of 1788. – Good PEWS of 1874, free classical. – Large FONT of coloured marble, given 1878. Contemporary FONT COVER in rich Victorian-cum-Wren style, designed and given by *Seddon*, who was baptized here. – ORGAN on the W gallery. By *Samuel Green*, 1791, in a five-towered case with Adamesque ornament (instrument rebuilt by *Henry Speechley*, 1867). – STAINED GLASS. A full sequence. E window, Agony in the Garden, 1788 by *James Pearson* from designs by *Nathaniel Clarkson*. Dark sepia painted glass, the style like Correggio. Indeed set like a painting in a round-headed frame with curtains of plaster; grisaille panels with figures inset below and either side. Pearson's lesser flanking windows were lost in the Second World War. The replacements are poor, in a clashing style. – N aisle, four windows of the Life of Christ by *Ward & Hughes*, 1886, in a very painterly style. – S aisle by *M. C. Farrar Bell*, 1955–8, four historical scenes in a story-book manner. – N gallery, three windows by *Ward & Hughes*, 1890; one of 1939 (w) by *A. K. Nicholson* (CS), bold, if old-fashioned. – S gallery, three windows made by *Lavers & Barraud* to designs of *Stephen Salter*, 1865. They came from St Matthew Spring Gardens, Westminster (dem.), in 1885, with one new window (Resurrection) to match (TS).

MONUMENTS. A good collection, mostly from the previous church. – Ann Packington †1563, a late example of a Gothic altar tomb. Quatrefoils etc. on the chest, and an enriched crested canopy with flattened arch. Against the back wall kneeling figures incised in the manner of a brass. The matrices indicate a Trinity and three groups of kneeling figures. – Christopher Tamworth †1624 and wife †1637, with cherub, skull and hourglass. – John Coston and family, dates to 1637. Tablet with three shrouded skulls. Attributed to *Humphrey Moyer* (GF). – Elizabeth Ashton †1662 and Lady Richardson †1639, both wall-monuments with frontal busts in niches, the latter attributed to *William Wright* of Charing Cross (GF). – Sir John Micklethwaite †1682 and Richard Chiswell †1711, cartouches. Attributed respectively to *Gibbons* and *William Woodman Sen.* (GF). – Elizabeth Smith †1750, by *Roubiliac*. Simple tablet, portrait medallion above. – Zachariah Foxall †1758 by *John Annis*, with putti holding a medallion; obelisk behind. – Catherine Meade, by *R. Cooke*, 1793, with mourner in relief. – Rev. William Webber, portrait relief by *Forsyth*, 1881.

The CHURCHYARD (Postman's Park) is entered from Aldersgate Street through good early C19 railings with a Gothic drinking fountain of 1870 attached. It was laid out as a park in 1880–90, together with the adjacent burial grounds of Christ Church Newgate Street and St Leonard Foster Lane. W of the church is a Japanesey LOGGIA, conceived in 1887 by the painter *G. F. Watts* as a memorial to civilian lives lost in acts of heroism and erected in 1899. As Watts wrote to *The Times* in 1887, 'the national prosperity of a nation is not an abiding possession, the deeds of the people are'. Timber, with a pitched tiled roof and on the rear wall fifty-three artistically lettered glazed plaques composed mostly by Watts or his widow, at once moving and unintentionally quaint. The latest is dated 1930. Central niche with a tiny wooden STATUETTE of Watts in robes by *T. H. Wren*, added *c.* 1907. In the garden also lots of fine trees, a fountain, and a bronze SCULPTURE of a minotaur by *Michael Ayrton*, erected 1973.

ST BOTOLPH ALDGATE

First mentioned 1125, but the dedication indicates a Saxon origin. Excavations inside the crypt at the S end in 1990 indeed revealed burials suggesting a C10–C11 foundation. Stow records a rebuilding in the early C16 by the patron, Holy Trinity Priory. The present church is by *Dance the Elder*, 1741–4. It is aligned N–S, so that it faces down Minories. Brick S (ritual W) tower, flanked by domed side entrances as at Wren's St Clement Danes. The rise of the tower is nicely separated from the façade proper by a pediment finishing the latter. Obelisk spire, with a clock stage. The short and broad church body gives it a sit-up-and-beg look. Side windows enriched by Gibbs surrounds, and in the middle of the W, E and the N (altar) sides, one Venetian window each. Drawings by Dance at the Soane Museum show external

St Botolph Aldgate, engraving by B. Cole

double staircases here (DF; date of removal uncertain). Below this on the W and E sides another tripartite opening, with round arches and rusticated inner jambs to the crypt door, a strangely unorthodox feature. On the E side discreet brick offices of 1987 by *John Phillips*.

The interior retains galleries on three sides resting on the pedestals of Tuscan columns that rise to the roof. But the general impression has been considerably changed by the redecoration undertaken 1888–95 by *Bentley*. Due to him is the remarkably original
54 ceiling in a kind of free Arts and Crafts Gothic – admittedly a style entirely out of keeping with Dance's. In the coving are lithe standing figures of angels in high relief holding shields; bands of square boss-like leaves. Bentley also lowered the galleries by some 18 in. and gave them white-painted balustraded fronts which do much to lighten the interior. He retained the flat C18 E (ritual) end rather than add an external chancel for the choir. In this and in the retention of galleries Bentley was deliberately respectful to C18 convention. Redecorated 1965–6 by *J. S. Comper* after a fire.

FONT. Circular, with nice domed cover. Some of the C18 font rails have been incorporated in a SCREEN. – ORGAN CASE probably by *John Byfield*, 1744, W gallery; ORGAN with pipework attributed to *Harris*, from an instrument given by Thomas Whiting, 1676 (restored by *N. Mander*, 1966). – REREDOS. Original, with Corinthian columns. On the panels, batik hangings by *Thetis Blacker*, 1982. – PULPIT. Simple, inlaid, *c.* 1745. The Sacred Heart and other details suggest it may not have been made for an Anglican church. – COMMUNION RAIL, C18, of wrought iron. COMMUNION TABLE. Late C17 with twisted legs, reconstructed. – SWORD REST, C18, heavy. – STAINED GLASS. E window by *Charles Clutterbuck*, *c.* 1850, after Rubens's Deposition. – Other windows by *Goddard & Gibbs*, 1969–72. The NE (ritual) chapel has engraved glass screens by *David Peace* and *Sally Scott*, 1988. – SCULPTURE. Sumptuous late C17 panel with King David surrounded by musical instruments. *Gibbons* style. From St Mary Whitechapel. – MONUMENTS. The best are in the baptistery (created under the tower during the restoration of 1965–6 by *R. Tatchell*). Thomas Lord Darcy put to death by Henry VIII, and others; tablet with emaciated recumbent effigy between Corinthian columns, *c.* 1560–70. – Robert Dow †1612 with bust in niche, made 1622–3 by *Christopher Kingsfield* (repaired 1675). – Bust of Sir John Cass by *Eric Winter*, 1966, after the full-length figure by Roubiliac in the Sir John Cass School, Duke's Place. – In the churchyard, abstract SCULPTURE: Sanctuary by *Naomi Blake*, 1985.

ST BOTOLPH BISHOPSGATE

First mentioned in the late C12, but almost certainly a late Saxon foundation like its City namesakes. Rebuilt in 1725–8 to a design by *James Gould*, by a consortium of masons: Gould's son-in-law *George Dance the Elder*, his father *Giles Dance*, *John Townshend* and *Thomas*
53 *Dunn*. A stately, solid, stone-faced E front faces Bishopsgate. The church is properly oriented, so that the altar is behind the street front beneath the tower, flanked by entrance lobbies. The centre has coupled Doric pilasters, a frieze, and a pediment. Above this rises the square tower: first a channelled stage with markedly Baroque

corner piers or pilasters carved with cherubs' heads, then a pilastered bell-stage more in the Wren manner, crowned by a circular cupola with ogee cap and urn. Quoins mark the corners. Sides and w end of red brick with windows in two tiers, the upper tier round-headed with keystones carved with cherubs' heads, and linked by a moulding at impost level. The steeple with its stone frontispiece derives from Wren; the free-standing site and the uniform treatment of the church body recall the later and cheaper of the 'Fifty Churches', e.g. the nearly contemporary St Luke Old Street (*London 4: North*). The parish had sought unsuccessfully to rebuild its church from the fund. Italianate s doorcase facing the churchyard added in restoration by *Bentley*, 1890–2 (DF) (earlier work by *A. T. Carter*, 1878). W window of Venetian form, a somewhat ungainly alteration of 1755. The church was restored after war damage by *N. F. Cachemaille-Day*, 1947–8, and again by *Kevin Stephenson* after bomb damage sustained in 1992–3.

The usual entrance is through the s door. The galleried interior has a barrel vault on giant Corinthian columns. Restrained plasterwork with motifs of mitres, crowns, cherubs' heads and bibles. The entrance lobbies flanking the tower have very domestic-looking gallery staircases with paired balusters and enriched strings. The interior was altered by *Michael Meredith* in 1821, and from that time dates the dome above the centre of the nave, with lantern lighting in a glazed drum, its unadorned forms and small panes from the outside startlingly like a fashionable architectural device of the mid 1990s. The chancel was remodelled by *Carter*, and again by *Bentley*; the NE chapel by *Joseph Hill*, 1929. In the chancel, large framed MOSAICS of the Life of Christ, 1892. – Original PULPIT, hexagonal and inlaid. The stair looks later. – COMMUNION TABLE of C17 type with twisted legs and lions' feet. – LECTERN, with little cherubs, by *Bentley*, sensitively done. – STALLS also by *Bentley*. – PEWS look like *Carter*'s work from 1878, in an enriched classical style not unsympathetic to the context. – FONT. 1720s. – ORGAN of 1764 by *John Byfield*, divided either side of the w window in 1893 (instrument rebuilt 1949). – Iron SWORD REST with arms of 1835. – STAINED GLASS. E window a Crucifixion, Renaissance style, designed by *F. W. Moody*, made by *Powell & Sons*, 1869. A w window of 1876 by the same artists was replaced after war damage by a window by *Hugh Easton*, in turn removed after bomb damage in 1993.– MONUMENTS. Plain tablet on the gallery stairs (NE) to Sir Paul Pindar †1650, whose early C17 house was in Bishopsgate nearby. Its façade is now at the Victoria and Albert Museum. – On the chancel arch, John Tutchin †1658, a skeleton holding up an inscribed cloth, attributed to *Edward Pierce* (GF); Andrew Willaw †1700, enriched cartouche. – Rev. William Rogers †1896, with portrait relief, designed by *Bentley*. – Mosaic WAR MEMORIAL by *William Glasby*, c. 1920, still in the Burne-Jones manner.

The large open space to the s is the old CHURCHYARD, one of the first to be made into a garden (1863). It extends nearly up to the old line of the City wall. The paved path across it passes under wrought-iron lanterns of the overthrow type. They look early C19. FOUNTAIN of 1972; Gothic memorial CROSS to Lord Kitchener, 1916.

The PARISH HALL w of the church was built as an infants' school

in 1861 in nice harmony with the style of the church (which was an
unusual thing at the time). It is a simple pedimented block in red
brick with stone dressings, with paired Doric columns within a
rusticated arch at the entrance. On this front two STATUES of
charity children, a boy and a girl, of *Coade* stone, put up in 1821 on
the former building in Peter Street. Round-headed windows face
the church, the central one of tripartite quasi-Venetian form. On the
other side an ornamented chimney stack. Converted to a Hall in
1905. Between 1952 and 1994 it doubled as the Fanmakers' Hall,
after further adaptation by *White Allom* (inside, panelling of 1726,
from a demolished house in Northants). – By its entrance the TOMB
of Sir William Rawlins †1838: a sarcophagus on lions' feet on an
elaborate table, enclosed with railings freakishly mixing Neoclassical
urns and torches with death's heads, heraldry and crucifix finials.

ST BRIDE
off Fleet Street

1671–8 by *Wren*, on medieval crypts excavated after the Second
World War. The church has the tallest of all Wren's spires, built in
1701–3. It stands 226 ft (69 metres) high, said to have been cut down
from 236 ft (72 metres) in 1764. The church was gutted in 1940 and
restored by *Godfrey Allen* in 1955–7. The outer walls remain, with
round-headed aisle windows (circular in the end bays), and oval
clerestory windows. E end with tripartite window under an open
pediment, the arch above the centre light concentric with the main
window arch. C18 views show the main aisle windows were similarly
mullioned. The church body is of five bays with slightly projecting
chancel. Pedimented NW doorcase. The craftsmen were *Joshua
Marshall* and *Samuel Fulkes*, masons; *Benjamin Leach*, bricklayer;
John Longland, carpenter; *John Grove*, plasterer.

Big impressive stone tower, slightly projecting, rather flatly articu-
lated on the W face. Pedimented W doorcase with columns. The
bell-stage has broad segmental pediments on pilasters, an unexceptional device but one not used elsewhere amongst Wren's towers.
Columns at the corners, the corners above them recessed. Eight
urns on the parapet. Four carved masks on each suggest *Hawksmoor*
had a hand in their design (PJ). The spire is of five octagonal stages,
telescoped and of diminishing height, a logical and original solution,
but not as satisfying to look at as other major Wren steeples. Its
resemblance to that on the dome of the Warrant design for St Paul's
(1675) was noted by Gerald Cobb. That the design was made before
1700 is also suggested by the diminishing stages (albeit apparently
square), sketched on top of the existing tower in Morgan's
panorama of 1682. The first three tiers are arcaded, with corner
pilasters. Engaged columns on the fourth stage, originally crowned
by eight little urns. Obelisk above. The spire's mason was *Fulkes*. It
has been much repaired: in 1764, 1803, and 1901–2.

The interior was remodelled by *Allen*. It has rather ungainly giant
Tuscan double columns (renewed), standing N–S. They carry
arches, above which rises a barrel-vault with penetrations from the
clerestory windows. The aisle bays are groin-vaulted. All this follows
Wren's design, including the ashlar-faced walls – an unusual fea-

ture. Margaret Whinney remarked on the similarity of the roof and (destroyed) galleries to Perrault's reconstruction of Vitruvius's Basilica at Fano, likewise of five bays. This was published in 1673, too late for St Bride. Did Wren discuss it with Perrault in Paris in 1665? The galleries seem to have been an afterthought, since the Vestry settled the design only in 1675. They used to cut clumsily across the columns of the aisles, an unsatisfactory arrangement which probably explains why Wren came to prefer double-height aisles, as at his St James Piccadilly, where the columns rise from the level of the gallery fronts. Allen replaced the galleries with stalls aligned E–W, screening the aisles. They have Wrenish carving. At their W ends big STATUES of saints by *David McFall*. – Free-standing REREDOS by *Allen*, after Wren's at the Chapel Royal, Hampton Court. STAINED GLASS in its central opening and illusionistic PAINTING around it by *Glyn Jones*, a juxtaposition so unsympathetic that it is a surprise to learn it was designed as an ensemble. The E end had been much altered: by *John Deykes*, 1822–3, *Champneys*, 1885–6 and 1892–3, and *H. M. Fletcher*, *c.* 1935; restoration also in 1863 and by *Arding, Bond & Buzzard*, 1875. – Other fittings also in Wren's style. – ROYAL ARMS carved by *Kenneth Gardner*. – FONT COVER with a model of a bell-shaped turret, after an early drawing for the tower. – SCULPTURE. By the font, two charity children from the former St Bride and Bridewell Schools in Bride Lane, probably of 1711; terracotta head by *Marjorie Meggitt*, *c.* 1985. – The S doorway leads to a Neo-Georgian RECTORY by *J. R. Stammers*, 1958.

ROMAN AND MEDIEVAL REMAINS. A staircase at the NW gives access to the CRYPTS, excavated by Professor Grimes in 1952–3. This constituted the first complete archaeological investigation in England of a parish church plan. It was followed up in 1992–3, and the accompanying display updated.

The red and yellow tessellated floors of two rooms of a late Roman suburban villa terraced into the hillside overlooking the

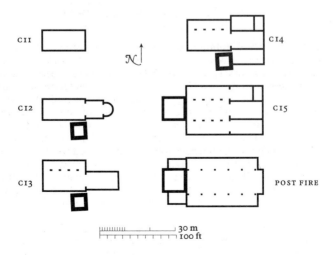

St Bride. Plans showing its development

River Fleet are displayed *in situ*, concealed from direct inspection by substantial medieval foundations, but visible in periscopic views via mirrors. The excavations also revealed two phases of Saxon work. The first, a modest masonry structure of the C6, cannot be firmly identified as a church, though the early Christianization of the Roman burial site may be posited (attested perhaps by the holy spring called Bridewell, which gave its name to Bridewell Palace to the S). The second was an apsed early to mid-C11 church, given an enlarged square E end late in the C12. The Norman church also had a campanile half-way down Wren's S aisle, not bonded in. A narrow N aisle was added in the early C13. A Lady Chapel was added to its E not long afterwards, adjoining the chancel on the N side. It was externally slightly wider than the N aisle, so a short W return wall joined them.

On display are some 30 ft (9 metres) of the chapel's N wall, and a three-bay rib-vaulted CRYPT inserted *c.* 1300. The N wall has chequered masonry of squared chalk and ragstone. At the W, remains of a former N entrance, blocked *c.* 1400 when the N aisle was widened. The crypt preserves traces of a N doorway into the church-yard and a splayed light-shaft in the E wall, made into a door in the 1950s. The change in coursing some two feet above the floor level marks the older foundations of the Lady Chapel proper. Chapel and crypt were thus originally self-sufficient, separately entered, and with their own Guild priest and services.

Wren reused the medieval foundations where possible, i.e. beneath the outer walls and beneath two S arcade piers, which rest on the N wall of the campanile. Sleeper walls for the arcades were built up with medieval material. Another VAULT built by Wren was found, tunnel-vaulted and running all along the S aisle, and another of 1750 with piers. There were also two bone-holes. In one of them the skulls and bones were arranged ornamentally in squares.

ST CLEMENT EASTCHEAP

Clement's Lane, N of King William Street

1683–7 by *Wren*, rebuilding a church first recorded by 1106. His craftsmen were *Edward Strong Sen.*, mason; *Israel Knowles*, carpenter; *William Grey*, joiner; *Doogood & Grove*, plasterers. The confusing suffix derives from Great Eastcheap, which extended to the S end of Clement's Lane before King William Street was built. Wren's un-assuming little church is of brick with stone quoins and dressings, its down-at-heel rendering and painted stucco at last under repair in 1997–8. The pedimented central bay of the W front projects slightly, with a large blocked round-headed window over a door in a concave round-headed frame. The SW tower stands on reused foundations, aligned to the street rather than the nave. Balustraded parapet, but no steeple or cupola. An alley on the N side leads E to the modest former churchyard, with a tree and railings of C18 type.

The interior too is plain, with a S aisle aligned with the tower and tapering to the E. It has Composite columns on octagonal plinths carrying a straight entablature. The space E of the S aisle represents an extension made after the Great Fire (PJ). Otherwise it is safe to assume that the nave occupies the space of the medieval nave and N aisle. The order continues around its walls in the form of pilasters, Wren's usual way of giving unity to a single-aisled space. They support groined arches piercing the coving. Above the aisle a clerestory of three lunettes. The N windows are blocked apart from three segment-headed upper lights, and since the s windows are also blocked the interior is dark. The ceiling was largely renewed in 1925 by *G. E. Nield*, to a simplified pattern. Only the central enriched elliptical panel is original. Alterations by *Butterfield*, 1872 and 1889, modified since mostly by *Sir Ninian Comper*, 1932–4. – The chief interest of the interior lies in its original WOODWORK, for which the parish paid *Thomas Poultney* for joinery and *Jonathan Maine* for carving. Butterfield and Comper have not left quite enough to save it from feeling underfurnished. – REREDOS in three pedimented parts with big engaged Corinthian columns and half-pilasters and flaming urns above. Reassembled and embellished by *Comper*, with gold-ground painted figures by *W. Butchart* in an unsuitably genteel Quattrocento manner, the frame painted blue and gilded to match. – The SEATING was rearranged by Butterfield. Old woodwork reused in the stalls includes parts of the former s gallery front. – COMMUNION RAIL with turned and carved balusters. – Noble ORGAN CASE (1696, by *Renatus Harris*). Placed by Butterfield in the aisle, but perched over the w doorcase in 1936. – Excellent big PULPIT, hexagonal with oval panel. Giant tester surmounted by festooned segmental pediments in the centre of each side and cherubs dancing on the angles. The balusters of the stair match the communion rails. – Four fine pilastered DOORCASES: three at the w; the best, to the NE vestry, otherwise similar but with a big broken segmental pediment. In the vestry an excellent contemporary OVERMANTEL with swags and festoons surrounding a fielded panel. – Carved in the panelling of the s aisle, a large GRAFFITO dated 1703. – ROYAL ARMS, Stuart, painted, s aisle. – BREAD SHELVES, now not normally displayed. – COMMUNION TABLE with coarsely carved cherubs as supporters. – FONT. Octagonal on an enriched baluster stem, of marble, by *Maine*. The pretty wooden cover (not normally on display) matches that at St Peter upon Cornhill (q.v.). – Iron SWORD REST, with painted mace and sword, probably c18. – From *Butterfield*'s work a few survivals, such as the polychromatic FLOOR TILES and good STAINED GLASS in the N clerestory. – No monuments of note.

39

ST DUNSTAN-IN-THE-EAST
St Dunstan's Hill, N of Lower Thames Street

The Gothic shell and steeple, set prominently half-way up the Hill, survived the bombs of 1941. The steeple is *Wren*'s, built in 1695–1701 (*Ephraim Beauchamp* mason). The rest by *David Laing*, 1817–21. This replaced the fire-damaged shell, patched up in 1668–71 without the aid of the Rebuilding Commissioners, following a private bene- faction. An excellent GARDEN with a fountain, made 1967–71 by the *Corporation of London Architect's Department*, now occupies Laing's shell and the surrounding churchyard. The C17 and C19 churches were both large, but smaller than the substantial medieval collegiate foundation here, probably of *c.* 1100. C12 and C13 carved stonework of high quality discovered in Harp Lane in 1974 may have come from this building. Before the Fire it had a leaded spire, and a S aisle rebuilt in 1381. *Henry Yevele* supervised the foundations, but there is no evidence that he designed the aisle.

25 Wren's new steeple must be among the 'some few examples' of Gothic churches in the E of the City he laid claim to in a letter to the Dean of Westminster in 1713. Payments were also made to *Hawksmoor*, who may have assisted with the design (PJ). *William Dickinson* supervised the work. The style was doubtless chosen to match the reused Gothic exterior, though as reconstructed this had Tuscan arcades inside. Soaring needle-spire, pierced below, carried on four steep flying buttresses – the principle of St Mary-le-Bow before the Fire, and also of St Nicholas, Newcastle, and Edinburgh Cathedral, both C15, but here carried up in a single visual sweep. The buttresses die into the spire in a strange stepped sequence. Lucarnes between. Big octagonal spire-like pinnacles on the angles of the square tower-top and a lesser intermediate pinnacle to each of the battlemented parapets. *Sir Herbert Baker & Scott* reconstructed the spire in 1953. The tower has three main stages of increasing height, with diagonal buttresses turning octagonal on the top. Typically post-medieval are the broad horizontal divisions made by the stringcourses between the stages. Tracery in the windows and belfry openings with lights cusped at the bottom as well as the top. Two-centred S and W doorways with crocketed hood-moulds starting oddly from incurved volutes. These crockets are in detail also by no means Gothic. Of the Wren period too the iron railings here, mixing Gothic and classical motifs (*James Ray*, smith). The tower was restored 1970–2 by *Seely & Paget Partnership* for use as a rectory, but now serves as offices.

Of Laing's church only the N and S walls, lower E wall and the shell of the NE porch remain. The tracery was restored *c.* 1970. According to Eastlake in 1872, the true designer was Laing's pupil *William Tite*, though the rebuilding accounts nowhere mention him. The huge expenditure of £36,000 is still palpable in the solid Portland walling with deep concave reveals, a more substantial treatment than the Commissioners could afford for their contemporary Gothic churches. Costly too the excellent cast-iron Gothic railings, E. Much detailing copied from greater medieval churches in a manner characteristic of the day: see e.g. the pinnacle reset in the N churchyard (mason and carver *Thomas Piper*), after Winchester Cathedral nave. Laing's nave had an impressive lierne vault of plaster.

ST DUNSTAN-IN-THE-WEST
Fleet Street

57 A Gothic octagon with a S tower, built 1830–3 by *John Shaw Sen.*, completed after his death in 1832 by his son, also *John*. The last of the medieval City churches to be rebuilt, and, for reasons of street widening, on a site N of the previous church (first mentioned *c.* 1170). Shaw's church looks so much at home in the street that its

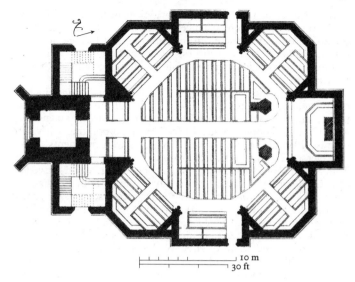

St Dunstan-in-the-West. Plan

unlikeness to most contemporary Anglican churches is easily over-looked. But the centralized plan (a consequence of the restricted site) went out of fashion *c.* 1800, and the combination of con-spicuous tower and concealed brick walls recalls Wren rather than the Commissioners' churches on their usual island sites.

Tower of Ketton stone, topped with a tall, delicate octagonal lantern designed on the pattern of All Saints Pavement at York, that is with long unglazed Perp openings and a lacy pinnacled parapet. Big pinnacles and chamfered corners make the transition from four to eight sides. The tower makes a fine, picturesque group with the CLOCK to its r. and then the statue of Queen Elizabeth. The clock was made by *Thomas Harris* in 1671 (for £35), saved in 1828 by Lord Hertford, and brought back to the church in 1935 from St Dunstan's, his villa in Regent's Park. On a black and gold bracket, but now without its C17 carved surround. Above this in a wooden Ionic aedicule two figures of men l. and r. of a feigned door, belabouring two bells – the arrangement familiar from Italian clocks, e.g. in the Piazza S. Marco in Venice and at Padua. The STATUE of Queen Elizabeth was made probably in 1586 (modern inscription) by *William Kerwin*, for the Ludgate, demolished in 1760. The AEDICULE with its decorated pilasters and open segmental pedi-ment is also from Ludgate, of *c.* 1667, but still very impure in its forms. Also from Ludgate, decayed STATUES of King Lud and his sons, kept in the vestry porch. Outside the church the NORTHCLIFFE MEMORIAL of 1930, obelisk designed by *Lutyens* with bust by *Kathleen Scott*.

The octagonal space inside is treated on principles not of, say, English chapter houses but of classical centrally planned churches. The four main axes have pointed plaster tunnel-vaults with trans-verse ribs, the four diagonal recesses also with rib-vaults. The main vault is star-ribbed above a clerestory of eight identical windows. The structure is of iron. Chancel on the N, i.e. the church is not oriented. Another entrance from Clifford's Inn Passage in the W vessel, balanced by the vestry doorway on the E. The SE and SW recesses, which originally housed galleries, have decorations by *F. H. Fowler*, 1881.

FITTINGS of the 1830s, designed by *Shaw Sen.* or *Jun.*, include the PEWS, made by *W. & L. Cubitt* (shorn of their poppy-heads), FONT, and PULPIT with linenfold panelling. – ALTAR SURROUND with Gothic canopies made by *Swaby*; incorporating early C16 Flemish Flamboyant woodwork. – STALLS with fragments of late C17 pierced carving. – ICONOSTASIS, in the NE chapel. Brought from Antim Monastery, Bucharest, in 1966. Of limewood, carved by *Petre & Mihai Babic*, *c.* 1860, with paintings in a wholly Renaissance idiom by *Petre Alexandrescu*. In the other recesses, altars dedicated to other Eastern churches. – ORGAN by *Joseph Robson*, 1834, in a case probably designed by *Shaw Jun.* – STAINED GLASS. Walton Window by *Kempe*, 1895, behind the iconostasis.* – (Ritual) E window by *Gerald Smith* of *A. K. Nicholson Studios*, 1950. Tracery lights from *Willement*'s window of the 1830s, otherwise destroyed in 1944. – SE and SW windows by Messrs *Taylor*, 1881–2. – Iron SWORD REST, frame type, 1745.

MONUMENTS in the chapels. Nothing very spectacular, but varied, and rewarding close attention. Clockwise from the entrance: brass to Henry Dacres †1530 and wife, kneeling figures, reset. – William Morecroft †1657, jowly frontal bust, characterful but somewhat gauche. In niche with looped curtains, altered above the cornice. Attributed to *Joshua Marshall* (AW). – Edward Marshall, the master mason, †1675, and wife, tablet with weeping cherubs, *c.* 1678 by the *Marshall* workshop (AW). Edward Marshall had rebuilt much of the old church in 1661–2. – Gerard Legh †1563, small tablet of good quality, flanked by male and female caryatids suggestive of French influence. – Cuthbert Fetherstone †1615, frontal bust in gristly circular niche. – Sir Richard Hutton, by *Nicholas Stone*, 1640. Small Michelangelesque tablet in black and white stone. – Richard Peirson †1718 and others, high up, reset in a Gothic frame. – Elizabeth Moore †1668, attributed to *Joshua Marshall* (AW). – Hobson Judkin †1812 'the honest solicitor', circular tablet with tiny skulls: 'Go reader and imitate Hobson Judkin'. – Concealed behind the iconostasis: Elizabeth North †1612, the usual kneeling figure, with dainty strapwork decoration; Thomas Valence †1601, with enriched frame. – Thomas White, founder of Sion College, early C17 style; designed by *Blomfield*, 1877. – Kneeling male figure, late C16. – Margaret Talbot †1620, slate incised with kneeling figure in perspective-box architectural setting; alabaster frame. – Albert Faber †1684, signed by *John Settle*. – Damaris Turner †1703, big cartouche. – Sir Richard Hoare, by *Thomas Stayner*, 1723. Tablet with scrolly surround and no effigy; two putti on top. – Sir Richard Hoare †1754, much larger. Sarcophagus with carved fluting. On it a putto with portrait medallion. – Edward James Auriol, drowned in the Rhône in 1847. Bust of white marble in a niche, lying on a pillow as if asleep; hand on heart. Very naturalistic; young features; hardly of English work-

---

* Augustus Hare, *Walks in London* (1901), gives it to *Bacon*.

manship. – Over the entrance from the porch, John Shaw †1832; circular tablet with angels, a naïve but pleasing Romantic composition, doubtless designed by *Shaw Jun.*

ST EDMUND THE KING
Lombard Street

First mentioned by 1157–80. The present church of 1670–4 is almost certainly by *Hooke*. The evidence is a drawing of the w front in his hand, initialled by Wren and inscribed 'With his M(ajes)ties' Approbation' (*Wren Soc.* IX, pl. 15). It differs from the present church in having carved garlands along the side pieces and on top a balustrade and little low turret, later replaced. The craftsmen were *Abraham Storey*, mason; *Maurice Emmett Jun.*, bricklayer; *George Clisby* and *Henry Wilkinson*, carpenters; *Thomas Whiting*, joiner; *Daniel Morrice* and *John Sherwood*, plasterers. It lies N–S and the s front is developed boldly into a ritual w end. According to the *Parentalia* this alignment was due to the high value of land in the street; but the medieval predecessor also lay N–S. Three-bay façade with quoins. Arched windows with key blocks carved with cherubs' heads, under straight hoods on brackets. Strangely gauche mullioned windows to l. and r. below. Quoined slightly projecting middle bay, carrying a small pediment. Above this rises the tower and spire. The outer bays send up to the tower concave pieces in the Italian façade tradition. At their outer ends and on the tower parapet urns and pineapples. Behind this parapet an octagonal leaded lantern and a slightly concave-sided short spire, completed as late as 1706–7 (mason *W. Kempster*, carpenter *Richard Jennings*, plumber *Joseph Roberts*). It was stripped *c.* 1900 of twelve flaming urns in two tiers. A drawing for this steeple exists in the hand of *Hawksmoor*. So here, it seems, is a 'Wren' church designed by two other architects, albeit under his supervision. Projecting CLOCK on the tower, *c.* 1810. The best view of the spire is from George Yard, adjoining part of the former churchyard, NE. N and E walls, originally of brick with a wooden cornice, were refaced excessively trimly by *Caröe & Passmore* 1929–32, when the Yard was opened out. Of this date also the churchyard RAILINGS.

Entrance is made via a circular domed lobby beneath the tower. The interior is spatially without interest (rearranged by *Butterfield*, 1864 and 1881). No subdivision, just an oblong with a flat ceiling on the usual coving. Nave ceiling crudely replaced after bomb damage in 1917, with a mechanically detailed plaster frame to the big central panel and an ugly little central skylight, first made in 1725. Round-headed recesses around the walls, pierced with windows on ritual s and E. Small projecting chancel with pendentives and semicircular ceiling, which replaced a tall timber lantern-cum-clerestory some time after the mid C18. On the ceiling now a ruined PAINTING, probably from Butterfield's work. Excellent WOODWORK (*Thomas Creecher*, joiner). PANELLING of the walls, complete except for a NE recess, apparently contrived by Butterfield as an organ chamber. – Flanking the chancel two fine Corinthian DOORCASES with broken pediments, palm fronds, and flaming urns added after 1707 (carver *Henry Swarbrick*). – Matching urns on the REREDOS were formerly on the S door. Otherwise flat and simple with a segmental pediment on half-pilasters, but with plenty of good foliage carving. On it PAINTINGS of Aaron and Moses by *Etty*, 1833. – COMMUNION TABLE with big scrolly legs. – COMMUNION RAILS with balusters of unusual form, tapering symmetrically from a carved central ring. – CHURCHWARDENS' PEWS with carved fronts. – Other SEATING with reused panelling. – LECTERN. The same. – PULPIT. Of the usual type, but specially good quality. No tester, but STAIRS with balusters matching the communion rails. – Nicely carved ORGAN CASES, one of 1701–2, the other a replica of 1880. One is set over the entrance, the other near the pulpit. – Six mysterious carved POSTS or piers on the wall of the tower. – FONT. Marble with acanthus decoration and within a good, solid rail with twisted balusters on a semi-elliptical plan (the COVER, with small figures of apostles, is not normally displayed). – ROYAL ARMS. Late C17. From St Dionis Backchurch Fenchurch Street (dem.). – SWORD REST. 1753. – STAINED GLASS. E window, Christ in Glory, said to have been made in Munich for St Paul's in the late 1860s but rejected, installed in St Bartholomew Moor Lane, and brought here *c.* 1905 after that church was demolished. – Flanking windows by Messrs *Taylor*, 1886. – Royal Fusiliers Memorial window by *Percy Bacon*, *c.* 1922. – MONUMENTS. Dr J. Milles, President of the Society of Antiquaries. Standing figure of Hope by an obelisk, leaning on an urn and pointing upwards. By the elder *Bacon*, 1786. – E. Ironside †1753. Substantial sarcophagus and obelisk in coloured marble. – Susan Horne †1835, by *Baily*.

ST ETHELBURGA
Bishopsgate

In 1993 a terrorist bomb destroyed the W end and most of the N wall of St Ethelburga: the greatest loss to the City's churches since the Blitz. Only 55 ft (17 metres) long, it was a unique survivor of the smaller medieval City churches, mostly lost in 1666. Its atmosphere was, unforgettably, that of a sleepy village church. The unique dedication to this C7 saint suggests great antiquity, but the first mention is only in 1250. A carved base of *c.* 1200, found reused in the walls, may be from the first church, which was wholly rebuilt in the late C14. No tower, though the entrance bay, W of the aisle, was separated from the nave by an arch like a tower arch. Its S respond remains, with S wall and arcade, E wall, and the lower E part of the N wall. The four-bay S arcade has piers with four shafts and four hollows, and two-centred double-hollow-chamfered arches. Two late C14 PISCINAE, one each in chancel and aisle. Late C15 five-light E window, renewed probably in *R. J. Withers*'s restoration, 1861–2. In the S aisle four plain pointed windows.

Opinion on the future of these remains has been divided. *Blee Ettwein Bridges'* competition-winning scheme, rejected in 1996, proposed for them a giant glazed enclosure like a reliquary, intended as a memorial to victims of terrorism, with offices to the E. A rival scheme for complete reconstruction was proposed by *Rothermel Thomas* and *Richard Griffiths* (structural advisers *Alan Baxter & Associates*). In 1997 it was announced that the church will be reconstructed as a Centre for Peace and Reconciliation by the firm of *Purcell Miller Tritton*. Their greatest challenge will be to re-create convincingly the funny little Bishopsgate front, which sat impudently between towering C20 offices. It was of ragstone like the rest, with a late C14 doorway and a broad three-light late C15 window, off-centre. Its brick upper parts and plain parapet replaced a crow-stepped gable probably in 1835 (by *William Grellier*); the square timber bell-turret dated from rebuilding in 1775, replacing a short C15–C16 spire. A weathercock dated 1671 survived the blast. Before 1932, the front was rendered and very picturesquely half-hidden by timber-framed shops, dated 1570 and 1613.

FITTINGS. A surprising amount was salvaged. Of the pretty furnishings by *Comper*, 1912, the PARCLOSE SCREEN survives. – FONT. Gothic, C18 or C19. – Fine FONT COVER from St Swithin Cannon Street, by *Kedge*, 1687. – WALL PAINTING. Crucifixion by *Hans Feibusch*, 1962, over the altar. – PAINTING. Christ healing; Flemish, early C16; attributed to *Peter Coeke van Aelst*. Only fragments remained of the STAINED GLASS: by *Kempe* (E window, 1878), *L. Walker* (1928–30, four windows showing the adventures of Henry Hudson), and *Hugh Easton*, 1936; also some good C17 heraldic glass.

ST GILES CRIPPLEGATE
Barbican

A large church mostly of *c.* 1545–50, i.e. at the end of the medieval church-building tradition. Much restored in the late C19 and again by *Godfrey Allen* after severe bomb damage (reopened 1960). It now serves as the centrepiece of the Barbican Estate's main open space. Overshadowed by massive concrete forms and paved right up to the walls, it looks in its situation by the lake almost as if dismantled and brought from elsewhere; but it also anchors the late C20 environment in the wider urban context – in part by marking the true ground level, something visitors to the Estate may find elusive – and in an older history.

The church is recorded as having been built by Aelmund the priest *c.* 1102–15. According to Stow, the former vicarage stood on the site of an earlier church further w, but this may only have been a wayside shrine (by tradition the church marks the resting place of the body of King Edmund Martyr outside Cripplegate in 1010). The addition of guild chapels to the church on the present site in the C14 culminated in its complete rebuilding in 1390. The C16 rebuilding, following a fire of 1545, is thought to have reused the C14 plan, which tapers markedly from w to e with the tower slightly off axis. Substantial late C14 work survives in the chancel walls, better visible since cleaning in 1994. C14 work also remains in the base of the tower, which has angle buttresses to the outer corners, a big NW stair-turret and two-light windows. Brick top stage with panelled parapet and stubby pinnacles, added by *John Bridges* in 1682–4. Its two-light tracery differs from that of the restored lower apertures, but its forms are also late C19 and not 1680s Gothic. The pretty open cupola is a post-war restoration. Otherwise, the church was refaced in ragstone by *F. Hammond* (s side 1884–5, redone after the fire damage in 1897; N side 1903–5).

8   Inside, the nave and aisles are of seven bays with a partly project-ing chancel, the ritual chancel extending also to the two bays furthest E. The stone piers have a moulding of four shafts connected by deep hollows with thin filleted diagonal shafts. The hollows con-tinue around the arch. Aisle windows of three lights with simple panel tracery, on the N simpler than on the S. Fine shafts up to the roof between depressed-arched windows. The carving of corbels, stops etc. is renewed. The E end was much altered in the C18, and the chancel arch dates only from 1858–9 (galleries removed 1862). The Perp E window is post-war, based on late C14 traces discovered during restoration (replacing a large *œil-de-bœuf* window of 1704 with glass of 1791 by *Pearson*). A two-light N chancel window was opened up at the same time; the answering S window remains blocked. The post-war roof is arch-braced. Traces survive of the ROOD-LOFT DOORWAY (S wall), battered double SEDILIA with near-equilateral arches (restored with salvaged Roman tiles), and PISCINA in a square-headed surround. They look late C14.

Few FITTINGS survived the war and the church has been re-furnished, partly with items from elsewhere. The big new W GALLERY by *Cecil Brown* has tall Composite columns. On it an ORGAN CASE, from St Luke Old Street, of 1733 by *Jordan & Bridge*; rebuilt in 1970 by *Noel Mander*, with casework of 1684 from St Andrew Holborn (behind). – FONT with elegant stem and bowl with acanthus leaves, and domed COVER, with pilasters and garlands, both from St Luke Old Street. – SWORD REST. C20. – STAINED GLASS. E window, Crucifixion by *A.K. Nicholson Studios*, 1957. – Armorial W window by *John Lawson* (*Faithcraft Studios*), 1968. – SCULPTURE. Four busts of *c.*1900 (Milton and Defoe by *Frampton*; also Cromwell and Bunyan), on loan from the Cripplegate Institute. – Bronze statue of Milton (who is buried here) by *Horace Montford*, 1904. It formerly stood N of the church, facing the old line of Fore Street (its battered pedestal, designed by *E.A. Rickards*, stands outside, minus Montford's reliefs). – MONUMENTS. Thomas Busby †1575, damaged bust from a once large monument. – John Speed †1629. Bust, damaged in the war, restored 1971 in a replica of part of the old surround. Attributed to *John & Matthias Christmas* (AW). – Elizabeth de Vallingin †1772 (part), with circular plaque of a female mourner, pyramid and urn. – Thomas Stagg †1772, tablet abruptly inscribed: 'that is all'. – Bust of John Milton, by the elder *Bacon*, given by Samuel Whitbread in 1793. The pedestal has a little carving of the serpent and apple. – Bust of Sir William Staines †1807, by *Charles Manning*, from a large monument destroyed by bombing.

Around the church is a brick-paved area planted with trees, partly on the site of the pre-war churchyard. The late C19 GAS LAMPS, scattered about like saplings, were brought here from Tower Bridge. Some early C19 tombstones of rounded-coffin type, with other slabs reused as seats. The huge monolith of the Stanier vault (S side) is worth looking at. A church hall is accommodated below ground level E of the chancel.

ST HELEN BISHOPSGATE

Great St Helen's, E of Bishopsgate

An unexpected relic hidden behind the massive office buildings of Bishopsgate, facing a little churchyard with two tall trees. It is the fragment of a Benedictine nunnery, with the nuns' church completely preserved. The nunnery was established *c.* 1200–15 by William, son of William the Goldsmith, in connection with an existing parish church (known possibly before 1010, certainly by *c.* 1140). Hence the odd arrangement of the present church, with twin naves of almost equal width, i.e. the nave of the former nuns' church (now N aisle) built against and parallel to the nave of the parish church, with its S transept with C14 E chapels. Most of the reliable external features date from *c.* 1475. The next date is *c.* 1632–3, when the exterior was embellished and the interior refurnished. Minor later restorations 1807–9 (*Robert Chapman*), between 1831 and 1845 (*Tite*); major work in 1865–8 (*J. F. Wadmore*), 1874–5 (*E. B. I'Anson*), and 1892–3 (*Pearson*). St Helen was damaged by the terrorist bombs of 1992 and 1993, and was restored and drastically reordered by *Quinlan Terry*, 1993–5, who swept away most of Pearson's work.

EXTERIOR. Walls are of random rubble, of which some C12 fabric remains in the parish nave S wall, perhaps also in its E wall. Of the C13 the whole W and N walls of the church, most of the E wall, and the S transept. The W front is exceedingly pretty, with two low-pitched embattled gables, and in lieu of a tower a timber bell-turret with square dome and open lantern between. This was first made 1568–9, but the present structure looks *c.* 1700 (repairs were mentioned in 1696; see however its casing, inside). W windows of *c.* 1475, with the usual depressed arches. No tracery, and – unusually – no cusping. The N and S halves of the building do not quite match here: the l. window only has a (C19) transom and a C16 doorway below; the r. doorway is early C14. The placing of the middle buttress indicates the slightly greater width of the nuns' church. 7

On the S side some visible C13 features: two non-matching lancets in the transept W wall (one blocked), and remains of three more in the S transept wall. One of those in the W wall has been partly destroyed by *Terry*'s ornate eared doorcase, dated 1995. A first-floor piscina on the transept W wall, S end, remains from a vanished two-storey appendage built *c.* 1400; traces of squints have also been found. Much brick patching to this wall, perhaps from 1807–9; more in the main S wall. This was heightened in the late C15, with three-light windows. Traces also of a blocked two-light window of *c.* 1400, E. Further W a pedimented stone doorway dated 1633, amongst the earliest examples of a rather Mannerist mid-C17 style which flourished in the City and the counties NE of London and is connected with the architect-bricklayer Peter Mills. Frame with ears, half-pilasters outside it, and other weird angular forms; doors to match (cf. the contemporary SW door). Summerson suggested as the designer the carpenter *Anthony Lynnett*, who was busy at the time at the Leathersellers' Hall to the N. Two chapels were added to the S transept some time before 1374, in line with the main E wall. They have Dec windows, largely of 1874–5. C14 parapets of banded stone and flint. In the main E windows, tracery of 1865–8 18

(S, Perp) and 1993–5 (N, curvilinear Dec, replacing geometrical work of 1865–8).

More C13 remains in the N wall of the nuns' church, visible from a narrow passage behind the buildings of St Helen's Place: one lancet at the W end, remains of three more beyond. The present windows here are C15, of varying heights to be clear of the former conventual buildings. Beneath the sills at the W end runs the weathering course of the former cloister, remains of which were uncovered and destroyed in 1922. The other buildings opened off it in the usual way. The E range lasted until 1799, latterly as the Leathersellers' Hall. Though greatly altered, it retained the vaulted crypts of the C13 dorter and chapter house. All that remains is a stub of the former W sacristy wall, with blind arches and a vault springer beyond. Further E a plain double-chamfered C13 doorway into the choir, and three squints.

INTERIOR. Until the restoration of 1993–5, the nave and S transept floors were several steps lower, with steps up to the two separate chancels: mostly the work of *Pearson*, who lowered the nave and fitted up the S chancel with screens and stalls. The precise medieval arrangement is unclear, although the transept was undoubtedly much lower than now. *Terry* remade the floor at one indiscriminately high level throughout. Walls are rendered and painted cream, except in the SE chapels. The inspiration seems to be the scrubbed, light-filled church interiors of C17 Holland, as painted by artists such as Saenredam. The remodelled interior is intended to allow flexible use for the church's current preaching-based services, which it undoubtedly suits better than Pearson's compartmented High Church arrangement. But few church interiors were less suited to such root-and-branch treatment. The restoration shows no sense of a creative dialogue between past and present, for all its Neo-Georgian trimmings. The loss to the viewer's perception of the unique early history of the church is also grave. The effect of the uniform floor level on the S transept is particularly unhappy, as a glance at its truncated central pier will show. The even sea of stone flags also laps absurdly close to those of the standing monuments which remain at the previous floor level.

The arcade between the two churches has, towards the W, four fine slim bays which allow access between the N aisle (former nuns' nave) and parish nave. The piers have four attached shafts with capitals, and double-wave mouldings in the diagonals without capitals. They date from c. 1475, paid for in part by Sir John Crosby's bequest. Between the two chancels are two arches opened up at different periods: the W arch early C14, the broad and low E arch c. 1420. A late C15 moulded doorway in the N wall leads to a narrow staircase in the thickness of the wall, probably the night stair from the dorter. Twin arches of c. 1475 open to the S transept and chapels. The pier between the chapels, of c. 1375, has four sturdy shafts and small diagonal hollows. The Gothic S window of the transept is early C17 (can it be c. 1633?). Ogee-headed NICHES on the chapel E walls, late C14, much renewed, in three vertical pairs. Two PISCINAE of the same date below, with square heads and shelves, now at floor level. The ROOFS throughout contain original material. They are of low pitch and tie-beam construction. All but that of the SE chapels were partially ceiled in 1993–5. The wagon-

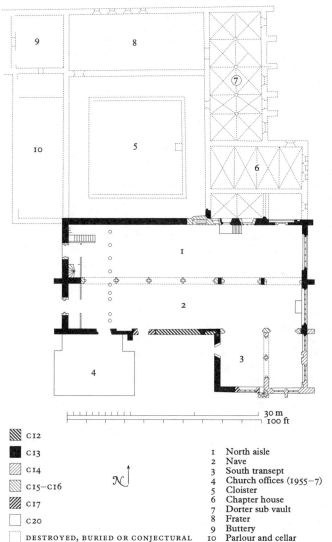

	C12			1	North aisle
	C13			2	Nave
	C14			3	South transept
	C15–C16			4	Church offices (1955–7)
				5	Cloister
	C17			6	Chapter house
	C20			7	Dorter sub vault
				8	Frater
	DESTROYED, BURIED OR CONJECTURAL			9	Buttery
				10	Parlour and cellar

30 m
100 ft

St Helen Bishopsgate. Plan

roofed s transept has a pretty c19 timber clerestory with Gothic windows.

OTHER FITTINGS. Much reordered in 1993–5, with movable seating arranged to face the PULPIT on the s wall. This is a glorious piece of carpentry, richly decorated with architectural forms, and with a large tester with bay-leaf frieze. It may be of c. 1633. c18 alterations to the back-board. – DOORCASES. An outstandingly good c17 example against the parish nave s wall. It is probably that paid for in the early 1630s, though it is more advanced in style than the contemporary fittings. The style derives from Inigo Jones and Nicholas

Stone and leads to the late C17 style favoured in the City. The use of fluted columns is the most telling feature. Swan-necked pediment, with standing lions flanking a tall attic block. Its inscription ('the gate of Heaven') is emphasized by the doorway motif in the cresting and in the *trompe l'œil* panels of the DOORS: a nice conceit. A second doorway in the S transept, a made-up piece, was moved from the W end in 1993–5. It has strapwork pilasters still of Jacobean type. Broken segmental curly-ended pediment, with reclining angels and a shield, formerly part of a reredos (*see Survey of London* Vol. 9, 1924). The different styles of all this joinery may reflect different dates, or the patronage of different livery and trading companies in a single campaign of embellishment. – COMMUNION TABLE. Early C18. Twisted legs, inlaid top. From St Martin Outwich. – SCREEN. Across the S transept, the former 1890s chancel screen, delicate late Gothic, by *Pearson*. – REREDOS by *Pearson* (cut down), triptych with gilt and polychrome relief of the Resurrection. – CHOIR STALLS. Thirteen C15 stalls from the nuns' choir, with grotesque arm-rests; no misericords. Supplemented by C19 fittings. – W GALLERY by *Terry*, extending across both naves. Neo-Georgian, with Doric columns. Sections of *Pearson*'s parclose screens reused in the lobbies below. On the gallery a mahogany ORGAN CASE by *Thomas Griffin*, 1742–4, with three towers and serpentine flats (instrument rebuilt by *Goetze & Gwynn*, 1995).– Alongside, pretty rusticated timber CASING of the W bell-turret, with pilasters. – POOR BOX, late C18, on a bearded caryatid probably of *c.* 1632. – FONT. 1632. Of baluster type, black and red marble. Contemporary COVER with ogee top. – BAPTISTERY by *Terry*. Hexagonal, for baptism by immersion, sunk into the parish nave floor. – EASTER SEPULCHRE in the N wall of the nuns' choir, doubling as the monument of Johane Alfrey †1525. Square-headed, crested recess with four-centred splayed and panelled arch: a design used for other early C16 London tombs (e.g. at Lambeth and Hackney). Not well preserved. Its special feature is below: instead of the usual quatrefoiled chest, an arcade of cusped pointed lights, open behind as a squint for the nuns to look into the church from the sacristy. – SCULPTURE. Excellent small seated female figure, *c.* 1600 (S transept). Alabaster; style of *Colt*? – TILES. Medieval and C19 tiles are preserved at the old floor level around the SE chapels, in a boarded-over trench. – SWORD RESTS (nuns' church). Two, one wrought iron of the frame type, C18. The other is a great rarity. It is of wood and bears the remarkably early date 1665. Two elegantly twisted columns carry an entablature with a coat of arms above flanked by two angels. – STAINED GLASS. Shakespeare window, nuns' nave, 1884. – C15–C17 fragments in adjoining windows. – Clear glazing replaces the destroyed E windows (1866–7, by *Powell*, N, and *Heaton & Butler*, S).

MONUMENTS. St Helen has the best pre-Fire collection of any London parish church, augmented in 1875 by several from the demolished St Martin Outwich, Bishopsgate (marked ᴹ). First the BRASSES (to be reset in the SE chapels). John Leventhorp †1510, in armour. – Civilian and wife, *c.* 1470. – Nicholas Wotton †1482,ᴹ rector of St Martin Outwich; small figure. – Another priest, *c.* 1500.ᴹ – Thomas Wylliams †1495 and wife, in civilian dress. – Robert Rochester †1510, in armour. – Lady in stiff cloak, *c.* 1535. – Other monuments. The mighty tomb of Francis Bancroft †1727, 9 ft (nearly 3 metres) square, 'like a house', was alas removed in 1892. Listed topographically: nuns' choir: Johane Alfrey (†1525), *see* Easter Sepulchre, above. Free-standing in front of it, Sir Thomas Gresham, the creator of the Royal Exchange, †1579, a remarkable tomb-chest 16 in the manner of an antique sarcophagus. No effigy on the black marble slab. Fluted sides with excellently understood classical details above and below the fluting, and big coats of arms. More restrained even than his Exchange's relatively pure Northern Renaissance, it speaks eloquently of the informed personal taste of a well-travelled merchant prince. – By it, under the first arch between nuns' church and parish church, Sir William Pickering †*c.* 1574, much more typical of Elizabethan exuberance. Recumbent effigy under six-poster, an early appearance of the type. Coffered arches, transverse lesser arches with guilloche; achievement on top like a locket. Attributed to the *Cure* workshop (AW). Inscription on a separate tablet, parish choir N wall. Contemporary iron RAILINGS with knobs on twisted finials. – E wall: Sir Andrew Judd, merchant, †1558. Tiny, with kneelers. The inscription tells of his travels 'To Russia and Muscova/To Spayne Gynny without fable'. – N wall, from the E: William and Esther Finch, †1672 and †1673, grand tablet with columns and oval wreath. Attributed to *W. Stanton* (GF). – Peter Gaussen †1788, obelisk with relief of cherubs and a woman holding a portrait relief; much agitated drapery, not well done. – William Bond †1576 and family, of the usual type, with kneelers. Attributed to *Gerard Johnson Sen.* (GF). – Martin Bond †1643, military relief in a frame with columns, seated pensively inside a tent with assistant figures on guard: a monument with much atmosphere. Bond appears as in youth, when he commanded the trained bands raised against the Armada. Other figures poignantly in Civil War dress. Attributed to *Thomas Stanton* (GF); freely copied from Sir Charles Montagu's monument (†1625), Barking, Essex. – Valentine Moortoft †1641. Pedimented tablet with black marble columns, a common type. Attributed to *Nicholas Stone* (AW). – Elizabeth Thompson †1828. Stereotyped mourners in relief. – Lady Lawrence †1682. Urn on a chest, incomplete. Attributed to *Bushnell* (GF). – Hugh Pemberton †1500,ᴹ stately Purbeck tomb-chest with canopy, straight-topped and crested. Three cusped depressed arches on the front, one each on the W and E sides, each with a crocketed blank ogee gable. Little niches on the diagonals of the canopy piers. Chest with the usual quatrefoils with shields. Brasses partly remain against the back wall. – Alderman Robinson †1599 (W gallery). Two pha- lanxes of kneelers between columns. – Free-standing beneath the second arch from the W, *William Kerwin*, the City Mason, †1594. Miniature railed tomb-chest without effigy. Inscribed figures on the sides. In the inscription he says of himself: 'Aedibus attalibus Londinum decoravi'. What buildings were these?

Parish nave, from W: Sir John Spencer, Lord Mayor, †1609 and wife (S wall). Standing wall-monument, with on the tomb-chest two tall flanking black obelisks, a kneeling figure, and two recumbent figures. Against the wall two shallow coffered arches and fine ribbonwork framing the inscriptions. Big achievement on top (cf. such monuments in Westminster Abbey as that of the Countess of Hertford, 1598). Attributed to *Nicholas Johnson* (AW). – Richard Staper †1608ᴹ (S wall). The kneeling figures are more ambitiously treated in perspective than usual. – Between parish chancel and S transept Sir John Crosby †1476 and wife. Crosby Hall was close to Great St Helen's. Purbeck tomb-chest with quatrefoil panels separated by double buttresses. Excellently carved alabaster effigies, he in armour, she with a head-dress fashioned as a smooth block. S transept: John de Oteswich and wife, late C14M. Alabaster effigies with narrow parallel folds in the draperies. The chest is modern. – Sir Julius Caesar (Adelmare), a judge in the Court of Admiralty, †1636, by *Stone* (paid £110). Plain tomb-chest, black marble top, and in lieu of the effigy the rare conceit of a flat parchment document with seal, carved in white marble as if it were lying on the black slab. It bears in self-consciously archaic black letter a testimony that Sir Julius was ready at any time to pay the debt of nature. Moved to the nuns' choir in 1875; moved back and repaired after severe damage sustained in 1992. – Rachel Chambrelan †1687. Elaborate upright tablet with standing cherubs. Attributed to *Gibbons*. – W. Bernard †1746, a large and clumsy architectural construction.

In the CHURCHYARD, altar tomb to Joseph Lem †1686: the master bricklayer of that name? The Neo-Georgian brick RECTORY, S side, replaced *Pearson*'s vestry here in 1966–8. Free-standing CHURCH OFFICE at the NW, by *Kenneth Lindy, J. Hill & Partners*, 1955–7, likewise Neo-Georgian, with a copper mansard.

ST JAMES GARLICKHITHE

Garlick Hill, N of Upper Thames Street

First mentioned *c.* 1170; made collegiate in 1481. The size of the pre-Fire church is reflected in the scale of *Wren*'s replacement of 1676–82. The mason was *Christopher Kempster*, bricklayer *Thomas Warren*, carpenter *Israel Knowles*, plasterers *Doogood & Grove*, joiner *William Cleere*. The tower, finished 1685, projects at the W. W doorway arched, with a cherub's-head keystone, and demi-columns overlapping pilasters carrying a pediment. Square tower with round-headed openings (ashlar-faced in 1944; later repairs by *D. Lockhart-Smith* and *Alexander Gale*, 1954–63). Then a pierced parapet with delicate uprights fashioned like hourglasses, and bulgy corner vases. Recessed, a delightful spire added in 1713–17 to a design possibly of *c.* 1700 in which Hawksmoor may have had a hand (*see* Introduction p. 34). It belongs with those at St Stephen Walbrook and St Michael Paternoster Royal, all three carried out by *Edward Strong Jun.*, mason, and *Richard Jennings*, carpenter. First stage square with diagonally projecting coupled colonnettes standing in front of pilasters. Each pair carries a projecting entablature, with more vases and a flattened angle scroll on top. Above, a tiny square stage, then a tinier concave stage with a finial. The CLOCK on the tower, dated 1682, is a replica of 1988 of one destroyed in the Blitz. RAILINGS in front given by the Vintners' Company, *c.* 1965.

The W front itself has paired close-set arched windows flanking the tower, with the returned clerestory walls rising above and segmental half-pediments with volutes joining them to the tower: an unusual composition. Lesser doorways beneath the windows. Plainer S and N fronts, of brick, the key blocks of the windows uncarved. Each has five arched windows, the middle one considerably higher. These middle windows acquired their circular shape and cast-iron tracery probably in 1866 (other restorations 1815, 1838, 1854, 1883–5). Traces of Wren's original round-headed mullioned window may be seen on the N side, above a blocked square-headed doorway. The S front was originally built against, with a light-well to the central window, but widening along Upper Thames Street in 1973 has exposed it. The stucco and blind window outlines here were added c. 1981 by *Michael Biscoe*. The centre of the S front was reconstructed again (by *Biscoe & Stanton*) after a freakish accident in 1991, when a crane fell on to it from across the street.

The interior explains the tall windows of the N and S walls. It is an ingenious minor version of one of the ideas of St Stephen Walbrook – a combination of longitudinal and central planning, but with the dome left out. Nave of five bays, very high, with flat ceiling on broad coving with penetration from segment-headed clerestory windows (central panels painted with clouds c. 1992). The coving rises on a straight entablature carried by the tall Ionic columns of the nave. The narrow aisles are lower and flat-ceilinged. Projecting chancel between pilasters, with windows on N and S. It is narrower than the nave; the proportions such that the chancel is one-third of the total width and the aisles one-sixth each. The middle bay of the nave is wider than the rest, and the entablature is not carried through but returned to the outer walls so as to form central transepts in line with the blocked N doorway outside.

Post-war restoration has erased Victorian traces (e.g. of *Champneys'* redecoration, 1886), and the church is now an orderly showcase for the unusually fine ensemble of Wren period WOODWORK (parochial joiners *Fuller* and *Robert Layton*; carver *W. Newman*). Rich COMMUNION TABLE by *Fuller*, with scrolled legs and doves perching on the feet. – COMMUNION RAILS with twisted balusters. – Big, exceedingly finely carved PULPIT from St Michael Queenhithe, with big flat-topped tester and elegant staircase with twisted balusters. – REREDOS. Tripartite, with two Corinthian columns between pilasters and a straight entablature. A pediment was removed in 1815 to accommodate the PAINTING of the Ascension by *Andrew Geddes*, whose brother was the curate here: splendidly Rubenesque in colouring, but somewhat weakly drawn. – STALLS with back screens from St Michael Queenhithe. – CHURCHWARDENS' PEWS, W, carved by *Newman*. On them HAT STANDS of iron. – WAINSCOT, painted dark blue c. 1992. No grand doorcases; instead, Corinthian pilasters flank doorways to E and (in the vestibule) to W. – Octagonal FONT by *Kempster*, a common type. The plain ogee cover is no longer displayed. – Two iron SWORD RESTS, each with carved LION and UNICORN supporters (one set from St Michael Queenhithe, perhaps of 1681). – ROYAL ARMS. Large piece in S transept, from St Michael; smaller one belonging to St James's, early C19, on the N wall. – WEST GALLERY of c. 1714 on openwork iron stanchions with Corinthian capitals. On it an ORGAN by *Knopple*, called 'lately erected' in 1719. Trumpeting cherubs with palm branches on the case, which has four towers rather than the usual three. On the summit the scallop shell of St James. – Generous double STAIRCASE from the vestibule, with swept ends and twisted balusters. – BUST of Thomas Cranmer by *Mary Quinn*, 1989, on the screen of the stalls. – CHANDELIER of glass, remade after the 1991 accident to original designs of 1967 by *Arnold Montrose*. Based on an C18 example at Emmanuel College, Cambridge. – MONUMENT. Peter Jones †1694, with cherubs holding back drapery. Apparently by *Thomas Cartwright Sen.*, a version of his Thorold monument at St Andrew Undershaft (GF).

ST KATHARINE CREE
Leadenhall Street

The most important church in London between Jones and Wren – a building of 1628–31, a rare period for churches. Creechurch means Christchurch, and Christchurch refers to the priory of Holy Trinity within the precincts of which St Katharine stood. It may have begun as a cemetery chapel, but became fully parochial in 1414. The new church was under the patronage of Bishop Laud and was consecrated by him. Only the SW tower of *c.* 1504 goes back to the Middle Ages. Doorcase and circular cupola with columns of 1776. E of the tower the C17 S side faces Leadenhall Street. Squared ragstone, the reused foundations of the previous S wall visible. Odd three-light cinquefoiled windows to aisle and clerestory, straight-headed, with the centre light a little higher than the others. Aisle windows eared, with eared aprons. A similar window at St Mary, Goudhurst, Kent, where the London mason *Edmund Kinsman* was busy in 1638, makes him a possible designer (Colvin). The present straight parapet, C18, replaced segmental pediments above the centre and end aisle windows, as well as wavy cresting on the clerestory, tower, and E and W walls. A fragment of the latter survives against the tower, facing Creechurch Lane (W). Thinly pedimented large W window (blocked 1686), above a doorway without Gothic reminiscences. On the S aisle wall a delicate SUNDIAL of 1706.

20 Inside, Gothic returns in full strength in the E window. Above five plain lights is set a sixteen-light rose inscribed in a square with pierced spandrels: a French device, imitated at Old St Paul's retrochoir (begun 1256), which may be the model here. The interior is of six bays, truncated by the skewed W wall. Corinthian columns carry arches without intervening entablature, a remarkable departure from Perp traditions at the time (cf. the wholly Gothic arcades of Lincoln's Inn Chapel, *c.* 1619–23). The arch soffits are coffered. Above the clerestory a flat, spidery rib-vault (of plaster) with ridge-ribs and one pair of transverse tiercerons. The two chancel bays are treated more ornately than the rest. They have big bosses like badges, mostly with arms of the City companies. The vault responds rise from corbels roughly like Ionic capitals. The aisles are rib-vaulted as well.

Reminiscences of the church's narrower C15 predecessor may be seen in the narrowness of the NW aisle bays (C15 walling here) and in the surviving respond of the old S arcade (W tower wall). The latter betrays the C17 raising of the floor, indicated by excavations in 1928 to have lain previously 5 ft (1½ metres) below. Victorian restoration in 1878–9 by *R. P. Notley*; post-war repairs by *Marshall Sisson*, 1956–62, reconstructing the vaults and S aisle. Formerly home to the Industrial Christian Fellowship, housed in flimsy offices in the aisles; since 1997 home to the City Churches Development Group.

FURNISHINGS. FONT. Octagonal, marble, doubtless of *c.* 1631, still with strapwork etc. Contemporary ogee-domed COVER. – REREDOS. Modest, with Corinthian pilasters; probably of 1728. – COMMUNION TABLE. Finely carved, *c.* 1780. – PULPIT. Elegant work of 1732, the tester much inlaid. – LECTERN. Made up of C17 parts. – ORGAN. 1686 by *Father Smith.* Beautifully carved CASE with three towers and cherubs on pedimented flats between. – DOORCASE to NW vestry, dated 1693. – Two iron SWORD RESTS, with arms of 1787 and 1820. – ROYAL ARMS. C17. – STAINED GLASS. In the E window rose, foliage etc. of 1630, repaired by *Pearson,* 1777. Lower lights of 1878. – N aisle: Transfiguration, by *Kempe, c.* 1890. – S aisle: Christ walking on the waters, by *M. C. Farrar Bell,* 1963. – MONU-MENTS. Sir Nicholas Throkmorton †1570. Oblong; recumbent figure between Tuscan columns with heavy entablature. Elaborate strapwork cartouche at the back. Attributed to the *Cure* workshop (GF). – Bartholomew Ellnor †1636, with robed mourners. Attributed to *Humphrey Moyer* (GF). – Richard Spencer †1667, with black marble columns. Attributed to *Thomas Cartwright Sen.* (GF). – Samuel Thorp by the elder *Bacon,* 1794. Standing woman bent over an urn. – Ralph Clay †1815, by *Sherwood* of Derby. – Some good early C18 cartouches, e.g. Sir W. de Bouverie †1717. 13

In the churchyard (entry from Mitre Street, N), a Portland stone DOORCASE dated 1631, formerly facing Leadenhall Street E of the church. Ionic half-pilasters; in the pediment a cadaver. Built by William Avenon, Goldsmith. It frames a fountain of 1965, when the churchyard was laid out as a garden by *D. W. Insall & Associates.*

ST LAWRENCE JEWRY
Gresham Street

1671–80 by *Wren,* on the site of a church recorded by *c.* 1190. Restored by *Cecil Brown* in 1954–7 after it was gutted in 1940. It stands proudly and conspicuously between Gresham Street and the extended Guildhall Yard. Wren's craftsmen were *Edward Pierce,* mason, *Thomas Newman,* bricklayer, *John Longland,* carpenter, *Thomas Mead,* plasterer. It cost £11,870, an unusually high sum. The whole church is stone-faced as befits its isolated site, less common in the C17 than now.

Facing King Street, the newly made processional route to Guildhall, Wren provided a spectacular E front. Four attached Corinthian columns on a podium carry a pediment set against a big attic storey. The flanking bays have Corinthian pilasters at the corners and eloquent arched niches in round-headed surrounds. Similar niche in the centre bay, with large arched windows in the bays to either side. The impost mouldings run across the front between the columns and all five bays have rich carved festoons above. The side towards Gresham Street is also treated as a façade: five arched windows in the centre, flanked by straight-headed entrances with circular windows above, the bays unevenly spaced. In the attic small segment-headed windows.

The W tower has tall obelisk pinnacles and a balustraded parapet. The bell-chamber below has on each face a round-headed opening in a shallow square-headed recess. The restored spire, of glass fibre, faithfully reproduces the four pedimented faces and octagonal spirelet of its leaded predecessor. Weathervane of 1732 in the form of the saint's gridiron. Quoined w front, far more modest than the E, with irregular windows N of the tower, where the vicarage is now accommodated. The plainer treatment here and on the rubble-faced N front is explained by their original setting facing narrow lanes. The w front is not square with the N and s sides, as is betrayed by the spire, which is a true square in plan. The visual effect on the tower seen from the w resembles that of distortion in a camera lens.

The interior is particularly spacious but was never of exceptional architectural interest. It has a wide nave six bays long, with a N aisle (the present Commonwealth Chapel) that stops one bay short of the E end: the result of the Corporation having taken the old NE bay to widen Guildhall Yard after the Fire (PJ). The N gallery here was removed by *Blomfield*, 1866–7. Corinthian pilasters to the nave, with four columns marking the aisle. Clerestory on the N and s sides, supplemented by a single circular light piercing the coving above the altar. Wren made the E wall of uneven thickness so the inside could be square with the N and s walls, as the differing depth of the window jambs shows. The ceiling is evenly divided by enriched ribs, faithfully following the old form.

Brown restored St Lawrence as a Guild church to provide a setting for Guildhall ceremonies, hence the unusual degree of pomp and circumstance in the new fittings. They were all to his design, which gives a welcome feeling of unity, in contrast to the bittiness of some restored City church interiors. The old church was noted for its glorious woodwork (by *Pierce* and *Kedge*), and the dark oak and ornate forms of the new PULPIT, REREDOS, N SCREEN etc. were intended as a C20 equivalent. In style they are traditional rather than explicitly Neo-Wren or modern, with devices unknown to C17 City joiners, such as the winged angels on the screen. – ROYAL ARMS and CHANDELIERS, also by *Brown*. – ORGAN. Older instrument adapted by *Noel Mander*, 1957, in a near-copy of *Harris*'s late C17 case with its later additions. – ALTARPIECE of St Lawrence, by *Brown*. – 64 STAINED GLASS by *Christopher Webb*, dated 1959–60. A complete sequence of windows with historical figures in an academic fancy-dress style with lots of plain glass: unobtrusive, but less successful than the new fittings. – Ironwork SCREENS to the N aisle, the central one given in 1974, flanked by later additions made by *REME Workshops*. – Simple FONT of *c*.1620, from Holy Trinity Minories. – Good PEWS from Holy Trinity Marylebone, probably from the restoration there by the elder *Somers Clarke*, 1876. – MONUMENT. John Tillotson, Archbishop of Canterbury, †1694, with a portrait relief above weeping cherubs, much restored. Attributed to *Gibbons*. – PAINTING. Martyrdom of St Lawrence, C16 Italian, in the entrance lobby. – Off here to the N, a narrow CHAPEL in a former stair-lobby. It perpetuates that made here in 1943, also designed by *Brown* with glass by *Webb*. A vestry further N was until 1940 exquisitely fitted up with carved panelling and ornate plasterwork, all by the artists of the church, with a painted ceiling by *Isaac Fuller II*: a very great loss.

ST MAGNUS THE MARTYR
Lower Thames Street

Begun by the parish in 1668 (mason *George Dowdeswell*); completed by *Wren*, c. 1671–84 (cupola added 1703–6); the body of the church much altered in the 1760s and later. Wren's craftsmen were *John Thompson*, mason; *Matthew Banckes Sen.* and *Thomas Lock*, carpenters; *William Cleere*, joiner; *Doogood & Grove*, plasterers. The Westminster Charter, a C12 document spuriously dated to 1067, mentions a church here, but an early C12 foundation is more likely. The church lies well below King William Street and the London Bridge approach, its w front almost touching the foot of that huge square cliff Adelaide House. Curiously enough, the conjunction of the vigorous and imaginatively detailed steeple with the tree close to it and the sheer wall of the C20 building is entirely successful.

The tower is big, massive and square, with paired pilasters on the top stage and a pretty pierced parapet. Above rises a large and solid octagonal lantern of stone, arcaded and pilastered. On it a lead-covered dome with little lucarnes and a concave obelisk spire, the whole 185 ft (56 metres) high (cf. the Jesuit church, Antwerp, 1614–24, of which Wren's office had a drawing). *Samuel Fulkes* was mason, *Abraham Jordan*, carpenter, *Joseph Roberts*, plumber. The model for it was made as early as 1684. – CLOCK projecting from the w tower wall, by *Langley Bradley*; dated 1709 on the face, 1700 on a benefaction board inside. Its present plain pediment made by 1807, replacing ornamental statuary.

The rest has a problematic history. When Wren took over the job, the parish had already raised part of the N front. Responsibility for the present N wall, of seven bays, cannot now be apportioned, though it has Wren's familiar cherub's-head keystones and straight hoods on brackets. Before the 1760s it was of nine bays, embracing the tower at the w. A broad three-bay pediment emphasized the centre, where the front breaks forward. In the middle bay here is a blocked doorway below a circular window, straight architrave and carved garland. But between 1762 and 1768 the two w bays were demolished for a pedestrian route through the tower, allowing the roadway on to old London Bridge to be widened. The tower's lowest storey thus became an external porch. Its N and S entrances are in concave-arched niches, apparently C17, with paired pilasters etc. added to the w pier to match Wren's applied temple front on the w face. The architect was possibly *Dance the Elder*, who made designs for the widened road. The N aisle pediment and tall flanking parapet were removed probably in 1782, when *J. Tricker* made the other windows round. So the upper parts now look a bit raw. Scrolly brackets reset against the tower, over the aisles, mark the parapet's original level. The S wall was rebuilt in 1803 by *Samuel Robinson*, who omitted key-blocks from the round-headed windows. Rendering here and on the E front of c. 1980, by *Laurence King & Partners*; until the later C20 both were built against in whole or part. Low SW RECTORY (former Sexton's House), of brick and stone with tripartite windows. Perhaps by *Robert Smirke*, who built the previous rectory on King William Street, 1833–5. The bay next to the church

has a round-headed window in a splayed frame, typical of *c.* 1850: an
addition?

The original form of the interior is even more problematic, since
no entirely reliable illustration survives from before 1760. In that
year a fire caused the upper parts to be reconstructed by *Peter Biggs*,
the work completed according to Godwin's *Churches of London*
(1839) before the passage beneath the tower forced further
alterations. Aisles and chancel fit into a near-rectangle, the s aisle
tapering to the E. Slender Ionic columns with cabled fluting rise
from octagonal pedestals. The aisles have flat ceilings, the tunnel-
vaulted nave deep transverse penetrations from oval clerestory
windows, out of alignment with the aisle windows. The clerestory is
difficult to date. Preliminary drawings by Wren show two treatments:
one like the present arrangement but with segment-headed lights
instead of oval ones; the other, apparently a preliminary version,
with a flat ceiling resting on upright walls with rectangular windows.
The oval lights are therefore almost certainly a later introduction.

A related mystery concerns the spacing of the columns. Wren's
preliminary version shows seven columns, aligned with the bay
divisions of the N wall. But the plan of St Magnus in Ogilby and
Morgan's map (1676–9), usually a reliable guide, has columns
irregularly spaced to form a double bay in line with the blocked N
door. This implies the presence of an internal transept of some kind
(cf. St James Garlickhithe, q.v.). The arrangement of the bays was
altered in the 1760s when the first bay W of the tower was taken to
make a lobby under the organ, and again during *Martin Travers*'s
restoration of 1924–5, when an extra pair of columns was inserted in
the double bay. So now there are six not quite regular bays in all,
including the organ bay. The present clerestory pays no regard to
any cross-axis, or to the spacing of the aisle bays generally. This is
consistent with a date in the 1760s, by which time the N entrance
had fallen out of use. Why, then, was the double intercolumniation
perpetuated, when the clerestory entablature is continuous? Nor is
a date in the 1760s entirely plausible for the clerestory; its sober
plasterwork, intermittently fluted and coffered, looks half a century
later. Might it not date from 1814, when *The Beauties of England and
Wales* tells us that the church was 'beautified'? It is certainly a long
way from anything Wren might have employed.

The especially sumptuous WOODWORK, though altered, is still
one of the richest remaining ensembles in the City (joiners *William
Grey* and one *Massey*). *Travers*'s additions of 1924 and later are
interesting examples of the extreme High Church taste for the
Continental Baroque. – Towering two-storey REREDOS, divided into
five by Corinthian columns. Carved pelican over the centre, with
PAINTINGS of Moses and Aaron on each side. The upper stage was
reconstucted by *Travers*; photographs indicate the reredos was partly
reassembled *c.* 1890. Surrounded by carving in the central roundel
is a painted Glory, doubtless that mentioned in 1708, repainted
perhaps in 1814. Carved urns with wriggling flames. To either side
sit fine Baroque carved angels, not mentioned in 1708, but recorded
by 1810. Crucifixion group on top by *Travers*. – SIDE REREDOSES:
SE, C17, made up of *Massey*'s former doorcase in the N wall; NE altar
by *Travers*, with reused C17 woodwork framing a PAINTING of the
Virgin and Child after Van Dyck. – COMMUNION TABLE, C17,

modest, SE. – Magnificent W GALLERY with a projecting centre, 40
reached from the W lobby by matching dog-leg staircases with finely
twisted balusters. Its date is probably 1712, which would match the
ORGAN by *Abraham Jordan Sen. & Jun.*, the first 'swell-organ', it is
said (instrument since rebuilt. DF). It has a boxy case, the top
treated as a big interrupted pediment, richly carved below with trophies of musical instruments. On the parapet four iron COLUMNS as
standards for lights, with Queen Anne's monogram. Repairs of 1886
recorded on the gallery front may have been by *I'Anson*; there was
work by *E.B. I'Anson* in 1893 (Colvin). – Corinthian SCREEN and
DOORCASE by *Massey*, 1677, set against the W lobby wall. – Lobby
SCREEN with nice octagonal glazing, doubtless of *c.* 1760, with C17
carved work reset below. – CHURCHWARDENS' PEWS at the W end.
– PULPIT by *Grey*, with rectangular panels. The massive TESTER
has inverted segmental arches, with carved garlands between vases
sweeping along the top.

Iron COMMUNION RAILS with repoussé ornament, probably of
c. 1705. – FONT. Octagonal gadrooned bowl given in 1683, on a later
stem of Greek-cross plan. Ogee-shaped COVER with four pedimented faces. – BENEFACTORS' BOARD by the font, late C17, with
carved garlands. On it a PAINTING of the Baptist by *Alfred Stevens*,
after Murillo. – Iron SWORD REST of 1708. – BENCHES in Bavarian 47
Rococo style, and SCULPTURE of St Magnus, both by *Travers*. –
AUMBRY. Late C16 Flemish, with diminutive carved caryatids. –
STAINED GLASS. N aisle, armorial windows by *A.L. Wilkinson*,
1953–60. – S aisle by *Lawrence Lee*, 1949–53, still in the genteel
manner of his master Travers (CS). – NW window with armorial glass
dated 1671, from the former Plumbers' Hall off Cannon Street
(demolished 1863). – MONUMENTS. A good collection especially of
the C18 and early C19. – Thomas Collet †1704. Sculpted cherubs
hold aside curtains. – Robert Dickins †1705, draped cartouche with
cherubs' heads. Attributed to *Thomas Cartwright Jun.* (GF). – Sir
James Sanderson †1798. Grand sarcophagus and trophy on an
obelisk. – Miles Stringer †1799, with columns, obelisk and urn, and
tiny sculpted figures in the frieze; by *Simpson* of London Bridge. –
Thomas Preston †1826, by *Reeves & Son* of Bath. Urn and weeping
tree, like a bookplate in high relief. – Miles Coverdale memorial,
Gothic, by *George Sharp* of Gloucester, 1837.

ROMAN REMAINS. Beneath the tower is a sorry-looking fragment of
dried and blackened timber, one of many massive oak baulks used in
the construction of the early Roman embankment N of the line of
Thames Street. It was found on the other side of Lower Thames
Street in 1931. The tower itself marks the point where the later
Roman riverside wall was likely to have been breached by a monumental gateway leading from the bridge into the city. W of the tower
also some VOUSSOIRS from the C12 London Bridge, found in 1921
during excavations for Adelaide House.

ST MARGARET LOTHBURY

First mentioned *c.* 1185; rebuilt *c.* 1441 and again by *Wren* 1683–92
(tower completed 1698–1700). Wren's craftsmen were *Samuel*

Fulkes, mason, *John Longland*, carpenter, *William Cleere*, joiner, *Henry Doogood*, plasterer, and *Matthew Roberts*, plumber; on the tower, *Samuel Fulkes*, mason, *John Longland*, carpenter, *William Knight*, plumber. In plan an irregular oblong with the tower rising in the SW corner. Restoration work in 1978 (by *Gerald Dalby* of *D. W. Insall & Associates*) revealed medieval foundations to the N and E walls. They indicated that the C12 church was extended E in the C15, on a large foundation arch across a tributary of the Walbrook.

1 Stone-faced S front towards Lothbury. Unusually grand S doorcase in the tower, with pediment on free-standing columns. The tower bay is balanced at the E by the vestry windows. Three windows between, arched, with ears, the parapet above them pierced with balustraded sections. The tower is square and plain and crowned by an uncommonly pretty lead spire, an obelisk on a square-domed base. Paul Jeffery attributes its design to *Hooke*. The E front, visible from a narrow passage, has Wren's favourite composition of three large round-headed windows, the central one larger, the lesser ones to each side with lower sills and circular windows over. All are now blocked. On the N the church faces the little St Margaret's Court. Vestry and parish room here added 1908–10 by *H. C. Ingram*, son of the rector A. J. Ingram.

The interior has a nave with a S aisle which runs between the E face of the tower to the W face of the vestry (gallery removed 1881). The plan suggests retention of the old foundations, including the S entrance through the tower, characteristic of medieval London (*see* Introduction p. 20). Corinthian columns to the aisle, matching pilasters to the other walls. Coved ceiling, intersected by groining from the round clerestory windows. Modest circular panels in the central section. The E wall is markedly skewed. – Exceptionally fine FURNISHINGS, including many from demolished churches installed 1890–8 by *Walter Tapper*, who was then in *Bodley & Garner*'s office.

45 – FONT from St Olave Jewry (q.v.). Baluster stem and round bowl with cherubs' heads and between them reliefs of Adam and Eve, Noah's Ark, Baptism of Christ, and Baptism of the Eunuch – of great finesse. Gibbons's font at St James Piccadilly is carved with the same scenes, but there is no evidence he worked here. – SCREENS.

37 Chancel screen from All Hallows the Great (dem. 1894). It was made in 1683–4 and carved by *Woodruffe* and *Thornton*. By tradition the gift of a German merchant called Theodore Jacobsen; but recent research shows that it was a parochial commission.[*] It is one of two surviving Wren screens in City churches (the other, at St Peter upon Cornhill (q.v.), is similarly composed but less delicate and ornate). It runs right across the church and has four divisions on each side of the middle entrance. They are separated by tapering twisted openwork balusters. The pilasters of the entrance are also pierced. They carry a wide open segmental pediment filled with the royal arms. Below the pediment a big eagle with spread wings forming the arch. The effect of the piercing is exquisite but undeniably top-heavy. – Pretty S aisle screen, made 1891 to designs by the rector's brother *W. Rowlands Ingram*. The base is the reused COMMUNION RAIL of St Olave Jewry. The upper stage has slender close-set balusters alternately of wood and wrought iron. – COMMUNION RAIL also

---

[*] *See* Paul Jeffery, 'The great screen of All Hallows the Great', *T.A.M.S.* 37 (1993).

with two-strand openwork twisted balusters, and acanthus carving along the top. – COMMUNION TABLES. Two, with twisted legs, that in the s aisle from St Olave Jewry. – REREDOS. Sumptuous piece with Corinthian columns carrying two segmental pediments with urns. Openwork foliage volutes at the sides. The blank panel above it marks where a mediocre and intrusive relief of the Ascension (by *W. R. & H. C. Ingram*, 1910) has been plastered over. – Flanking the reredos, in the former NE and SE windows, big PAINTINGS of Moses and Aaron, *c.* 1700 (from St Christopher-le-Stocks). – REREDOS in the s aisle, simple, with broken segmental pediment, twin pilasters, and hanging garlands; incongruously painted 1908 with an Annunciation by *Sister Catherine Weeks*. From St Olave Jewry. – PULPIT. Splendidly carved, the flowers, fruit etc. partly openwork. The very large and grand TESTER is from All Hallows the Great, given to that church by Theodore Jacobsen. On it dancing cherubs, an eagle etc. – W GALLERY. CI8, surprisingly simple, with Doric columns. On it, modest ORGAN, 1801 by *G. P. England* (restored by *Bishop & Son*, 1983–4). – READING DESK and other miscellaneous pieces incorporating woodwork of the Wren period. In the NW vestry, PANELLING from demolished churches. – Two SWORD RESTS, CI8, of iron. – Two CANDELABRA from All Hallows the Great, brass, dated 1704 and 1760, in the chancel. The rest copies of 1962. – STAINED GLASS. Post-war armorial windows, some by *Goddard & Gibbs*, 1969.

MONUMENTS. In the s aisle Ephraim Skinner †1678, Sir Nathaniel Herne †1679, similar tablets with columns and broken pediments, both from St Olave Jewry. Attributed to *Thomas Cartwright Sen.* (GF). – Also in the s aisle, two fine BUSTS: Alderman Boydell (of the 'Shakespeare Gallery'), designed by *Banks* in 1791 and carved by *F. W. Smith*, 1820, for St Olave Jewry; Ann Simpson by *Nollekens*, 1795; her plain sarcophagus-tablet nearby also signed by him. – Rev. Watts Wilkinson †1840 by *Wyon*, with severe full-length figure in high relief. – Many other large but plain tablets. – A large bronze bust of Sir Peter le Maire attributed to *Le Sueur*, 1631, from St Christopher-le-Stocks, is no longer displayed.

ST MARGARET PATTENS
Eastcheap

First recorded in the CI2, and rebuilt as late as 1538 after the old building collapsed. Stow thought the name derived from nearby pattenmakers, but it may commemorate one Ranulf Patin, canon of St Paul's and a parish landowner. The present church by *Wren*, 1684–7. His craftsmen were *Samuel Fulkes*, mason, *Thomas Woodstock*, carpenter, *William Cleere*, joiner, and *Doogood & Grove*, plasterers. Since 1954 it has been a Guild Church.

West front to Rood Lane, of stone, tripartite, with a large round-headed central window above a doorcase, flanked by two lesser and lower ones with circular windows above. The s front, of brick with early CI9 rendering, has a mixture of circular and round-headed windows. The NW tower has square-headed bell louvres and one of the most remarkable of the late spires (of 1698–1702): polygonal and lead-covered, as if it were medieval, but with equally needle-shaped corner pinnacles at the foot of the square tower top. Balustrade between these pinnacles. The group of five needles is very effective, though a little harsh; more so since the spire lost the little urns which originally crowned the second of its three stages of apertures. The mason was *Fulkes*, with *Abraham Jordan*, carpenter, *Matthew Roberts*, plumber, and *Jonathan Maine*, carver. Paul Jeffery suggests it may be by *Hawksmoor*; he points out payments by the parish to 'Sir Christopher Wren's clerk'.

The interior is a plain rectangle with a N aisle and small projecting chancel, lit by circular clerestory windows cut through the coving. Corinthian pilasters around the walls turn into full columns across the aisle (now the Lady Chapel). A N gallery and a W gallery are separated by the tower. The N gallery, reached by a pretty staircase with twisted balusters, runs awkwardly across the columns one-third of the way up. It was converted into conference rooms in 1955–6 during restoration by *A. W. Moore & Son* (earlier renovation by *R. P. Day*, 1892). Much original WOODWORK survived reseating in 1879–80: twin canopied CHURCHWARDENS' PEWS (W), one dated 1686, for the parishes of St Margaret and St Gabriel Fenchurch, once not uncommon in the City churches, but surviving only here; BEADLE'S PEW, NE corner; low CHANCEL SCREEN with reused carved work; REREDOS with Corinthian columns and a broken segmental pediment, narrow to fit the chancel but of excellent quality (gilded 1886); COMMUNION RAILS with twisted balusters; lesser REREDOS in the N aisle, made from a former doorcase; simple hexagonal PULPIT, testerless, with an iron hourglass stand. – Two
43 sets of Stuart ROYAL ARMS; that above the entrance exceptionally fine. – C17 HAT-PEGS, N aisle. – W SCREEN below the gallery, 1791. – WAINSCOTTING in the lobby, 1834. – ALTARPIECE. Christ at Gethsemane, attributed to *Carlo Maratta*. – In the N aisle a *Della Robbia* TONDO, installed by a late C19 neo-Jacobite rector, J.L. Fish. – ORGAN. 1749 by *Thomas Griffin* (much rebuilt), in a fine three-towered contemporary CASE with carved trophies of musical instruments. – Two iron SWORD RESTS, the larger dated 1723. – FONT. Octagonal, carved with cherubs' heads and foliage on the bowl in the usual manner. The cover is no longer displayed. – The C19 copper CROSS and BALL on the S wall, copied from those at St Paul's, were formerly on the spire.

MONUMENTS. Sir Peter Vandeput and family, cartouche erected 1686. Attributed to *Jasper Latham* (GF). – Susannah Batson †1727; a charming small piece with cherubs' heads. Attributed to *Robert Hartshorne* (GF). Both are convex and applied to columns. – Sir Peter Delmé †1728, by *Rysbrack* (erected 1740), a big hanging architectural monument with reclining cherubs on a pediment and terminal scrolls with female heads, the forms fashionably Kentian. – John Birch †1815, large with weeping cherubs and urn by *Charles Regnart* (W gallery). – Mary Ann Graves †1843, bad relief of seated figure, by *John Ely Hinchliff*.

ST MARTIN LUDGATE
Ludgate Hill

On a site adjacent to the former Lud Gate, and first mentioned
c. 1138. Geoffrey of Monmouth's fantastic claim that Cadwallader
founded the church in 677 may yet be evidence for a pre-Conquest
foundation. The present church of 1677–86 is by *Wren*, or perhaps
Hooke, whose diary records 31 visits before and during construction.
It cost £5,378 (*Nicholas Young*, mason; *Allan Garway* and *Thomas
Horn*, bricklayers; *Henry Blowes*, *Robert Day*, *Matthew Banckes Sen.*,
carpenters; *Doogood & Grove*, plasterers; *William Draper*, joiner;
William Emmett, carver; *John Talbot* and *Peter Read*, plumbers). St
Martin suffered the least air-raid damage of any City church and is
generally in an excellent state of preservation.

The pre-Fire church stood clear of the City wall, with a tower up
against it pierced by an arch. Wren's church lies further w and incorporates part of the Roman town wall in its w wall. As at St Edmund
the King, the alignment is N–S, and the S front is here treated 29
similarly as a three-bay stone-faced composition with central tower
slightly projecting. Three tall windows (here segment-headed), all
with the usual straight hoods. Doorway below the middle window.
Volutes above the side windows curve up to the tower. Smaller
volutes ease the transition between the square tower and a short
octagonal stone stage. From this rises a charming Dutch- or
Scandinavian-looking lead spire, with an octagonal bell-shaped
dome, iron balcony, and then an open-arched stage supporting the
tall leaded spirelet: a nice foil to St Paul's when one looks up
Ludgate Hill. The modest brick N front, facing the courtyard of the
Stationers' Hall, has a projecting central bay with a blocked
entrance.

   What appears to be a ritual w end proves inside to be the façade to
a s narthex with a gallery above, allowing the church proper to be
correctly oriented, besides insulating it from street noise. The
double stairs to l. and r. date probably from *Ewan Christian*'s
generally restrained restoration, 1892–5 (earlier restoration by
Edward Cresy, 1824. DF). Previously a single flight rose immediately
within the door. The plan is otherwise similar to St Anne and St
Agnes, though taller in its proportions: square, with a smaller central 31
square on four Composite columns and a rich, deep cornice. The
central square is groin-vaulted. Tunnel-vaulting to the main axes.
Pilasters mark off the remaining lower corner sections, which are
covered with flat ceilings. All this is divided from the narthex by
three arches on broad pillars. The arches are coffered but otherwise
unmoulded.

   FITTINGS. Within the s arches a GALLERY, which has a superb
panelled substructure with three pedimented DOORCASES of the
richest design (joiner *William Grey*, carver *William Emmett*). Ionic
half-columns to the central doorcase, which has within the pediment
carved cherubs holding a wreath and crown. Plainer Corinthian
doorcases, flanking, not *in situ*: probably from the former outer
lobby. Above, reset fronts from the old gallery, which projected
further. More good woodwork in the other fittings (joiners *Athew*,
Draper and *Poulden*; carvers *Cooper* and *W. Newman*). w GALLERY.

Set well back from the crossing piers. The stairs have twisted balusters. – REREDOS rather flat, with pilasters only. Raised centre with segmental arch and pediment. – PULPIT with oval panels, of the usual Wren type, but with stairs with exceedingly slender twisted balusters (i.e. probably later). – COMMUNION RAILS, three-sided, with twisted balusters. – COMMUNION TABLE with thick twisted legs. – CHAIR for two churchwardens, typical of its date (1690) and with cane seat and back. – Miscellaneous other contemporary woodwork, e.g. in the PEWS and STALLS, some of it from St Mary Magdalen Old Fish Street. – FONT. 1673, from the 'tabernacle' (*see* Introduction p. 34). Bulgy baluster and fluted bowl with palindromic Greek inscription. Behind it a C17 carved marble pelican. – FONT RAILS. 1703. – ORGAN of 1847, by *Theodore Bates* of Ludgate Hill. – ROYAL ARMS. Early Victorian; perhaps a C17 piece repainted. – CHANDELIER. Very large, of brass. The central one brought from St Vincent's Cathedral, West Indies, *c.* 1777. – SWORD REST. C18, much restored. From St Mary Magdalen. – PAINTING. Large picture of the Ascension by *Robert Brown*, 1720, brought in 1890 from St Mary Magdalen. Also some Old Master copies of *c.* 1900. – STAINED GLASS. By *Powell*, late C19. – MONUMENT. Little brass of Thomas Beri, 1586 (N wall). From St Mary Magdalen. An identical brass is at Walton-on-the-Hill, Lancs. – Not normally displayed are carved BREAD SHELVES from St Mary Magdalen and the ogival FONT COVER.

ST MARY ABCHURCH
Abchurch Lane, s of King William Street

First mentioned in the late C12 and probably named after a benefactor such as Abbe or Abbo. A vaulted chamber below the churchyard, said to be of the C14, was revealed after bombing in the Second World War. It must have formed the undercroft of a lost chantry chapel. The present church is by *Wren* and dates from 1681–6. It cost £4,974. *Christopher Kempster* was mason, *John Bridges* and *John Evans* bricklayers, *Thomas Woodstock* carpenter, *Doogood & Grove* plasterers and *Thomas Dobbins* plumber. Red brick with stone dressings; almost as homely as St Benet Paul's Wharf. Three bays each to s and E, with round-headed windows with circular lights over, flanking a large segment-headed window (the E one blocked). Hipped roof. To the s an open space, the former churchyard, prettily paved to a pattern by *E. I'Anson* in 1877. NW tower with quoins, carrying on a square ogee-domed base a small pierced lantern and then the sweetest lead obelisk-spire (slightly altered 1884). The church room was added to the N in 1914–15 by *W. Campbell-Jones*, in connection with his adjacent Gresham Club in Abchurch Lane.

The interior is a surprise, for although the area is small, Wren made it look very spacious indeed by giving it one big dome on eight arches. There are no aisles; all that he did was to groin the corners so as to lead on to the base of the dome, which has a hemispherical profile continued below the cornice in pendentives on Corinthian pilaster-capitals. At the sw the dome rests on a pilaster and a full column, which carry it across a gallery. Font enclosure below. The
33 PAINTING of the dome is unparalleled by any other Wren church. It

was done in 1708 or shortly after by *William Snow*, for £170. It represents the Name of God in Hebrew surrounded by rays, clouds and heavenly choir in colour above, divided by a painted cornice from architectural motifs with seated figures of Virtues in monochrome around the four oval windows. The most recent of many restorations were in 1946–53 by *W. Hoyle* and *E. W. Tristram* after severe bomb damage, and in 1994–5 by *Tom Organ* and *John Burbidge*. The rest of the church was restored by *Godfrey Allen*, 1945–57.

FURNISHINGS. Huge REREDOS by *Grinling Gibbons* himself, 38 1686. Two original requests for payment for the 'olter pees' were found in 1946. Reassembled 1948–53 after it was blown into two thousand pieces in 1940. Tripartite, the centre with coupled Corinthian columns, carrying sections of a segmental pediment. Behind and above, an attic with four vases and a raised, concave-sided centre crowned with a Garter monogram: a device not found elsewhere. Limewood pelican, garlands etc. exquisitely carved. – COMMUNION TABLE, made in 1675 by *Almandy Howart* for the temporary 'tabernacle' (*see* Introduction p. 34) and unusually small. – Late C19 COMMUNION RAILS. – Other woodwork by joiners *William Grey* and *Thomas Creecher*, carver *William Emmett*. The most intact set surviving, for Victorian alterations (by *I'Anson*, 1878–9) were modest, and little has come from elsewhere. – PULPIT. 1685 by *Grey*, thickly carved, with large tester with upswept sides and garlanded urns on a square Ionic pillar. Still at its original height, with intact wine-glass stem and stairs complete with twisted balusters and big curved platform. – FONT of marble by *William Kempster*, 1686, a fluted octagon on a slender stem. Wooden FONT COVER by *Emmett*, square and strongly architectural, with statuettes of the Four Evangelists under curvy pediments. It is raised by a spiral wooden screw like a narwhal's tusk. – FONT RAILS with twisted balusters and enriched square piers. – PANELLING to the walls. – W GALLERY with oval and circular panels and cherubs' heads. Late C17 GRAFFITI inside. – ROYAL ARMS by *Emmett* on the gallery front. – Richly carved DOORCASES by *Emmett*, that to the s especially fine, with segmental pediment on Composite pilasters, garland frieze with a central shell, urns and cherubs. That facing it on the N a little plainer, with a gilded copper pelican (by *Robert Bird*) which was the weathervane until 1764. – Some of *Creecher*'s original PEWS, N and S, with openwork panels of carved foliage, very tall so that one sits high up inside. Also two churchwardens' pews (w). – LION and UNICORN on the front pew. – SWORD RESTS. Two, of iron, with arms of 1812 and 1814, but probably older. – Unusual CANDELABRA on the pews, made 1957 using mahogany columns from Lockinge House, Berks. – ORGAN CASE of 1717, from All Hallows Bread Street, replacing that lost in 1940. Flanking screens by *Lord Mottistone*. Instrument by *Mander*, 1954. – POOR BOXES. Two, square on square pillars, made 1694 by *Creecher*.

MONUMENTS. Sherwood family †1690–1703, with twisted columns and lots of cherubs. Attributed to *William Woodman Sen.* (GF). – Sir Patience Ward †1696. Good tablet with mourning putti, and, at the top, between urns, an allegorical figure (Patience?) on a tall concave-sided pedestal. Attributed to *Thomas Cartwright Sen.* (GF). – Benjamin Eaton †1730 and wife †1741, by *Sanders Oliver*. –

Matthew Perchard †1777, also by *Oliver*. – Martha Perchard †1787, with carved female mourners or virtues. – Some good floor slabs, exposed by the removal of I'Anson's raised floor in 1954.

ST MARY ALDERMANBURY

See Churchyards p. 141

ST MARY ALDERMARY

Queen Victoria Street

First mentioned *c*. 1080, but almost certainly much older: Aldermary is thought to mean the elder Mary, i.e. the oldest City church so dedicated. The present church is the chief surviving monument of the C17 Gothic revival in the City, and – with Warwick – the most important late C17 Gothic church in England. It is also the most mysterious of the City churches.* Rebuilding began in 1510 following a bequest by Sir Henry Keeble, and the body was probably finished shortly after 1528, when another bequest was made for roofing the nave. Further work in 1626–9 completed the tower, after a further bequest requiring it to follow the 'ancient pattern... [of] the foundation of it laid 120 years since'. After the Great Fire, the church was, unusually, rebuilt with money from yet another bequest. There is no evidence for the tradition that its benefactor Henry Rogers specified that the new church should copy the old: his will stipulated only that the money go to a City church, and it was his niece Anne Rogers who selected St Mary. The choice of style appears to have derived rather from the reuse of substantial medieval remains.

First the body of the church, which is an aisled and clerestoried rectangle with Perp windows throughout. The rebuilding was carried out in 1679–82, supervised by the *Wren* office (*Edward Strong Sen.*, mason; *John Longland*, carpenter; *Thomas Creecher*, joiner; *Henry Doogood*, plasterer; *Jonathan Maine*, carver). It was surveyed by *John Oliver*, but not necessarily designed by him, for such work formed part of his routine duties. Indeed, Wren's authorship is as likely here as at any other undocumented City church. However, the appearance of the exterior is due largely to refacing in stone by *Charles Innes* of *Tress & Innes* in 1876–7, after the making of Queen Victoria Street exposed the S and E sides. Innes exaggerated the Perp details of buttresses, etc., and added the doorcase, quatrefoil parapet (partly surviving), octagonal corner buttress and NE vestry wall.

It is with the windows that the difficulties begin. The aisle windows may follow in detail those of their C16 predecessors. Reused Caen stone, still visible in the S window reveals in the C19, suggested that the medieval walls were retained in the C17; but, when the ashlared N wall to Watling Street was exposed in the 1830s, traces of exterior buttresses were found surviving only to sill level, and out of alignment with the blind windows inside (opened up in 1840 by *Tress*). These windows were themselves aligned with the arcades and with the S aisle windows. So either the church begun in 1510 was much less regular than was then usual, or the spacing of

* *See* H. M. Colvin, *Architectural History* 24 (1981).

the bays was altered at the C17 rebuilding, reusing only the lower medieval walls and resetting some window mouldings for economy. This interpretation guarantees that the window outlines conform to the pre-Fire ones, even if they may be in new positions, although Wren's big E and W windows, no less correctly Perp, were apparently made without reused stone. S. Lockwood's study of the church draws attention to the cast-iron trusses inserted in the aisle roof space by *Samuel Ainger* in 1825. Ainger was awarded the Society of Arts' Gold Medal for his work.

The big SW tower was not reconstructed until 1701–4, with Coal Tax money (*John Clarke*, mason). Repairs of 1674–5 suggest it had survived the Fire well, but subsequent refacing makes it difficult to distinguish any earlier work. The lowest stage at least looks authentically Perp, with its four-light window and panel tracery. The big bulky polygonal buttresses, too, should probably be accepted as an original feature. Gerald Cobb noted their similarity to those of the C15 drawing for the campanile of King's College, Cambridge. They have paired panels grouped in five tiers of three (two on the lowest stage), moulded rings on the shafts at the angles, and smaller shafts at the angles of the big polygonal pinnacles. These – a characteristic feature in the City skyline from many points – are attributed by Sir Howard Colvin to *William Dickinson* on the strength of his drawing for a central tower at Westminster Abbey, which has similarly bottle-shaped pinnacles. (Kerry Downes gives the tower to *Hawksmoor*, though it was Dickinson who had charge of the City churches office by 1701.)

Much of the interior seems at first straightforward Perp: six bays, slim piers with the familiar four-shafts-four-hollows section, four-centred arches, three-light Perp aisle and clerestory windows under four-centred arches. But the piers stand on reused medieval rubble (proved during rebuilding in 1935), so they must have been Wren's work. The walls may be similarly deceptive.

Above the arcades, however, all is clearly C17. Wren's ceilings are plaster fan-vaults, in the nave as well as the aisles. They rest on 36 vaulting shafts, in their turn starting from entirely Wrenish cartouches in the spandrels. They display the arms of Henry Rogers and of the patron, Archbishop Sancroft of Canterbury. Fan-vaults for a whole parish church is something unheard of, though not for major monastic churches such as Sherborne or Bath. Such fan vaults did not of course have the oversized central roundels, which are sunk like shallow saucer-domes. But supposing Wren was imitating a vault of 1629 and not of *c.* 1520? Fan-vaults, most commonly non-structural, were still in use in the early C17: a similar example is at the 1630s Convocation House in Oxford which, as Kerry Downes points out, Wren would have known. Still, the value of Wren's work lies not in the extent to which it copies accurately, but in its very originality, the freedom with which he treated precedent, and the fun which he evidently had in playing with Gothic forms (see the enriched panelled barrel-vault made over the short projecting chancel, with its skewed E wall).

FITTINGS. Carved Gothic STALLS, PEWS, W SCREEN etc. of *c.* 1876, with PANELLING of 1886: a near-complete ensemble of good quality but uninspired design. – Carved wooden REREDOS of 1914, designed by *J. Douglass Mathews & Son.* – COMMUNION

TABLE. *c.* 1700, of oak, with white marble top. – The late C17 PULPIT survives: of the usual type, with cherubs' heads, on a base of 1876. Made by *William Grey*, probably carved by *Jonathan Maine*. – FONT. Fluted bowl on baluster, dated 1682. Enclosed in RAILS with twisted balusters, probably reused communion rails. – SWORD REST. A rare example of oak, 1682, tall, with superbly carved flowers, fruit etc. and the royal arms on top. – DOORCASE, a sumptuous piece with Corinthian pilasters and broken pediment, from St Antholin Watling Street (dem.). – POOR BOX on a flat twisted stem. – Brass LECTERN. Eagle type, unusually elaborate, *c.* 1876. – ORGAN last rebuilt in 1908 (*Norman & Beard*), with pretty stencilled pipes. – PAINTING. Transfiguration, in the blind window in the N aisle. Probably by *Clayton & Bell, c.* 1876. – STAINED GLASS. E window, Crucifixion, by *Lawrence Lee*, 1952. – W window, risen Christ, by *John Crawford*, 1952. – Other windows by *Lee, c.* 1955. All unattractively pale. Lee followed the outlines of designs by the late *Martin Travers* (CS). – MONUMENTS. John Searle †1714, above average. Time and Death suspend drapery held open by cherubs. By *William Woodman Sen.*, the drawing now in the V and A Museum (GF). – René Baudouin †1728. Big gristly cartouche with pediment and weeping cherubs. Signed by *Joseph Pasco* (GF). – In the chancel, tablet with wreathed urn, signed by the younger *Bacon* but otherwise uninscribed. – MEMORIAL. Relief of St Antholin Watling Street, 1880 by *C.H. Mabey*, from the former site (N porch).

ST MARY-LE-BOW
Cheapside

By *Wren*, 1670–80, with an C11 crypt from the medieval church. The tower stands out some distance to the N because Wren found here a Roman gravel roadway, which made an admirable new foundation. Behind it is a vestibule, and only S of that the church, built on an enlarged site 1670–5 (mason *Thomas Cartwright Sen.*, bricklayer *Anthony Tanner*, carpenter *Matthew Banckes Sen.*, plasterers *John Grove Sen. & Jun.*). The vestibule is continued to the E by the rector's lodging. Of the church only the modest outer walls of brick with stone dressings survived the war. The interior was rebuilt by *Laurence King*, 1956–64, reproducing Wren's design (Victorian restorations by *J. L. Pedley*, 1867, and *Blomfield*, 1879). The W side is a three-bay façade with a big pediment connected with the aisle fronts by small curved pieces. Central doorway with segmental pediment on carved brackets. Large arched central window, smaller lower arched side windows each with a circular window above, and an oval window in the pediment. As restored, they have gratingly inappropriate metal mullions. Corresponding E front. The S front has a projecting centre with another doorway and a circular window above; the other windows are arched.

But the glory of the church is its steeple, the proudest of all Wren's steeples, and at 224 ft (68 metres) second in height only to St Bride (q.v.). It was raised in 1678–80, the first true steeple made after the Fire, and cost £7,388 as against £8,033 for the rest of the church. The square tower is especially broad and high. Entrances from the

27 street and churchyard by big doorways each lying back in a rusti-

cated niche, with little angels on top flanking an oval window: motifs
taken from J. Hardouin Mansart's Hôtel de Conti, as Viktor Fürst
pointed out. Each doorway has Tuscan columns and a heavy
triglyph frieze, like those of Wren's Trinity College Library,
Cambridge (1676). The room under the tower has a vault with a
circular opening in the centre. It is a triumph of the skill of the
tower's masons, *Thomas Cartwright Sen.* and *John Thompson*, that it
withstood the fire inside the steeple and the crashing down of the
bells in 1941. The iron balcony facing Cheapside is said to be a
reminiscence of the temporary grandstands (called 'silds' after low
market structures of the C12–C14 here), from which tournaments
were viewed. The bell-stage above has coupled Ionic pilasters.
Above this is a balustrade with openwork angle pilasters in the form
of volutes moving up to the top. Between them the spire rises, with
a conical core but a splendid architectural dress. First a rotonda of
free-standing Corinthian columns. If the steeple has a fault, it is
their excessive slenderness; but their order follows the proper
vertical sequence. On them a second balustrade, then again volutes
moving up to the graceful top stage, which is of a Greek-cross type
with further projections in the re-entrant angles. It carries twelve
Composite colonnettes (renewed in granite by *George Gwilt Jun.*,
1818–20), to correspond to the twelve columns below. Obelisk to
finish; on it a very large copper WEATHERVANE, a dragon, made by
Robert Bird in 1679 from the wooden model of *Edward Pierce*.

Below the church lies an exceptionally important CRYPT. It dates
from *c.* 1077–87, when the church was rebuilt by Lanfranc of
Canterbury as the London headquarters of his Archiepiscopal fee.
There are certain affinities with contemporary crypts at Canterbury
Cathedral, St Augustine's Abbey, Canterbury, and Rochester. If one
accepts a date after the fire of 1087 for the crypt, then a further connection between the Canterbury workshop and the rebuilding of
that date at Old St Paul's may be implied. It may be the vaults here,
and not the flying buttresses on the pre-Fire steeple of 1512 at the
sw, which gave the church its suffix *de arcubus* (of the arches or
bows). About sixty per cent of the material survives, compromised
by Wren's repairs and post-war insertions. It consisted originally of a
nave and two aisles, separated by heavy unmoulded piers with
Roman brick reused in the outer order of voussoirs. The s aisle has
been fitted up as a chapel, entered from the churchyard via a w
extension built in connection with the medieval sw tower. The nave
and N aisle are reached from the vestibule beyond the tower.
Converted to a restaurant in 1989, so little feeling of antiquity
remains. The nave, now partitioned at the w, was originally subdivided into three parallel vessels by columns with single-scallop
capitals, some of which survive. Each bay was groin-vaulted. Thus
there were altogether twelve vaulting bays in the nave, and four
larger ones in each aisle. Only the N aisle retains C11 vaulting.
Blocked round-headed windows in the aisles and larger recesses in
the E wall indicate the crypt originally stood above ground, perhaps
as the lower part of a two-storey chapel in the Carolingian
tradition.* The upper part of an C11 newel staircase found in 1959 in

---

* *See* Richard Gem's reconstruction of the crypt, in *B.A.A. Conference Transactions*
1984 (1990).

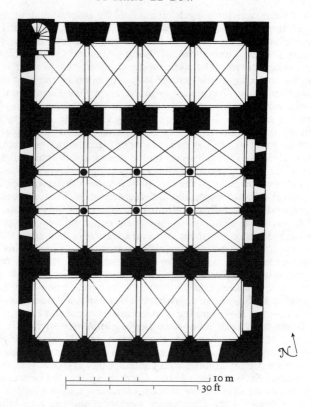

St Mary-le-Bow. Plan of the crypt

the NW corner may have led to the upper level. It probably also served a tower on the N which collapsed in 1271, when damage to property here is recorded. On the newel behind, two star-shaped GRAFFITI in C11 style. Two PIER BASES of early C13 pattern, found in 1955 and displayed in the vestibule, are the only evidence for a rebuilding of that date. Their form suggests the use of Purbeck shafting, unusual in a parish church.

The church itself has an almost square nave of three wide arches on piers with attached Corinthian demi-columns. The ghost of a cross-axis appears in the greater width of the central bay, in line with a long-blocked S doorway. The *Parentalia* identifies this arrangement of bays and columns as derived from the Basilica of Maxentius in Rome. More demi-columns support dosserets and an ornamental feature over the E window. The piers carry the transverse arches of an elliptical tunnel-vault, pierced by segment-headed clerestory windows. The narrow aisles have transverse tunnel-vaults. Keystones are carved with the heads of those involved with King's restorations.

The new FURNISHINGS, designed by *King*, are mostly of oak, some explicitly Neo-Georgian, others plainer but still traditionally detailed. Two PULPITS; BISHOP'S THRONE behind the altar, with

REREDOS made by *Faithcraft Studios* (CRUCIFIX on it by *Simon Robinson*, 1994); SACRAMENT HOUSE in the s aisle; ORGAN CASE at the w end, made by *Dove Bros.* – Hanging ROOD designed by *John Hayward*, carved by *Otto Irsara* of Oberammergau. – Good STAINED GLASS also by *Hayward*, 1964, but with colours and forms too hot and strong for the gilt and pastel gentilities around it. The NE window shows the bombed City churches. – Wrought-iron aisle SCREENS made by *Grundy Arnatt*. – RELIEF of St George and the Dragon by *Ragnhild Butenschøn*, 1966, N chapel. – BUST of Admiral Philip by *C. L. Hartwell*, 1932, formerly on St Mildred Bread Street. – SCULPTURE, Virgin and Child, in the vestibule. – At the entrance to the s crypt, etched glass SCREEN by *Hayward*, 1960.

ST MARY-AT-HILL

Between Eastcheap and Lower Thames Street

First mentioned in the late C12. The town house of the abbots of Waltham adjoined it. The present church is a mixture of periods outside and in, preserving the plan and much of the fabric of *Wren*'s rebuilding of 1670–4 (*Joshua Marshall*, mason; *Thomas Lock*, carpenter; *John Grove*, plasterer). Wren reused the medieval w end (in turn rebuilt 1787–8 by *George Gwilt Sen.*) and the N and s walls, which he heightened. In 1694–5 *Wren* or his office had added a lantern to the previous w tower. His E end, facing the street called St Mary-at-Hill, has a mullioned and transomed Venetian window (blocked 1767) and an open broken pediment. In it a semicircular window, made during alterations by *James Savage*, 1826–7, and blocked in 1848. Carved festoons above the side windows were chiselled off before the 1830s. Another festoon probably stretched below the central window. The fabric of Wren's N wall, facing the little paved churchyard, was revealed to be substantially medieval by investigations in 1984 and again in 1990–1, following a serious fire in 1988. Rebuilding of the aisles is recorded *c.* 1487–1504, which tallies with the N wall's ashlared Kentish rag (partly exposed) and traces there of segmental-arched pointed windows, retained and modified by Wren. *Savage* put in the present iron-framed round-headed windows in 1826–7. *Gwilt*'s w tower and flanking bays to Lovat Lane are of plain yellow brick (bricklayer *John Harrison*, mason *Thomas Piper*). Domestic-looking fanlights to the doors; crenellated parapet. The s wall may be inspected from the narrow Church Passage (called Priest's Alley in the C15). Beneath the rendering this is also chiefly medieval. It also had Perp windows until 1826–7. Densely built-up surroundings prevent these disparate parts from being easily visible together, so that St Mary presents a completely different character whether approached from the W or E.

The plan is one of the most interesting among remaining Wren churches. It derives directly or indirectly from the Byzantine quincunx plan, i.e. it possesses a square domed centre resting on four free-standing columns. The plan may have been suggested by the form of the old church, which had transepts formed within the space of the aisles. Cross-arms of even (or nearly even) length and lower flat-ceilinged sub-centres in the four corners (cf. St Anne and

St Agnes, and St Martin Ludgate). Until alteration in the 1820s the cross-axis served doorways on the N and S, traces of which are hidden by the wainscot. The columns are a curious variant of the Corinthian order, described by Hatton (1708) as 'the workman's own invention', but in fact taken from Serlio (PJ). Vaults and ceilings were renewed in 1826–7 by *Savage*. His also are the pilasters on the N and S walls. The 1820s plasterwork juxtaposes delicate repetitive patterns with passages in a fleshier Neo-Wren style (e.g. the pendentives). The shallow dome is coffered. Its C17 plasterwork was plain, the lantern very much larger. *Savage* returned in 1848–9 to add the dome's central cupola and the windows piercing the chancel vault. The roof and ceiling, burnt in 1988, have been excellently restored on a new laminated timber structure by *The Conservation Practice*, 1990–2.

Most of the notable WOODWORK remains in store in 1998. Its full restoration is an urgent priority. It is partly late C17 (joiner *William Cleere*), admirably altered and added to by *W. Gibbs Rogers* in 1848–9. His work can hardly be distinguished from that of the C17 joiners, a feat which few would expect from an Early Victorian craftsman. Until the fire of 1988, the ensemble survived intact but for tinkering to enlarge the chancel in 1881. In situ in 1998: *Rogers*'s W SCREEN and the lower part of the W GALLERY right across the W arm and W sub-centres, minus *Rogers*'s carving. Probable dates for the gallery are 1692–3 (centre), extended in 1787 to just beyond the columns, in 1849 to the N and S walls. – STAIRCASE up to it from the NW lobby to a DOORCASE bearing the date 1672. – C17 COMMUNION TABLE, smaller than usual. – Two SANCTUARY CHAIRS given 1845, C17 style and incorporating C17 work according to the RCHME. – FONT. With reeded octagonal bowl. – STAINED GLASS. Only narrow decorative borders survive from *Willement*'s scheme of *c*. 1850. The rest was removed in 1967–9 during redecoration by *Seely & Paget*. – CANDELABRA. Six modern pieces in C17 style. – MONUMENTS. John Harvey †1700, cartouche signed *William Kidwell*. – Thomas Davall and his wife Anna †1700. Big, with urns and arms. Attributed to *Francis Bird* (GF). – Henrietta Vickars †1713, draped cartouche with cherubs' heads. – Rev. W. J. Rodber †1843, with bust by *Nixon*. – Some other pieces from St George Botolph Lane (dem.). – In the NW vestibule: Isaac Milner †1713, with columns and weeping cherubs, by *Edward Stanton*. – William Smyth and family †1723–52, urn on obelisk. Attributed to *Sir Robert Taylor* (GF). – Also in the lobby, SCULPTURE. Relief of the General Resurrection, *c*. 1600, damaged (cf. St Andrew Holborn; also St Giles-in-the-Fields, Holborn, Camden). Formerly at the Billingsgate Ward Schools in St Mary-at-Hill; doubtless originally over the churchyard entrance.

In store: REREDOS with Corinthian columns to the raised centre, good carving and nice open finials on top. Grander than that described by Hatton (1708), so probably extended later in the C18. – Fine PULPIT with stairs and tester, perhaps a C17 fitting embellished by *Rogers*, 1849, perhaps wholly new then. He signs the backboard. – Also by *Rogers* the carved LION and UNICORN, and ROYAL ARMS from the W gallery. – ORGAN by *William Hill & Son*, 1849. – COMMUNION RAIL, C17, with twisted balusters. – C17 ROYAL ARMS, from St George Botolph Lane. – BOX PEWS and CHURCHWAR-

DENS' PEWS, the only complete set from a Wren church. – Ogee-domed FONT COVER. – Six SWORD RESTS of wrought iron, specially elaborate. Two came from St George. Dated between 1770 and 1854, but most are probably older.

Projecting from the SE corner of the church, a pedimented CLOCK on a rich bracket. S of this corner a carved C17 DOORWAY with pediment, decorated with skull and crossbones made for a former entrance into the N transept, superseded when the W end was rebuilt. It leads beneath a two-storeyed C17 vestry to Church Passage. Adjoining the vestry, *Savage*'s gaunt brick RECTORY of 1834 has clumsily irregular fenestration suggestive of later alterations.

ST MARY SOMERSET
Upper Thames Street

The tower only of *Wren*'s church, in a brave little garden on the N side where the traffic thunders into the tunnel under Peter's Hill. Known from *c.* 1150–70 and named possibly from one Ralph de Sumery. Rebuilt on a smaller, regularized site, 1685–94 (mason *Christopher Kempster*, bricklayer *John Evans*), one of the last group begun after the Fire. The rest of the church, a simple aisleless rectangle with round-headed windows, was demolished in 1869, but an Act of Parliament saved the SW tower, which projected to make a feature on the E corner with the lost Old Fish Street Hill. Segment-headed doorways and alternating circular and round-headed openings above, then eight wildly Baroque pinnacles (restored 1956), flanked with little scrolls and crowned alternately with square fluted vases and panelled obelisks. These taller obelisk-pinnacles stand not at the corners in the Gothic manner, but centrally on each face. Magically varied silhouettes result.

ST MARY WOOLNOTH
Corner of Lombard Street and King William Street

1716–27 by *Nicholas Hawksmoor*, replacing a fire-damaged medieval church partly rebuilt in 1670–5. That work was apparently directed by *Sir Robert Vyner*, not Wren; called 'Modern Gothick' by Hatton in 1708.* First recorded 1191; Woolnoth probably commemorates an C11 founder named Wulfnoth. Hawksmoor's was one of the so-called Fifty New Churches, strictly intended to serve new areas of London. *John James* assisted with the drawings, but the results are plainly Hawksmoor's own. Here he created the most original church exterior in the City of London, very different from his big, isolated churches elsewhere – a difference due in part to the demands of a cramped site. At £16,542 it cost more even than St Mary-le-Bow (chief mason *Thomas Dunn*; carpenters *William Seagar*, *John Meard*, *Thomas Denning* and *James Grove*; plasterer *Chrysostom Wilkins*).

*See David Cast, *J.S.A.H.* 43 (1984).

The w façade has a projecting centre with banded rustication and cylindrical Tuscan columns at the angles also banded with the same rustication – a very ingenious and wholly successful motif. Semicircular steps (added in *Butterfield*'s restoration of 1875–6), up to a round-headed doorway in a rusticated niche. The semicircular window above lights the ringing chamber. The tower rising above this is in plan much broader than it is deep (cf. Hawksmoor's Christ Church, Spitalfields). First a broad base with three completely unmoulded square windows. The principal storey above is treated in three bays with attached Composite columns so as to give the impression of two w towers that have merged. Indeed the top of the façade is split into two square turrets. The effect is of powerful forces firmly held in check. The lower part of the façade has curious affinities with Vanbrugh's Seaton Delaval (Northumbs), begun 1718, i.e. designed at about the same moment as St Mary. Hawksmoor and Vanbrugh had already collaborated for years, at Castle Howard (North Yorks) and Blenheim (Oxfordshire), but in the second decade worked independently from one other. Low doorways flanking the tower are for external access to the galleries, as stipulated by the Fifty Church Commissioners. Good iron RAILINGS of *c.* 1900, extended l. and r. *c.* 1992 when curved screen walls housing entrances to the Underground were removed. Crypt and plinth of the church were used most ingeniously in 1897–1900 as a booking hall for the Underground, requiring the insertion of steel girders beneath floor and walls (engineers *Sir Benjamin Baker*, *Basil Mott* and *David Hay*).

51 The N elevation has three very large round-headed frames, heavily rusticated. Inside the frames blank niches framed by columns set diagonally. They carry a straight entablature curving boldly back into the wall – a motif as personal as any in the Italian Baroque or at Baalbek. Blockish sills on big brackets intensify the feeling of great depth. Surprisingly delicate central balustrade above the corbel-cornice, marking the width of the clerestory behind it. The absence of windows insulated the interior from the noise of Lombard Street. The remarkable and quite unexpected difference between this and the fenestrated five-bay s elevation is to be explained by the fact that, before the construction of King William Street, the s wall could be seen only in steep foreshortening, from a narrow and therefore quieter alley. The lower part is now masked by the single-storey former Underground station by *Sidney R. J. Smith*, 1897–8. This has a Hawksmoorish rusticated centrepiece, let down by mediocre flanking figures in low relief. Through the arch, l., one of Hawksmoor's bays may be inspected to full height: rusticated lowest aperture like those on the N, then a tall round-headed recess with a blind rusticated opening below a round-headed window high up (in this bay only also blind). Also hidden from the outside is Hawksmoor's little low SE VESTRY with its Venetian window.

The interior (altered by *Butterfield*) is much more monumental than the exterior would make one expect: completely centralized, with a square high space carried by four groups of three giant Corinthian angle columns. Above the straight entablature the clerestory has big semicircular windows. Kerry Downes notes its derivation from an earlier design by Hawksmoor, based on the Egyptian Hall as described by Vitruvius, with evenly spaced columns and rectangular clerestory lights. Square ambulatory, formerly with galleries reached by doors in the w angles. Redecorated in sober white and cream, 1996.

The WOODWORK is as original as its setting, though not necessarily to Hawksmoor's designs. GALLERY FRONTS, set back against the walls by *Butterfield*, with big openwork brackets, on odd outward-tapering PIERS (actually the former square columns cut in half). Made by *John Meard*, carved by *Thomas Darby* and *Gervase Smith*. – The W ORGAN GALLERY survives. ORGAN CASE dated 1681, instrument attributed to *Father Smith*, adapted 1727 by *Gerard Smith*. Second organ in the N aisle by *Hill*, 1913. – BALDACCHINO with beefy twisted columns and a richly ornamented canopy, much grander than the compositions in relief of reredoses in Wren's churches. Made by *Meard*, carved by *Gabriel Appleby*. Butterfield's raising of the chancel has jammed it up into Hawksmoor's elliptical chancel arch. – Polychromatic PAVING by *Butterfield*, of graduated richness from plainish central aisle to coloured marble chancel. – COMMUNION TABLE with marble top, 1720s. – PULPIT of mightily bulging shape, made by *Darby* and *Smith* and inlaid by *Appleby*. The TESTER, on tall square columns, echoes the shape of Hawksmoor's ceiling. – LECTERN, PEWS and STALLS with reused woodwork. – COMMUNION RAILS of wrought iron (*John Robins*, smith). – ROYAL ARMS of 1968. – HELM, GAUNTLETS, etc., of Sir Martin Bowes, *c*. 1550, in a case by the altar. – MONUMENT. W. A. Gunn †1806, in the gallery. Woman seated by an urn.

ST MICHAEL CORNHILL

A lively mixture: classical body of 1669–72, Gothic tower of 1715–22, and porch and other alterations of 1857–60 and later. After the Fire, the church except for the tower was rebuilt on parochial initiative. The rector consulted 'skilful workmen' in 1669, and a model or design was shown at the vestry in that year (*Wren Soc.* XIX). So there is no reason to suppose Wren's office was responsible for the design. The craftsmen were *Nicholas Young*, mason; *Anthony Tanner*, bricklayer; *Thomas Gammon* and one *Miller*, carpenters; *William Cleere*, joiner; *John Grove*, plasterer. The speedy completion suggests the reuse of much medieval work. In 1715–22, the old tower of 1421 was finally taken down and rebuilt in the Gothic style with big angle turrets and pinnacles. A lost drawing of tower and spire before 1421, preserved in a late C16 copy, shows octagonal buttresses suspiciously like those of the present tower: did its lower stages survive to influence the form of the C18 work?* There were two phases of work. The first, to 1717, reached the shallow machicolated cornice. Designer probably *William Dickinson*, who was in charge of winding down Wren's City Church Office; mason *Samuel Fulkes*. The much richer bell-stage and tall pinnacles above were built in 1718–22 by *Hawksmoor* for the Commissioners for the Fifty New Churches. They have panelled buttresses and masks alternately young and old (mason *Edward Strong Jun.*, carver *Joseph Wade*). The

---

*For what may be earlier designs by *Hawksmoor* for a new tower, *see* Paul Jeffery, *Architectural History* 36 (1993).

pinnacles echo the forms of the C15 spire. The break in building was because the City Church money ran out, and a new Act was needed to divert funds from the New Churches' coffers.

Then in 1857–60 St Michael became the first City church to be p. thoroughly remodelled to High Victorian taste, at the hands of *Sir* 41 *George Gilbert Scott* (with the parish architects *W. A. Mason*, then *Herbert Williams*). According to his *Recollections* (1879), Scott 'attempted by the use of a sort of early Basilican style, to give a tone to the existing classic architecture'. But the elaborate porch to 60 Cornhill is Gothic, taking its cue from the tower, though in a rich and defiantly inharmonious Continental manner. Tympanum sculpture by *J. Birnie Philip*, Michael Disputing with Satan about the Body of Moses. The style recalls such medieval Italian artists as the Pisani or Lorenzo Maitani. WAR MEMORIAL by the door: small bronze group by *Richard Goulden*, 1920. St Michael drives away War. Scott added Lombardic tracery and ornate surrounds to the windows, best seen from the former churchyard to the S with its two trees. The round-headed aisle windows are Scott's restoration of the C17 design; they had been made circular by *George Wyatt*, 1790. Also Lombardic is Scott's little vaulted cloister between the churchyard and St Michael's Alley, where it is dated 1868. The E side of the churchyard is made by the tall RECTORY and VESTRY of 1913–14 by *Charles Reilly Sen.*, crudely done in brick.

The entrance is from Cornhill. The C17 interior is simple, with aisles of four bays and slightly projecting chancel, and groined vaults on tall Tuscan columns carrying arches. Egg-and-dart carving to the capitals. The N aisle is windowless. In the aisle vaults circular skylights, of uncertain date. *Scott*'s transformation remains immediately obvious despite well-meaning post-war attempts to tone it down. 'The great ugly stable-like circles of the clerestory become roses under his plastic hand', wrote the *Ecclesiologist*. These survive only in the tower bay, the rest having been made plain *c.* 1952. Angel corbels below the cross-ribs carved in timber by *Birnie Philip*, with other stone-carving. Scott's polychrome wall decoration was replaced in 1960 by genteel blue, gold and white.

FURNISHINGS. Scott made a clean sweep of these. His replacements are of exceptional interest and quality. – REREDOS by *Scott*, Italianate, of Derbyshire alabaster with Cosmati-type marble inlay. It incorporates C17 PAINTINGS of Moses and Aaron by *Streeter*.* – COMMUNION TABLE. Late C17. – COMMUNION RAILS from Scott's campaign, with fine sinous wrought-iron foliage. – Fine PULPIT, on a stocky marble column, and eagle LECTERN, carved by *W. Gibbs Rogers*, 1859. – PEWS also by *Rogers*, 1859–60, loosely medievalizing, with highly individual carvings (e.g., SW, a scapegoat after Holman Hunt's painting of 1856). – FONT. Octagonal gadrooned bowl of 1672 on a stem of 1860. – ORGAN. Much rebuilt; on it four cherubs' heads from the case of the *Renatus Harris* organ of 1683–4. – SWORD REST. C18. – SCULPTURE. Large wooden 49 figure of a pelican and its brood (W end). Ferocious-looking, like a pterodactyl. Carved by *Joseph Glazeley* for the former altarpiece, 1775. – Bronze head of Christ by *J.-B. Clésinger*, 1868, a salon piece

*The C17 reredos and communion rails survive at St Lawrence, Great Waldingfield, Suffolk (K. E. Campbell, *London Topographical Record* 27 (1995)).

(S aisle). – STAINED GLASS. An important early scheme designed for Scott by *Clayton & Bell*, 1858, and probably made by *Heaton & Butler*. The excellence of the ensemble in design and colouring may still be seen in the big E oculus (Christ in Glory). The S aisle ₅₉ windows (Life of Christ) were cruelly deprived of their decorative backgrounds in 1952. The W window (Crucifixion) is part of the same scheme. – DECORATION. Stencilling in the surround of the E window is all that remains of Scott's decorative scheme, executed by *George Trollope & Son*. Here also four roundels with sculpted heads of Evangelists.

MONUMENTS. A good selection of mostly medium-sized pieces: John Vernon †1615 (remade after the Great Fire), demi-figure elegantly gesticulating. Attributed to *William Woodman Sen.* (GF). – Several substantial late C17 tablets, including: Sir William Cowper †1664 and wife †1676; Sir Edward Cowper †1685 (large and unimaginative, with twisted columns); John Huitson †1689. Attributed respectively to *Jasper Latham*, *Thomas Cartwright Sen.*, and *Edward Pierce* (GF). – Platt monument, 1802, with cherub, by *Richard Westmacott Sen.* – Mrs Asperne †1806, concave drapery with cherubs' heads: of *Coade* stone.

The vestry has reset PANELLING from its late C17 predecessor. Fine carved OVERMANTEL here, the delicate swags etc. suggesting a date *c.* 1700.

ST MICHAEL PATERNOSTER ROYAL

College Street, N of Upper Thames Street

First mentioned *c.* 1100. Named from the rosary (paternoster) makers, who worked nearby, and from La Reole, a tenement known from the mid C13, named after a town in Gascony and popular with merchants from that province. Dick Whittington, whose house was next door, rebuilt the church in 1409 and in his will founded a college attached to it, in College Hill, N. The present church by *Wren*, 1685–94 (*Edward Strong Sen.*, mason; *William Cleere*, joiner; *Thomas Denning*, carpenter; *Henry Doogood*, plasterer). In plan a plain oblong with SW tower, the W front slightly out of true. This and the S front are stone-faced and balustraded, with arched windows with winged cherub's-head keystones. The S entrance is through a segment-headed doorway adjoining the tower. N and E fronts partly of brick, the E vestry a post-war replacement of a C17 structure. Until the war the raised centre of the parapet above it had a triangular pediment.

The tower is plain but crisply finished, with matching arched windows and a pierced parapet. In 1713–17 the beautiful steeple was added (mason *Edward Strong Jun.*, carpenter *Richard Jennings*), one of the group of three also comprising St Stephen Walbrook and St James Garlickhithe, designed possibly as early as *c.* 1700, perhaps by *Hawksmoor* (*see* Introduction p. 34). It is as light and graceful as its fellows. First a recessed open octagon with eight columns set in front of the angles, each with its own little projecting piece of entablature surmounted with a square urn, then a smaller open octagonal stage with urns, and a little circular solid stage on top. Blast damage in 1944 imperilled the church, and many furnishings were lost, but in

1966–8 it became the final City church to be restored, by *Elidir Davies*, for the Missions to Seamen. (Earlier restorations by *James Elmes*, 1820, a thorough job by *Butterfield*, 1866, and by *Ewan Christian*, 1894.)

Inside, the Mission's offices occupy the tower space, the former w vestibule and the first w bay, truncating the reconstructed church interior. This makes a spare and cool setting for the surviving fittings and the new stained glass. The new ceiling is shorter by one bay but follows Wren's simple coved pattern. – Original REREDOS, tripartite with four engaged Corinthian columns and some good carving. Two flaming urns above, the pediment removed probably in 1820. – Flanking stone SCULPTURES of Moses and Aaron, from All Hallows the Great (dem. 1894). They have a fine Baroque swagger, far above the quality of the average (and more common) painted figures. Aaron formerly held a censer, but his hands were lost in the Blitz and have been restored in a gesture of blessing. Moses formerly held a rod pointing to the Decalogue. Was the use of sculpture at All Hallows inspired by that at James II's short-lived Whitehall Chapel (1686)? – PULPIT, original, of the usual type and with good carving. Shallow TESTER, made up of the upper part of the cornice only. – Chunky FONT given 1865, with coloured marble columns and inserts in the style of *Butterfield*, and probably designed by him. C17 COVER of two stages, big but plain. – ORGAN CASE. Post-war replica of *Jordan*'s case from All Hallows the Great, 1749, incorporating some fragments from it. Instrument by *N. Mander*. On the organ gallery, good ROYAL ARMS of William III, original. – COMMUNION RAILS with some reused carved work. – LECTERN. Of wood, also incorporating carved work. The attached figure of Charity trampling Avarice, 1992, replaces a C17 piece from the w gallery of All Hallows the Great, refixed here but later stolen. – Also from All Hallows the very large brass CHANDELIER, with three diminishing tiers each of twelve arms. – STAINED GLASS. E windows by *John Hayward*, 1968. Big dramatically posed figures with strong diagonals and bold colours. The sw window showing Dick Whittington also by *Hayward*. Other windows are plain with irregularly-patterned leading. – SWORD RESTS. Two, of iron, one very large, both probably C18 but remade. Also a HAT RACK of iron. – MONUMENTS. Jacob Jacobsen †1680, enriched cartouche, from All Hallows. Attributed to *Jasper Latham* (GF). Thomas Coulson †1713, convex with pilasters and pediment. Attributed to *Robert Hartshorne* (GF). – Sir Samuel Pennant †1750, by *Rysbrack*. Tablet with Palladian details, and bust above.

ST NICHOLAS COLE ABBEY
(COLE ABBEY PRESBYTERIAN CHURCH)
Queen Victoria Street

A *Wren* church of 1672–8, conspicuously exposed on the N side, higher up and at a slight angle to the street. Used since 1982 by the Free Church of Scotland. First recorded *c.* 1130; the name is a corruption of Cold Harbour, a shelter for travellers. Wren's craftsmen were *Thomas Wise Sen.*, mason, *Henry Blowes*, carpenter,

William Cleere, joiner, and *John Sherwood* and *Edward Martin*, plasterers. Medieval work has been traced in the s and w walls. The rebuilt church seems to be wider than its predecessor, however, perhaps to accommodate parishioners from St Nicholas Olave, with which the parish was united after the Great Fire (P J). Reordered 1874, partly restored 1928–31, and burnt out in 1941. Reconstruction was by *Arthur Bailey*, 1961–2. The upper part of the N W tower was rebuilt, the hexagonal leaded spire remade taller than before, but retaining the trumpet shape and delicate iron balcony near the top. On the summit a weathervane of a ship from St Michael Queenhithe (formerly in Upper Thames Street).

The body of the church is a balustraded stone box with quoins. It has Wren's favourite arched windows under straight hoods on brackets. Wren built it with main fronts to Fish Street (the present Distaff Lane), N, and Old Fish Street Hill, E. Three similar but slightly larger windows here. W wall, originally facing a narrow alley, of rubble and brick. The four E windows on the s side were opened up *c.* 1874.

The interior, light and somewhat cold, is a completely straightforward rectangle with a flat, uncoved ceiling and Corinthian pilasters. Wren's swags of plaster over the E windows have been re-created, as have small pendants at the junction of the ceiling beams, first made in 1884. A few original fittings were saved (*Richard Kedge*, joiner). They have been bleached to match new panelling, seating etc. in the Wren style. – FONT COVER. By *Kedge*, very handsome, with foliage carving and openwork scrolls supporting a crown. The FONT is a modern copy, without the black marble stem of the old piece. – PULPIT. Late C17 too, not large, with rectangular panels and the usual festoons, swags and cherubs' heads; without its tester and on a modern base. – COMMUNION RAIL. With twisted balusters; late C17, surviving in part only. – ROYAL ARMS (W gallery). Large, C17, formerly on the reredos. – WOODWORK from the reredos is reset on the s doorcase; other pieces in the w gallery (two gilded cherubs), etc. – SWORD REST of 1747. Wrought iron, frame type. — CHANDELIER. Of brass, with 24 branches in two tiers; mid C18. – ORGAN by *Noel Mander*, 1962. – CARVING. A medieval carved stone head found during restoration is preserved behind panelling by the s door. – STAINED GLASS. E windows by *Keith New*, 1962. Dark 65 and rich in colour and painterly in style, showing the influence of Chagall. The theme is the Extension of the Church. – No monuments, but in the N W vestry shattered ledger-slabs laid crazy-paving-wise. Here also a STATUE of St Nicholas, gilt metal, from the overthrow of the gateway to Queen Victoria Street, made *c.* 1874; its walls, gates and stairs remain there.

ST OLAVE HART STREET

Corner of Hart Street and Seething Lane, E of Mark Lane

A modest church, and, since the bombing of St Ethelburga in 1993, the smallest of the City's intact medieval churches. St Olave also has most interesting work of the late Commonwealth and the years of Anglican Restoration just before the Great Fire. Walled churchyard to the s, remarkably secluded and atmospheric, with headstones and a big central lime tree alongside the SW tower. A church is first recorded here in the late C12. The dedication suggests the presence of Scandinavian traders in the area. The present building preserves some fabric in the W end from *c.* 1270, including a crypt. The aisles and tower date from mid-C15 rebuilding, for which money was left by Richard and Robert Cely, skinners. Ragstone walls, with much original masonry visible especially at the E. The aisles run through to the E front, i.e. there is no structurally separate chancel. Restored E window, curvilinear Dec, owing more to mid-C19 taste than fidelity to context. Due either to repairs by *Scott*, 1863, or restoration by *Blomfield*, 1871 (other repairs in 1823 by *J. B. Gardiner*, 1853, and 1891–2 by *E. Christian*). The restored E windows of the aisles are C15 (N), early C16 (S). Aisle and clerestory windows of early C16 type with three pointed lights under a depressed arch. The best exterior view of the rest is from the churchyard. Entrance from 19 Seething Lane is through a renewed GATEWAY typical of its date of 1658: round-arched doorway in a big eared frame, big segmental pediment carved with skulls and bones, and skulls either side, bristling with iron spikes along the top. From a design by Hendrik de Keyser (Roger Bowdler). The clerestory was rebuilt in the restoration by *E. B. Glanfield*, 1951–4, after the church was gutted in 1941. Also his the heavy parapets and the regrettable low stone porch by the tower, with weak Gothic detail. The tower has a SW stair-turret but is otherwise unbuttressed. Brick upper stages of 1732, by *John Widdows*. Each face has a round-arched belfry opening with stone impost and key blocks and a big circular opening above. The octagonal wooden lantern is a larger version of the pre-war one. Attached at the SE, a humble gabled brick VESTRY of 1661–2, i.e. contemporary with the gateway, though, lacking a model for imitation, it reverts to more vernacular forms: square W windows, tiny *œil-de-bœuf* S lights. A plaque on the S aisle wall marks the position of a former doorway to the gallery for the Navy Office in Seething Lane, contemporary with the vestry but removed in 1853.

The usual entrance is from Hart Street. The floor level is well below the street. Interior of three bays, in plan a near square of 54 ft (16½ metres) except that the E wall tapers to the S. Glanfield's restoration successfully retained an atmosphere both intimate and antique, aided by a number of surviving fittings. Of the C13 the W nave wall, behind the organ, and an adjacent section of wall to the N, W of the C15 N aisle. Beneath the nave here a two-bay C13 CRYPT, its W part in line with these walls. It is cross-vaulted, with single-chamfered ribs. A blocked lancet in its W wall shows it was formerly partly above ground. It housed a well, probably pre-dating the church's extension over it from the E.* Aisles of late C13 type, partly renewed 1951–4, with two-centred moulded arches on quatrefoil piers of Purbeck marble. Capitals have been made octagonal in the C15 fashion. The bays are regularly spaced but do not coincide with the line of the E wall, to which the arcades are joined by short spur walls. The N tower arch extends just W of the nave wall, indicating that a further W extension of the nave was intended. This would have given a plan of more orthodox proportions had the N aisle also been so extended. The roof is *Glanfield*'s, a renewal of one said to

---

* John Schofield suggests it may come from a C13 house.

have been of 1632 but more plausibly described by the RCHME as C15. Vestry doorway (SE), C15, with quatrefoils in the spandrels and a well-preserved original DOOR.

OTHER FITTINGS. PULPIT. Hexagonal with carved swags and cherubs' heads, c. 1685, from Wren's St Benet Gracechurch (dem.). – COMMUNION RAIL, late C17, with twisted balusters and deep embellished top rail. It rests on crouching lions. – REREDOS by *Glanfield*, of oak. – ORGAN likewise post-war, of oak. By *John Compton Organ Co.* – FONT. Post-war. – SWORD RESTS. Four, of wrought iron, two from All Hallows Staining (dem. 1870). The dates are 1715, 1736, 1741, 1781. – STAINED GLASS. E windows, prettified figures of Christ and Saints by *Arthur Buss* (of *Goddard & Gibbs*), 1954. Aisle windows also by *Buss*. Over the S porch a heraldic window by *John Hayward*, 1970. – MONUMENTS. A rich collection especially of the C16–C17, augmented from All Hallows Staining and St Katharine Coleman (dem. 1926), but depleted by wartime losses. The most notable are original to St Olave. – BRASSES: to Lord Mayor Sir Richard Haddon †1524, with kneeling figures of two wives and five children (S aisle); to Thomas Morley †1566, a palimpsest, the inscription in its Gothic frame worth reading; also several C17 brasses. – Sir John Radclif †1568, fragment of recumbent figure. – Lady Radclif †1585, kneeling figure only, mounted on the chancel wall. – Peter Cappone, Florentine merchant, †1582, with battered kneeling figure in pedimented aedicule. From All Hallows Staining. – Sir James Deane †1608, above the vestry door. A grand tripartite piece with kneeling figures of Sir James and his three wives. Corinthian columns between. At the top, achievements surrounded by strapwork. – Bayninge brothers †1610 and †1616, N of the altar, with kneeling figures at prayer. It swerves round the corner of the impost. Attributed to *Christopher Kingsfield* (GF). – Above, Mrs Pepys †1669, by *John Bushnell*, with good frontal bust in an oval niche, the surround partly destroyed in the war. Margaret Whinney described her expression 'as if admonishing her wayward husband'. She indeed looks towards the former Navy Office gallery, where he sat. – Sir Andrew Riccard †1672, swaggering standing figure in Roman dress, erected by the Levant Company of which he was chairman. Attributed to *Bushnell* (GF). – Elizabeth Gore †1698, with routine bust. – Matthew Humberstone †1694, cartouche with carved heads. – Sir William Ogborne, Master Carpenter to the Board of Ordnance, †1734, cartouche. He was much employed at the Tower. – Memorial tablet to Samuel Pepys designed by *Blomfield*, 1884, with portrait roundel.

VESTRY. A remarkable interior of great charm, of 1661–2. Plaster ceiling with central angel holding book and palm, surrounded by an oval bay-leaf wreath. In the spandrels cherubs' heads. The style is rustic by comparison with Wren's craftsmen's efforts in the next decade. Walls have plain PANELLING with a pilastered fireplace. Above it a grisaille painted OVERMANTEL, restored c. 1980. The subject appears to be profane: The Three Graces. It has been attributed to *De Witte*.

In Hart Street adjoining (w) is a substantial gabled RECTORY by *Glanfield*, 1954, vestigially Gothic in Portland ashlar. Carving of St Olave by the Norwegian artist *Carl Schou*.

ST OLAVE JEWRY
Ironmonger Lane, between Gresham Street and Cheapside

By *Wren*, 1671–9; demolished 1892 apart from the projecting w tower, w wall and part of the NW wall, which were converted into a rectory for St Margaret Lothbury. Excavations in 1985–6 uncovered, in the SW corner, foundations of a small C9–C11 predecessor, of roughly coursed ragstone and reused Roman brick. It had a nave and a w appendage, probably a tower. During removal of human remains in 1888–9, Wren's reuse of later medieval foundations was noted, including in the tower two responds of a C14 E arch and one of a C15 N arch, presumably connected with aisles documented in 1435–65. The tower overlooks a secluded railed garden made from the churchyard, the site until 1666 also of the little St Martin Pomary. Wren's mason was *John Shorthose*.

The tower has a Doric doorcase with segmental pediment, plain parapet, and tall obelisk corner pinnacles. In profile it is gently battered, the only one of Wren's towers so treated. The clock face is dated 1824, but its pedimented stone surround is Wren's. Nice ship weathervane, from St Mildred Poultry (dem.). In 1892 oval windows replaced half-pediments on the flanking w walls, and extra windows were cut in the N and S sides of the tower. The C19 E addition was replaced in turn in 1986–7 by the American architects *Swanke Hayden Connell*. The new brick round-arched walls resemble those of Wren's church, but stop short of Old Jewry. Wren's church had a coffin-shaped plan tapering out and then in towards Old Jewry, partly determined by the line of St Olave's Court on the S. The Old Jewry front was remarkably Palladian, pedimented, with quoins and a Venetian window with columns and full entablature. The obvious influence is Jones's Queen's Chapel, Westminster.

ST PETER UPON CORNHILL

Prominently sited on what is by a few feet the highest ground in the City. By tradition very ancient (Stow records a claim to C2 foundation); but it probably originated in Saxon colonization of the old forum, the courtyard of which may have served as its churchyard. The first definite mention is as late as *c.* 1127. By the mid C15 it had a stone-built school, repaired in brick by the executors of Sir John Crosby (†1475) of Crosby Hall, E of Bishopsgate. The church was substantially repaired *c.* 1630, and the parish made unsuccessful attempts to patch it up after the Great Fire.

The present structure, however, is of 1677–84, by *Wren*, probably assisted by *Hooke*. A drawing in Hooke's hand for St Clement Danes, Westminster, includes a version of St Peter's tower (AG). The craftsmen were *Joshua Marshall* and *Abraham Storey*, masons; *Thomas Warren*, bricklayer; *William Cleere*, joiner; *Thomas Woodstock*, carpenter; *Edward Freeman* and *Richard Howes*, carvers; *Doogood & Grove*, plasterers. It cost £5,647. The pre-Fire site was truncated by ten feet at the E to widen Gracechurch Street. St Peter is still surrounded by buildings on most sides, like many City churches before the C20, while its proximity to St Michael Cornhill reminds one of the former density of churches within the walls. From Cornhill may be seen only a porch with inset Ionic columns and part of the upper wall, rising at an angle above C19 shops. Windows with sunk carved spandrels appear above. That on the r. is circular with imposts unusually returned round the bottom. The best view of the spire is from the churchyard to the s, which lost its plane trees in 1995. Here the steeple shows most happily: the plain brick tower ends in three close-set round-headed openings, above which a neat leaded dome supports a little lantern and an obelisk spire of copper. Original weathervane in the shape of St Peter's key. Below ground the tower rests on a reused vault, dated to the C14 or C15 (RCHME). The walls of the church are stuccoed, with three round-arched windows. The E view from Gracechurch Street, one of Wren's 'show fronts', is grander: ground floor of five uniform arched windows separated by pilasters, the central three bays slightly broken forward to support the upper floor of one arched and two circular windows, topped by a broken pediment. The upper floor is connected with the wider lower floor by curved pieces in the Italian façade tradition.

The interior (restored 1872 by *J.D. Wyatt*) is of five bays. The nave is tunnel-vaulted, the aisles with transverse tunnel-vaults pierced by cross-arches from pier to wall. The pillars have attached Corinthian pilasters towards the nave, with shorter Doric pilasters rising to the springing of the arcade arches. The pillars are distorted slightly and skilfully in section to hide the irregular plan. Excavations in 1990 confirmed that Wren had reused the medieval pier foundations, probably mid C15. Kerry Downes suggests that Wren's roof was made unusually shallow to reduce the load on these old foundations; and this may also explain the unusual lack of clerestory lighting. With the old WOODWORK (joiners *Thomas Poultney* and *Thomas Athew*) and stained glass this makes the interior darkly atmospheric. REREDOS. Unusually low, to avoid obstructing the windows, with simple Ionic pilasters, not specially ornate. – CHANCEL SCREEN right across nave and aisles. Introduced by the rector at the rebuilding, William Beveridge, who was greatly concerned with the sanctity of Communion. One of only two screens provided in Wren's churches; as the earlier of the pair it apparently served as the model for the other, now in St Margaret Lothbury (q.v.). The sections are divided by very slim shafts with pendants between. The centre curves up and is flanked by broad fluted Corinthian pilasters, with a carved lion and unicorn on either side of the central royal arms: an elegant, unacademic composition. Lesser pediments to the aisle entrances. – FONT. Marble, octagonal, with leaves growing up the lower stem; given 1681. Contemporary COVER with a carved dove enclosed in eight brackets with cherubs' heads (cf. St Clement Eastcheap). – PULPIT. Splendid big wooden piece with large tester. – The large W GALLERY and ORGAN CASE (by *Smith*, 1681–2) are also original. ORGAN by *William Hill*, in consultation with the Rev. H.J. Gauntlett, 1840 (rebuilt 1959), incorporating parts from Smith's instrument. – STAIRCASE to the gallery in the tower, of two flights. – DOORS and DOORCASES. Four, at W; of fine workmanship, with Corinthian pilasters and broken pediments. – COMMUNION RAILS with square Doric pillars for

balusters, similar to the shafts of the screen. Altered 1872. – COM-
MUNION TABLE. Top on Doric pillars, of the same style and date as
the communion rails. Enlarged 1872. – BREAD SHELVES (W wall). –
SANCTUARY CHAIRS, two, late C17. – CHURCHWARDENS' PEWS,
backs only, at the far W. – POOR BOX of wood. – Relics of the 1872
restoration include the brass LECTERN, polychromatic TILES, and
GAS JETS (W end). Victorian benches were unfortunately removed
c. 1990. – STAINED GLASS. Coarse E windows by *C. A. Gibbs*, 1872.
63   Obtrusive windows on martial themes in the aisles by *Hugh Easton*,
1951–60. One window by *A. K. Nicholson Studios*, 1950, S aisle. –
MONUMENTS. J. and I. Gale †1739 and †1741, big, with cherubs'
heads and winged skulls. – Woodmason children, 1782, with
cherubs' heads, said to be designed by *Bartolozzi* and carved by
Ryley. The children had perished in a fire. – Richard Gibbs †1864,
with portrait bust probably by *Weekes*. – A few C17–C18 tablets,
none special. – Wrought-iron GATE to the churchyard with figure
of St Peter, said to be of 1853 but looking C18. Churchyard land-
scaped 1997.

ST SEPULCHRE
Holborn Viaduct

First mentioned in 1137, when it was given to the Priory of St
Bartholomew. The dedication supplanted an earlier one to St
Edmund, apparently because the church stood outside the NW City
gate, like the Holy Sepulchre in Jerusalem. Grandly rebuilt in the
mid C15 by Sir Hugh Popham, Chancellor of Normandy, who
added the surviving S porch. The present church is essentially a
restoration of 1667–71 of the burnt-out C15 shell. C17 Gothic
windows were made round-headed in 1789–90, then mostly made
Perp again by *A. Billing*, 1879–80. His also are the S aisle buttresses,
but he left the bald C18 parapet alone. C17 SUNDIAL here. The big
round-headed main E window also survives, set uneasily between
the restored windows of the aisles. It may be of *c.* 1670 or *c.* 1790. To
6   the C15 belongs the big proud W tower, heavily restored by *W. P.
Griffith* in 1873–5. He Gothicized the window tracery and replaced
the already large pinnacles (remade 1712–14, probably by *Dickinson*)
with others still more oversized. The tower is embraced by the aisles.
Popham's three-storey S porch was also refaced by Griffith, without
feeling. His is the oriel over the door, where until 1790 there was a
statue of Popham in a niche. The wrought-iron GATE looks *c.* 1700.
5   The fine two-bay panelled and cusped lierne-vault survives, as does
a ribbed and pointed barrel-vault to the former first-floor priest's
chamber.
    The roomy, loose interior, largest of the post-Fire City churches,
exactly follows the outlines of the large C15 building. Seven bays,
with no division between nave and chancel. Groin-vaulted aisles
and a flat nave ceiling, on arcades of Doric columns standing on
tall octagonal plinths. Tiny figures of angels at the springing of
the vaults. No evidence connects this rebuilding with Wren (cf.
the prompt, parish-led rebuildings at St Michael Cornhill and
St Dunstan-in-the-East, both also with Doric or Tuscan arcades).
The likeliest designer is *Joshua Marshall*, mason to the rebuilding

(carpenter *Hodgkins*, plasterer *Blount*). Deeply coffered nave ceiling, made 1834 by one *Clark*, originally pierced by octagonal skylights. Clark also introduced the clumsy dentil cornice of the aisles. The three C15 tower arches may rest on older foundations, since they are not aligned with the outer walls. *Billing* restored the arches and also removed the galleries and pews. Round-headed windows of 1790 survive in the CHAPEL OF ST STEPHEN (now Musicians' Chapel), off the N aisle. Otherwise this contains more C15 traces than any other part of the interior: two niches l. and r. of the E window, a TOMB RECESS in the N wall with lozenge-panelled and cusped coving, and a PISCINA. Two more PISCINAE in S and N aisles (the latter best-preserved, with shelf and two arches). Near the chapel also a rood-loft doorway (N wall).

OTHER FURNISHINGS. FONT. Marble, baluster stem and fluted bowl with cherubs' heads, probably of 1670. Ogee-shaped COVER of the same date. – Second FONT COVER from Christ Church Newgate Street, also ogee-shaped, very grand, with four urns at the base and an angel on top. – Matching PULPIT and LECTERN, by *Pratt* of Bond Street, 1854, in the Wren style and extremely convincing. Since lowered, but still facing one another across the nave, early C19-fashion. – REREDOS. Tripartite with segmental pediment on Corinthian columns. It looks *c.* 1670. Hatton in 1708, however, reported a piece with Ionic entablature and two marble (marbled?) columns. – Late C17 ORGAN CASE, altered, but still magnificent. Five towers of pipes with segmental pediments between and angels on top. Parts of the gallery fronts remain below. The much-rebuilt ORGAN has parts from an instrument of 1675–6 by *Renatus Harris*. Formerly in the w gallery, removed to the N chapel in 1879, to the N aisle in reordering by *Sir Charles Nicholson*, 1932. – CHURCHWARDENS' PEWS, w end, with some C17 woodwork. – COMMUNION RAIL. Wrought iron; early C18. – SWORD REST. Also wrought iron; early C18. – ROYAL ARMS. Of 1714–1800, or else an earlier set repainted. – BENEFACTION BOARDS of *c.* 1700, with carved cherubs' heads (w vestry). – TILES, medieval, from Christ Church (N aisle at w). – STAINED GLASS. N chapel. Two good windows to Melba and John Ireland, by *Brian Thomas*, 1962–5. – Other windows by *A. K. Nicholson* (St Stephen Harding window, N aisle, 1932); *Gerald Smith* (A. K. Nicholson memorial window, 1938; Musicians' window, 1946; E windows, 1949–52); *Francis Skeat* (S aisle, 1968). In the N aisle a window of 1896, from the demolished Cordwainers' Hall. – MONUMENTS. Edward Arris †1676 and wife, with two frontal busts in circular niches. – Amongst the late C17 cartouches, those to Thomas Sawyer and family †1672–93 and Sir Thomas Davies †1679 are notable, the latter attributed to *Jasper Latham* (GF). – John Yates †1807, with urn and weeping figure.

DRINKING FOUNTAIN. Set into the churchyard wall at the SE, the central part of the first fountain erected by the Metropolitan Drinking Fountain Association, 1859. An elaborate Neo-Norman surround was dismantled in 1867, when the old churchyard was truncated for Holborn Viaduct. – By the porch, TOMB of Edward Chandler †1780, with both carved and *Coade* stone ornament.

WATCH-HOUSE. Facing Giltspur Street on the N side of the church. Of stone, bow-fronted, joined to the church by a single-storey vestry with Venetian window. A replica of 1962 by *Seely & Paget* of a structure of 1791, destroyed in the Second World War; according to Dorothy Stroud by *Dance the Younger*. On its wall a BUST of Charles Lamb by *W. Reynolds-Stephens*, 1935, from Christ Church. The watch-house was built to guard the churchyard from bodysnatchers. Good wrought-iron GATES alongside. They look late C18.

ST SEPULCHRE'S SCHOOL (former). Facing Snow Hill Court NW of the church, by a garden made from part of the churchyard, reached through *Griffith*'s splendid Gothic cast-iron railings. Built 1874–5, perhaps also to Griffith's design (contractor *William Pigsley*). Low, stuccoed, only just Gothic.

ST STEPHEN WALBROOK

First mentioned probably *c.* 1096, as part of the founder's gift to Colchester Abbey. It lay first on the W side of the street called Walbrook, but was rebuilt in 1429–39 on the E side. John Harvey gives the C15 architect as *Thomas Mapilton*. This pre-Fire church is recorded as having two lesser chapels and a cloister by the late C15. Its successor is by *Wren*, 1672–80. Masons were *Thomas Strong* and *Christopher Kempster*; carpenter *John Longland*; plasterers *Doogood & Grove*; plumber *Thomas Aldworth*; and joiner *Roger Davies*. It cost £7,652. Though on a smaller site than before the Fire, it is still amongst Wren's largest churches. It is also the one for which there is strongest documentary evidence of his close involvement: the parish paid him 20 guineas for his 'greate care & extraordinary pains taken in ye contriving ye designe of ye church & assisting in ye rebuilding ye same'. It is the most majestic of his parish churches, and in at least one essential point a try-out for St Paul's, where many of the craftsmen also worked.

The exterior was in Wren's time even more hemmed in than now, with houses built up against the N side of the NW tower and the whole S side. The N side originally faced the Stocks Market (the site now occupied by the Mansion House). Wren at one stage intended to accommodate the market in colonnades attached to the church, but the plan was abandoned. The present exterior with its rough masonry and brickwork hardly hints at the grandiose interior: on the contrary, the outside is of little interest from near by. Simple bracket-cornice to N and E walls, not carried round the other fronts. The central bays rise up through this cornice, originally flanked with carved scrolls, surviving on N and E. The copper-clad dome with its lantern and cupola is visible from some angles. From a distance the church is dominated by a spire added to the tower in 1713–15, which cost a further £1,838 (*Edward Strong Jun.*, mason, *Richard Jennings*, carpenter). Square urns on the tower balustrade date from the same time. The design is related to the contemporary steeples at St James Garlickhithe and St Michael Paternoster Royal, all three perhaps by *Hawksmoor*. Like them the design may date from as early as *c.* 1700 (*see* Introduction p. 34). It is among the most playful City church spires, far recessed behind the balustrade and with a main stage which is square with three columns set ahead of the square at each angle. The entablature is carried forward to follow these little bastions. The same motif is repeated, smaller and without columns, above, and then follows a tiny lantern. The tower seems additional to the building as it was originally conceived, as a glance at the plan immediately shows. Ogilby and Morgan's map (1676) shows the church without it. The lower stages accommodate a vestry. Ashlar facing has replaced much original rough masonry since the war.

The main entrance is s of the tower, up twelve steps inside a lobby. The doorway to the street has above it an oval window and thick garlands. The staircase leads into an exedra or w apse of the nave – the first unexpected motif. From this vantage-point the church appears at first longitudinal and of classical composition, ending, one can see, round the E altar, with just such another bay as that in which one is standing. A number of slender Corinthian columns accompany that procession on the l. and r. They are all of the same height – that is, the church is of the hall-church type. It consists, we can read at once, in this w part, of a nave with oblong groin-vaulted bays, aisles with square flat-ceilinged bays, and narrow outer aisles. But almost at once it becomes clear that the church is in fact not simply longitudinal, but leads to a splendidly dominating dome with a lantern to let in light from above. It is this ambiguity

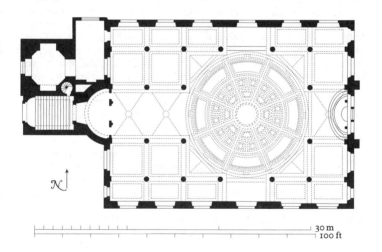

St Stephen Walbrook. Plan

between two interpretations of the space within what is really no more than a perfectly plain parallelogram that connects St Stephen with the international Baroque, in spite of Wren's English insistence on the cool and isolated columns and on classical decoration. The spatial ambiguity does indeed go much further, for, once the dome is reached, one sees that the church can also be understood in quite a different way – as a central building with a dome on eight arches of which four arches form the introduction to cross-arms of equal height and, it seems at the first moment, equal length. The transepts are actually a little shorter than the chancel. They come to an end very soon against the walls of the outer parallelogram.* And the nave consists of course of two bays, not of one. But the interaction of cross and dome – two central motifs – is all the same as potent a spatial effect as the interaction of longitudinal and central. That Wren wanted this double meaning is clear for instance from the way in which the chancel has the same groined vaulting as the nave, but the transepts are barrel-vaulted. The next complication concerns the fact that the dome rises over a square space. That in itself is nothing unusual, and in Italy and France pendentives would have been used as a connecting motif. But Wren wished his dome to stand not on solid piers but on slender columns. So instead of one pier in each corner he has three columns, spaced so as to make each corner clear as a corner. It is in point of fact only at the level of the entablature that the whole ingenuity of all this comes to life. The columns carry a straight entablature, and this traces for us first the length of the nave on the l. and r. (and in the E parts of course of the chancel), then turns and marks the corners of the central span, and then turns again to run to the l. and r. of the transepts against the N and S walls. This motif of the corners of a central space with straight entablatures and flat-ceilinged corner-pieces can – an additional interpretation – also be seen as a grander version of St Martin Ludgate. And now what happens above the entablature? Here again a motif of Baroque ambiguity is used to reach the circular base of the dome. The four arches of nave, chancel and transepts Wren had available without difficulty, but he needed four more of the same height and width in the diagonals, and to obtain these he threw arches diagonally across his corners. So below the arch the result is a triangular space, and Wren covered it with a half-groin-vault. All this is clearly in the spirit of St Paul's.

The other architectural features of the interior seem incidental to this brilliant ensemble. Kerry Downes has noted the similarity of the entablature to a drawing by Webb for the King's Cabinet at Greenwich, 1666. It has the same shallow architrave and frieze of continuous leaves, so Wren is likely to have been borrowing here. On the N and S walls it rests not on pilasters but on flat capitals with free motifs of cherubs, shells, and the arms of the Grocers' Company, who gave money for the rebuilding. The rich plasterwork on the main ribs of the vault, the spandrels, and above all on the coffered dome is especially enjoyable. The E window is arched with a transom. The two mullions are carried up above the transom as a smaller concentric arch. In the other windows there is a large variety of forms, round-headed and segment-headed, semicircular, circular, and around the outer walls repeated ovals.

So (largely) Pevsner described the interior in 1957. War damage to the dome and elsewhere had been made good in 1948–52, by *Gilbert Meadon* of the firm of *Duncan Cameron*, followed by *Godfrey Allen*. The interior has since been transformed again, in a controversial restoration conceived by Lord Palumbo and carried out in 1978–87 by *Robert Potter* of *Brandt Potter & Partners* (engineers *Ove Arup & Partners*). Its centrepiece is an irregularly rounded altar to a design

---

* Remains of a N doorway may be seen on the outer wall, giving a functional justification for the cross-axis. It was blocked as early as 1685.

commissioned by Lord Palumbo for the church from *Henry Moore* and carved from rough Travertine in 1972. In assessing the changes three things should be made clear. Firstly, subsidence caused by the Walbrook beneath had reduced the structure to a parlous state, and it has undoubtedly been saved from collapse by Lord Palumbo's generosity. Secondly, the repairs to the fabric have been carried out with great ingenuity and tact. A reinforced concrete ring has been inserted around the top of the walls, crossing the E window through the transom. Above this, a steel girdle now runs around the clerestory, visible only where it crosses the nave between the first and second W bay. The floor had to be remade in concrete and steel and is now evenly paved in polished buff stone. Thirdly, what was actually swept away was not of the Wren period but largely the result of refurnishings of the late C19 and C20. St Stephen was widely regarded from the beginning as Wren's masterpiece amongst the City churches, and repairs in 1791, 1803–4 (by *James Peacock*) and 1814 were generally respectful, culminating in 1849–50 in a restoration by *John Turner* who was required by the vestry to restore the church to 'the state in which it was left by Sir Christopher Wren'. But the vestry later thought it could go one better, and *Alexander Peebles* remodelled the interior in 1886–7. Apart from that which survives at the W there were no galleries to remove, but the church still had its high pews that rose to the level of the bases of the columns. Objections were raised by the Grocers' Company, patrons of the living and donors of most of the original fittings; but the plan was put to arbitration and, sad to relate, was largely approved by a committee of senior architects under *F. C. Penrose*. So the pews were replaced by movable seating on a new floor of mosaic, although in a compensatory gesture the octagonal pedestals of the columns were made square, in the (possibly mistaken) belief that this was the original form. This mosaic floor and the contemporary glass have now gone, as have *Keith New*'s E windows of 1961, and the new plain glazing at least is more in the spirit of Wren's day.

On the other hand – as visitors who have read this far will already have discovered – there is no doubt that the reordering around the new altar and its stepped plinth goes against the grain of the interior by emphasizing its centralizing tendencies at the expense of its longitudinal ones. The altar also obstructs one's natural desire to walk E along the central aisle and experience the unfolding nuances of Wren's interior. A central altar furthermore does violence to the origin of all Wren's churches as settings for the liturgy of the Restoration church, with its revival of the E position for the altar. And all this remains the case whether or not one admires the altar, its surrounding beechwood SEATING (by *Andrew Varah*), and the cool redecoration of the interior for themselves.

OTHER FURNISHINGS. Plenty of excellent woodwork of the Wren period survives, stained near-black (joiners *Stephen Colledge* and *Thomas Creecher*, carvers *William Newman* and *Jonathan Maine*). – REREDOS. Tripartite with Corinthian columns and rich carving below the cornice and again below the dado. By *Creecher*, assisted by *Newman* and *Maine*. The frieze closely resembles that on the church's own entablature. Between the columns, PAINTINGS of Moses and Aaron, late C17, probably those which *William Davies* was paid for in 1679. Segmental pediment of *c.* 1850, carved by *W.*

Gibbs Rogers after a drawing for the original by *Creecher*. (The original
pediment had been removed to make way for an altarpiece of the
burial of St Stephen by *Benjamin West*, painted in 1776 and not now
shown.) – Small COMMUNION TABLE and COMMUNION RAILS.
Both of unusual semi-elliptical form, calculated no doubt to suit the
domed interior. The table has scrolly brackets for legs and ball feet.
The rails have an enriched top and the usual twisted balusters. Both
also by *Creecher*, *Newman* and *Maine*. The altar steps and chequered
black and white paving also survive in their original form. – W
LOBBY with pedimented doorcase on Corinthian three-quarter
columns, below a glorious ORGAN GALLERY. ORGAN CASE above
by *England*, 1765. Trumpeting angels on the towers, with cherubs
between. Instrument of 1888, much rebuilt. – On the gallery good
carved ROYAL ARMS, Stuart. – PULPIT and TESTER. By the same
team as the reredos. Modelled according to the accounts on that at
St Lawrence Jewry (destroyed). Hexagonal, much enriched, with
inlaid panels. The staircase has strong twisted balusters of late C17
type, but the work looks later. A square Ionic column supports the
tester on which putti dance. Its sides have inverted segmental mouldings. The low ogee-dome is a reinstatement of 1987. – PANELLING
on the walls with the Grocers' arms. – The former front of the N
chancel STALLS, now by the font. A pretty design with circular openings and cherubs' heads in the spandrels. In the Wren manner, but
inscribed as by *Thomas Colley*, 1887. – DOORCASE to the E lobby,
pedimented. – FONT of stone, made 1679 by *Thomas Strong*, with
cherubs' heads and festoons. Its wooden COVER carved by *Newman*.
Octagonal, unusually tall, with carved panels between twisted
colonnettes below, little urns, and around the domed top seven
small figures of virtues and one C20 one of Christ – SWORD REST of
wrought iron, dated 1710, from St Ethelburga. – CHANDELIERS of
brass by *Potter*, *c.* 1985, late C17 style. – PAINTING. Adoration of the
Magi, not big, attributed to *Cigoli*, over the NW vestry door. – In the
vestibule, a MOSAIC panel of St Stephen, from the floor laid in
1887–8. – MONUMENTS. On the columns flanking the altar, two
convex examples: John Lilburne †1678 (S), with cherubs, small
figures of man and wife in contemporary dress, and on top others of
death and a maiden; Robert Marriott †1689 (N), with twisted
columns. Attributed respectively to *Jasper Latham* and *James Hardy*
(GF). Many tablets above the wall panelling. – Percival Gilbourne
†1694, with bust and urns; attributed to *John Nost* (GF). – Sir
Samuel Moyer †1716, with cherubs holding up inscribed drapery,
attributed to *William Woodman Sen.* (GF). – Deschamps family, 1776
by *S. Oliver*, a pretty piece. – Rev. and Mrs Wilson, 1784 by *J.F.
Moore*, also pretty, more ornate. – George Street †1786, draped urn.
56 – Thomas Stonestreet, founder of the Phoenix Assurance, 1803 by
the younger *Bacon*, with a ship's rigging and a hand-operated fire-
engine in delicate relief. – George Croly †1860, Italianate, with bust.
– John Dunstable, the C16 composer, monument in early
Renaissance style with coloured mosaic, by *Powell*, 1904. – Vanbrugh
is buried here, but has no monument.

ST VEDAST ALIAS FOSTER
Foster Lane, between Cheapside and Gresham Street

Probably a post-Conquest foundation, since the dedication – known elsewhere in England only at Tathwell, Lincs. – is to a Frankish saint. The present church is by *Wren* of 1695–1701. It is the second post-Fire church here, replacing one restored on parochial initiative from burnt ruins after 1669 and completed by the Rebuilding Commissioners in 1672. Wren was probably not consulted over this design, which was aisled with a central w tower. His new church has instead a sw tower forming a feature towards Cheapside, and combines in one space the former nave and N aisle leaving a single s aisle (cf. e.g. St Clement Eastcheap). Craftsmen were *Edward Strong Sen.*, mason; *John Longland* and *Philip Rogerson*, carpenters; *John Smallwell*, joiner; *Matthew Roberts*, plasterer. Cleaning of the s wall in 1992–3 revealed that medieval fabric had survived both rebuildings: ten feet of dressed ragstone rubble, with part of the jamb of a blocked doorway, possibly reset. The wall to the E may also be medieval but has lost its facing. Old rubble was also reused in the tower. The w front is oddly gauche, though no more so than, say, 23 Wren's Greenwich Observatory: plain parapet with round-headed windows flanking an excessively large three-light transomed window. A similar window on the E front was made round-headed in the 1850s. Segmental heads to the w doorway and belfry openings.

The main appeal is the spire added 1709–12 at a cost of £2,958, the most Baroque of all the City church steeples – in the sense of the style of Borromini. Above the Doric frieze of the tower, first a stage with closely-grouped diagonal pilasters of free Composite type and concave wall between, then a more recessed stage with convex wall between plain pilasters, and then the panelled obelisk spire with corner scrolls. The lower stages have big rectangular openings in each face. The light and shade effects of this arrangement are delightful. They cannot be described. The mason was *Edward Strong Jun.*, bricklayer *Matthew Fortnam*, carpenter *Richard Jennings*. (Rebuilt in 1837 by *Samuel Angell*, but not altered.) Was Wren the author? *William Dickinson* supervised the work, but there is no parallel for it in his other designs. Paul Jeffery argues rather that it is by *Hawksmoor*, perhaps designed some years earlier. While no documents tie Hawksmoor to the work, its simplified forms, the concave and convex games and the obelisk termination are indeed features one associates with him; furthermore, Wren's usual urns and vases are absent.

The quiet interior was reconstructed in 1953–63 by *S. E. Dykes Bower* after war damage. The coved ceiling and Tuscan s aisle arcade with cherub's-head keystones were re-created, but the aisle is now screened off except at the E. The walls are not parallel, at the E markedly so. FURNISHINGS. None of the original furnishings escaped the war (or *Ewan Christian*'s reordering of 1885–6), and the present set are from different sources, mostly Wren period. New woodwork is dark-stained to match. – FONT, octagonal with square base, by *Thomas Hill*, and FONT COVER with ogee-domed top, by 42 *Cheltenham* and *Page*, both from St Anne and St Agnes. – REREDOS. Modest, with Corinthian pilasters and segmental pediment, smaller than its predecessor. From St Christopher-le-Stocks; recovered from

St Mary Magdalen, Great Bursted, Essex. – COMMUNION RAIL. From the same source. – PULPIT. From All Hallows Bread Street. Richly carved, especially in the elaborate allegories and symbols up the angle-posts, with some modern work. – PEWS. New, and convincingly arranged college-chapel-fashion. PAVING of chequered marble, also new, adding to the collegiate atmosphere. – Excellent big ORGAN CASE by *Harris & Byfield*, 1731, made for St Bartholomew Exchange. Three towers, separated by serpentine flats. Instrument by *N. Mander*, 1955. – LECTERN by *Dykes Bower*. – ROYAL ARMS from St Matthew Friday Street (N wall). – SCULPTURE. Carving of Dove and Glory, with eight cherubs' heads, by *Edward Strong Sen.*, 1697. Formerly over the E window; now on the E tower wall, inside the aisle. – STAINED GLASS. Three E windows illustrating the life of St Vedast, by *Brian Thomas*, 1961. The close-patterned style, reminiscent of the C17, suits the restored Wren interior impeccably. – S aisle E window with panels salvaged from windows fitted by 1857, early work by *Clayton & Bell*. – AUMBRY in S aisle by *Bernard Merry*, 1992. – COMMUNION TABLE in S aisle, reconstructed late C17, from St Matthew Friday Street. – SWORD REST. From St Anne and St Agnes, plain and tall, of iron pole type. Probably of 1680. – MONUMENTS. William Fuller †1659, with scrolls. – William Hall †1680, convex cartouche. Attributed to *Jasper Latham* (GF). – John Davenport †1683, broken pediment on pilasters. – From St Matthew Friday Street: Sir Edward Clark †1703, with twisted columns and very rich emblematic carving; Rev. George Avery Hatch †1837, with bust by *Samuel Nixon*.

The associated buildings to the N make an engaging group. No. 4 Foster Lane is *Dykes Bower*'s RECTORY, completed 1960. Brick with stone dressings in shallow relief under a pediment, a pattern-making design evocative of Continental Neoclassicism. On the first floor, a large and highly-coloured MURAL of Jacob's dream, by *Hans Feibusch*, 1959. A passage between rectory and church leads to a charming paved courtyard with a wall-fountain, faced opposite by the little red brick CHURCH HALL, built 1691 as the school-house of St Leonard Foster Lane. Five cross-windows and modillion cornice, then a tiled roof and cupola with diagonal pilasters added in restoration by *Dykes Bower*. He also re-created the tiny two-storeyed wooden S cloister, with an open loggia below a sashed gallery linking hall and rectory. The loggia extends also along the front of the rectory making an L-shape. Around its walls are displayed part of a ROMAN PAVEMENT found in 1886 on the site of St Matthew Friday Street, a RELIEF of a head by *Epstein*, and two cherubs from a lost monument.

TEMPLE CHURCH

The Temple Church of St Mary is not a parish church; it is like Westminster Abbey a Royal Peculiar. It serves both Middle and Inner Temple. Built in two phases: nave and porch in *c.* 1160–85, chancel in *c.* 1220–40. C19 restorations in 1825–30 by *Sir Robert Smirke*, 1841–3 by *Sydney Smirke* in collaboration with *Decimus Burton*, following the dismissal of *James Savage*, and 1862 by *St Aubyn* (consultant *Sir George Gilbert Scott*). They refaced much

of the church in Bath stone, and generally left their marks every-
where. In addition in 1941 the church was severely damaged
and had to be thoroughly restored, by *Walter H. Godfrey* in collaboration with *Carden & Godfrey*, 1947–57. All Purbeck marble
members were replaced, and the church was completely refaced
internally.

The NAVE was consecrated in 1185 by Patriarch Heraclius of
Jerusalem, a fact recorded in an inscription destroyed in alterations
of 1695; but it was already in some sort of use in 1161. It dates from
the Transitional phase between Norman and Gothic. The PORTAL is
round-headed and of three orders of columns with intermediate
colonnettes, extremely richly decorated, with lozenge, reel, and
ribbed leaf motifs: all characteristic late Norman devices. The
capitals are partly waterleaf, partly of the trumpet-like scallop
variety, partly of other leaf formations. The design is related to that
of Dunstable Priory, Beds., and to a sculpted fragment surviving
from the Westminster Abbey Infirmary, probably all by one London
craftsman. Restoration in 1842 and again by *Caröe* in 1912 renewed
much, including the whole innermost order, and comparison with
original voussoirs now in the V and A Museum indicates that some
minor alterations were made.* The PORCH in front of the portal is
rib-vaulted with Gothic detail, and has a pointed archway. In the
C12 it apparently led on to a cloister to the S, a fact disguised by the
addition of gables to all three sides in 1862 by *St Aubyn*, who
removed a C17 block of chambers on top.

The nave itself is circular, as was the Templars' tradition, main-
tained in homage to the Sepulchre of Christ. Most of the medieval
circular churches known in England are connected either with the
Templars (here; the first Templars' church, Holborn; etc.) or the

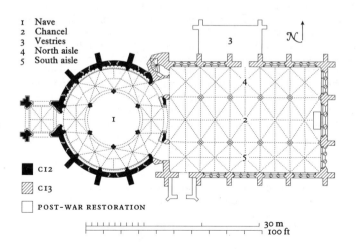

1 Nave
2 Chancel
3 Vestries
4 North aisle
5 South aisle

■ C12

▨ C13

□ POST-WAR RESTORATION

30 m
100 ft

Temple Church. Plan

*On the C19 restorations in general *see* J. Mordaunt Crook in *Architectural History*,
1965, and C. M. L. Gardam in *B. A. A. Conference Transactions 1984* (1990). On the portal in particular *see* George Zarnecki in *Essays Presented to Hans Wentzel* (1975).

Hospitallers (e.g. St John Clerkenwell, *see London 4: North*).*
Crenellations on top of the drum of the Temple Church nave
probably re-create an original feature thought appropriate to a
military order. Wholly reliable restored features include the stringcourse and corbel table; on the s side these are *Robert Smirke*'s work,
following an unaltered section of the exterior exposed when he
demolished the Chapel of St Anne (*see* below). The restored
buttresses are massier than the originals. The high ambulatory
parapet is post-war. It re-creates one added in 1695 and removed
in 1862, when *St Aubyn* restored the N side. Original C12 work
may be seen on the exterior only in several of the capitals to the
nook-shafts of the windows and in the small wheel window over the
porch.

3   The circular nave is 59 ft (18 metres) across internally. Six
grouped piers form a broad, rib-vaulted ambulatory with a triforium
above and a clerestory above that, with slim, round-headed
windows. The main piers are of Purbeck marble, the first known
architectural use of this material in London. They consist of two
strong and two slenderer shafts, arranged quatrefoil-wise and with a
big shaft-ring. The (recarved) capitals are mostly waterleaf. Above a
continuous bench around the ambulatory wall runs blank pointed
arcading, with billet motif in the arches and heads in all the
spandrels. Heads renewed by *Robert Smirke*, responds largely by
Savage. The ambulatory windows are slim and round-headed. The
triforium is essentially blind arcading of intersected arches with
Purbeck colonnettes, and open only in two small oblong doors or
windows for each bay of the arcade below. Intersected arches are a
Norman motif, but this motif apart, the fact to be realized about the
Temple Church is that it is one of the earliest Gothically conceived
and executed buildings in England. If one forgets the circular shape
for a moment and thinks of it as a normal design of nave and aisles,
it will at once be seen that it is much more consistently Gothic than
the Cistercian buildings of England of *c.* 1150–75 (except for Roche
Abbey, Yorkshire). At the same time it may well be earlier than the
Canterbury choir of William of Sens (begun 1175). It has excellently
detailed pointed arcade arches, vaulting-shafts starting immediately
on the capitals of the piers, and provision for stone vaulting with
wall-arches or dosserets (the sexpartite wooden vault is a post-war
re-creation of *Smirke*'s design). All this is perfectly up to date from
the French point of view. The replacement of a gallery by a triforium
is indeed so much ahead of its time that it will not fit into any system
of development based on the Île-de-France alone.

The chancel of this church was no doubt aisleless (as e.g. at Little
Maplestead). Foundations of a straight wall about half-way down
the present chancel were found during the post-war restoration.
Whether that tells in favour of an E end without an apse cannot yet
be said. Equally surprising was the discovery after the war of an
UNDERCROFT below the W half of the present S chancel aisle. It has
a bench along the walls, and short columns on the bench as if for

---

* The others are: Bristol; Dover; Aslackby, Lincs.; Temple Bruerne, Lincs.; Garway,
Herefs. (Templars); St Giles, Hereford; Little Maplestead, Essex (Hospitallers).
Cambridge and Northampton have circular parish churches dedicated to St Sepulchre.
Only the last three mentioned survive above ground, along with a ruinous circular
chapel at Ludlow Castle, Shropshire.

vaulting. The one capital still *in situ* looks *c.* 1170. No Purbeck
marble is used. The undercroft has a PISCINA and an AUMBRY, and
a staircase led into it from the chancel. If, as usual, the Temple
Church was built from the E, then a date *c.* 1170 for an addition of
this kind to the chancel is not surprising. But what was it used for?
Another CRYPT, from the former Chapel of St Anne, lies SE of the
round nave. This is early C13 work, with short strong shafts for
vaulting. *Smirke* demolished its superstructure in 1826–7.

About 1220 a new enlarged CHANCEL was begun. Henry III 4
attended its consecration in 1240. Though wholly refaced, the exterior is faithful to the C13 except in a few details (e.g. hoodmoulds
and stops of the 1820s–40s, lancet openings in the E gables of the
1840s). The low porch was added in 1953. The chancel was
designed on the hall principle, on the pattern of the Winchester
retrochoir and exactly contemporary with the Salisbury retrochoir,
that is with aisles of the same height as the nave. In its proportions,
however, it has none of the excessive slimness of Winchester and
Salisbury. It is in fact one of the most perfectly and classically proportioned buildings of the C13 in England, airy, yet sturdy, generous
in all its spacing, but disciplined and sharply pulled together. The
measurements are: height to vault 36 ft 3 in. (11 metres), to pier
capitals 20 ft 10½ in. (6⅓ metres). The aisles are narrower than the
central vessel. Tall Purbeck piers of the classic French Gothic
section (cf. Salisbury, begun 1220): circular core with attached
shafts in the main axes. Moulded capitals. Quadripartite rib-vaults
with elegantly moulded ribs. The transverse arches are as thin as the
ribs. Stiff-leaf bosses in the vaults. Tall lancet windows in stepped
groups of three. To the interior they are shafted with detached
Purbeck shafts. Only the E windows have in addition headstops, flat
dish-like bosses of stiff-leaf foliage, and, in the centre group, two
blank elongated quatrefoils above the lower windows. A similar
quatrefoil in the middle spandrel of the DOUBLE PISCINA. The two
arches here are trefoiled. At the W end of the chancel, in the bays
between the nave ambulatory and the chancel aisles, elaborate
(renewed) vertical stiff-leaf bands lead up to head corbels. Behind
the reredos and along the aisles remains of the blank arcading. A
curious feature is the penitential cell, housed in a NW turret with a
squint into the chancel.

REREDOS. Made in 1682–3 by *William Rounthwaite* under the
supervision of *Wren*, who refitted the interior. *William Emmett* was
paid £45 for carving it. Removed by *Smirke* in 1840 and exhibited
until 1953 at the Bowes Museum, Barnard Castle, Co. Durham.
Centre with Corinthian columns carrying a big segmental pediment.
Two Corinthian columns which supported the organ loft of 1680–2,
between the chancel and the nave, remain in the Bowes Museum.–
FONT. 1842, Norman style. – ORGAN by *Harrison & Harrison*, given
1954. CASE designed by *Emil Godfrey*, 1966, loosely based on the
C17 one by *Smith*. In a large chamber built out from the N wall. –
Other fittings (PULPIT etc.) in a loosely Neo-Wren style, the seating
arranged collegiate-fashion. – STAINED GLASS. The three E triplets
in the chancel have glass by *Carl Edwards*, 1957–8, among the best
post-war glass in London, intricate and delicate. Historical scenes in
roundels of C13 type alternate vertically with heraldic subjects. – In
the S aisle windows fragments from *Willement*'s E window of 1842.

Willement also decorated the vault with polychromatic roundels and foliate scrolls: an important and influential scheme, based according to the artist's plausible claim on traces of the original decoration (TS). – In the nave, good windows by *Ward & Hughes* in C13 style, 1853 and later (TS). – Some of Willement's excellent encaustic TILES have been relaid in the nave triforium. – BRASS of Edward Littleton, 1664, with vainglorious display of arms.

MONUMENTS. Of the famous series of C13 Purbeck marble
9 effigies of knights only one survived the war intact, the so-called Robert de Ros (†1227). The others were seriously damaged, but have been restored and re-dedicated. All had been heavily restored already, notably in the early 1840s by *Edward Richardson*, whose efforts were much criticized. They include William Marshall Earl of Pembroke †1219, his sons William (†1231) and Gilbert (†1241), and Geoffrey de Mandeville †1144. The others are unidentified. They represent not Templars proper but the order's most illustrious supporters. – S aisle of chancel: effigy of a bishop (Sylvester of
10 Carlisle †1255?), also of Purbeck marble. Well carved, typically mid-C13 drapery, blessing hand, in the other the crook with stiff-leaf decoration, head within a gable on projecting brackets. Two small figures of angels in the spandrels. – Between chancel and nave: Edmund Plowden †1584, Treasurer of the Middle Temple, recumbent effigy below thin coffered arch; very small obelisks l. and r.; against the back wall big strapwork cartouche. – Richard Martin †1615, Recorder of London. He kneels before a desk holding an open book, also below a coffered arch. – Mrs Esdaile attributed it to *William Cure II.* – Minor late C17–early C18 monuments: Sir John Williams †1669, attributed to *William Stanton* (GF); George Wylde †1679, signed *William Stanton;* Sir John Witham †1689, signed by *Thomas Cartwright Sen.* – In the triforium staircase, BUST of Lord Chancellor Thurlow †1806 by *Rossi*, formerly part of a monument.

In the raised CHURCHYARD, N, the mouldering monument of John Hiccocks †1726, with reclining figure in contemporary dress. Also the plain stone coffin lid of Oliver Goldsmith †1774. Nearer the Church several eroded medieval TOMB-SLABS.

ST MARY MOORFIELDS (R.C.)
Eldon Street, N of Finsbury Circus

1899–1903 by *George Sherrin*. Portland-faced façade, so much like street architecture that it is easily overlooked amongst its commercial neighbours (Sherrin also did Eldon House next door). Arched portal in a kind of free Flemish style of *c.* 1600, with sculpted Virgin and Child by *Daymond & Son* above and in character. The upper storeys house the presbytery. Steps down to the interior, aligned N–S. The simple nave is dimly lit from lunettes pierced through the barrel-vault. Four bays, with marble columns to a ritual S aisle and pilasters around the other walls. Details are really Quattrocento (carving of panelling and fittings by *Daymond*). Six columns around the apse come from the church's Grecian predecessor in Moorfields (hence the present name). Demolished in 1900, it was for much of the C19 the grandest Roman Catholic church in London: 1817–20 by *John Newman*, the E end designed by *G. B. Comelli* with columns framing a spectacular panoramic fresco of the Crucifixion by *A. M. Aglio*. A smaller version remained in the present church until 1964.* – HIGH ALTAR by *Comelli*. – FONT. *c.* 1820. – PAINTINGS. Uncompleted figure frieze by *G. A. Pownall*, 1925–6.

CITY TEMPLE (CONGREGATIONAL)
Holborn Viaduct

Little more than the street front survives from the building of 1873–4. By *Lockwood & Mawson*, best known for Bradford Town 62 Hall and other Yorkshire buildings. Of Bath stone, the centre recessed behind a two-storeyed portico, the bay to the r. continued upwards as a square tower topped by an enriched stone lantern with a cupola. (No answering tower was ever intended to the l.) The juxtaposition of portico and tower evokes St Paul's as if in challenge, and the paired columns of the turret also derive from Wren. But the eclectic admixture of motifs of the Venetian Renaissance etc. strikes the true High Victorian note, reminiscent of the grand civic Neo-Renaissance of the North rather than the Anglocentric 'Wrenaissance' of the next generation.

The Temple was built at the great cost of £35,000 for its charismatic minister Joseph Parker, who was determined not to forsake the increasingly depopulated City. The congregation traces its origins back to 1640. Its previous (but not original) home was in Poultry. On completion, it was second in size only to Spurgeon's Tabernacle in Southwark amongst the Nonconformist chapels of London. Schoolrooms, offices and the minister's house were in a large basement, reached from Shoe Lane: an example of the later C19 trend towards multi-functional Nonconformist buildings. But after bombing in 1941 all was rebuilt differently inside and out by *Lord Mottistone* of *Seely & Paget*, 1955–8. The result is a curious hybrid: the body of the church has a concrete frame, its verticals exposed and copper-clad, with stone panels between. The end bays of the old building are retained, like book ends. The cupola was given a more Wren-like profile and a squat attic was added to the far l. bay.

Inside, the vast principal hall has a deep gallery as in a theatre or cinema. The style teeters uneasily between traditional and 'contemporary', with strange Wedgwood-blue decorative bands on the walls and around the apse etiolated columns of cedar, framing a round window by *Hugh Easton*. The C19 interior was clerestoried and galleried all round, with a colossal central pulpit of inlaid marble. Instead of a clerestory, a floor of offices now sits above the auditorium. The new lower hall is reached from Shoe Lane. Alterations in 1971 by *Seely & Paget Partnership* created new offices etc. from part of the main hall. In the vestibule BUSTS of Parker by *C. B. Birch*, 1883, and of the Rev. Weatherhead (†1960) by *K. Wojnarowski*.

---

* *See* Ralph Hyde in *Country Life*, 182, 1988.

DUTCH CHURCH

Austin Friars, N of Throgmorton Street

The church of the Austin Friars was founded in 1253 by Henry III's Constable Humphrey de Bohun and rebuilt after 1354. At the Dissolution only its long, lean and spacious preaching nave was kept, given in 1550 to the Dutch Protestants. It was heavily restored in 1863–5 by *E. I'Anson* and *William Lightly* after fire damage, and destroyed in 1940 by a direct hit. One of its pier bases (four shafts, four hollows) is reset on the plinth of its smaller replacement, by *Arthur Bailey*, 1950–4. Bailey built offices on the E part of the old site (completed 1957). Together they make a pleasantly boxy group in Portland stone.

The church is symmetrically composed to the street, with a tall four-light window between low wings on a low rustic base. The entrance lies l. of this, carrying a thin, elegant lantern with a spirelet. On it a jaunty weathercock by *John Skeaping*. Carving by *Esmond Burton*. The entrance leads into a kind of raised transept, with steps down to a lower hall. The church interior is aisleless with a shallow coffered tunnel-vault and ashlared walls with fluted pilaster-strips. Tall two-light windows to N and S. Organ stair surmounted by a spindly tubular metal frame. – STAINED GLASS. Best in colour and design is *Max Nauta*'s large W window; other windows by *Hugh Easton* (NE), *William Wilson* (N transept), *D. Kok* (S, of *c.* 1962). More glass by Nauta in the lobby. – Large TAPESTRY, Tree of Life, by *Hans van Norden*. – Big brass CHANDELIERS of traditional type.

JEWIN WELSH CHURCH (PRESBYTERIAN)

Fann Street

By *Caröe & Partners*, 1956–61, replacing a bomb-damaged chapel of 1878–9 by *Charles Bell*. The name commemorates the chapel before that, in the old Jewin Crescent on the Barbican site. Solid brick rectangle with square SW tower and pitched copper-clad roof. On the tower a pyramidal copper roof with a big square urn finial. Half-heartedly Gothic W window with triangular head and tracery in diagonal lines. (Interior with the traditional U-shaped gallery and central pulpit before the organ. Pointed concrete arches support the roof. STAINED GLASS by *Carl Edwards* in W window and clerestory.)

SPANISH AND PORTUGUESE SYNAGOGUE

Off Bevis Marks, S side

The oldest surviving English synagogue, still very largely as built in 1699–1701. It succeeded the first synagogue of the Jewish resettlement, in nearby Creechurch Lane (1656, enlarged 1674). Jews were still forbidden from building in a high street, hence the position in a court, facing Heneage Lane on the E; yet by tradition royal favour was shown when Princess Anne (later Queen) gave one of the main beams. Another tradition is that its Quaker builder, the carpenter *Joseph Avis*, returned to the Congregation the difference between the cost and his higher estimate. The design may be his, or may follow a model supplied in 1694 by another carpenter, *Henry Ramsey*. It is an undemonstrative brick rectangle with windows in two tiers, round- or elliptical-headed. Even the plinth is of brick. The nice big lamp on iron brackets over the entrance looks late C18. NE vestry, C19, of no architectural ambition.

Inside, a flat ceiling with small rosettes, and a three-sided gallery 32 on twelve wooden Tuscan columns: that is, like the body of a contemporary established church or a superior Nonconformist chapel. The general arrangements also owe much to the Great Synagogue at Amsterdam (1675). The galleries have lattice fronts. At the corners square piers instead of columns. The FURNISHINGS resemble slightly plainer versions of those of Wren's churches. – Two-storeyed ECHAL or Ark with Corinthian columns, marbled and grained. It houses the Torah scrolls. The design is very similar to a tripartite reredos, but with big Baroque scrolls on the upper stage. On it the Decalogue in Hebrew, painted by one *Cordoueiro*. – Silver SANCTUARY LAMP, given 1876. – RAILS in front with twisted balusters, on the pattern of communion rails, but taller. Similar rails surround the elaborate BIMAH, the platform from which the Torah and Benediction are read. The stairs up to it, with straight balusters, were added *c.*1730. – Ten hefty brass CANDLESTICKS (for the Ten Commandments), on Bimah and Ark rails. – Dominating the central space, seven gorgeous BRASS CHANDELIERS hung low, representing the seven days of the week. One came from Amsterdam. – BENCHES, open-backed, very domestic-looking, with distinctive flat openwork uprights. They face inwards, according to the Sephardic rite. Hinged seats allow the storage of prayer books and shawls. Some plainer benches from the Creechurch Lane Synagogue. – More domesticity in the PRESIDENT'S CHAIR (*c.*1750) and CIRCUMCISION CHAIR (*c.*1790, Sheraton style). – Canopied CHOIR STALL, *c.*1830 (N wall).

Other treasures are kept in the S vestry, which is part of an office development by *Peter Black & Partners*, 1978–81, facing Heneage Lane. Four excellent MANTLES of *c.*1600, C17, and early C18; C17 and C18 PLATE (Scroll Mounts, Bells, etc.); and a PAINTING of the Tablets of the Law by *Aaron Chavez*, 1675. This came from the Ark at Creechurch Lane, but was rejected for the new Synagogue because its figures of Moses and Aaron contravened the Second Commandment.

CITY CHURCHYARDS*

The burial grounds of vanished parish churches may be seen throughout the City. They continued in use until the mid 1850s, when the City established its own cemetery at Little Ilford, then in Essex (*see London 5: East and Docklands*). Most of the survivors belonged to churches which were not rebuilt after 1666. Sometimes it is the site of the church which survives, sometimes that of the churchyard; a few preserve both together. Other churchyards are relics of later demolitions, including two casualties of the Second World War, St Mary Aldermanbury and St Swithin. Certain churches on constricted sites necessarily had burial grounds some distance away (St Dunstan-in-the-West, St Martin Outwich).

St Ann Blackfriars. Church Entry, between Carter Lane and Playhouse Yard. The churchyard of the former parish church, established on the site of the Dominican Friary in 1598 and not rebuilt after 1666. The churchyard occupies part of the former nave. A second burial ground lies SE, N of Ireland Yard [A].

St Botolph Billingsgate. Monument Street, N side, by the corner with Lower Thames Street. A hemmed-in burial ground, behind iron gates. The church, destroyed in 1666, stood nearby, s of Lower Thames Street [B].

St Dunstan-in-the-West. Bream's Buildings, N side. A fragment of the former burial ground, with mature trees [C].

St Gabriel Fenchurch. Fen Court, N of Fenchurch Street. Three C18 table tombs survive amidst benches and trees. The church stood in the roadway of Fenchurch Street until the Great Fire [D].

St John the Baptist. Cloak Lane (s of Cannon Street), N side. A stone monument erected shortly after 1884 on the site of the former churchyard, most of which was taken for the District Railway. The church was destroyed in 1666 [E].

St John Zachary. Gresham Street, N side (Goldsmiths' Garden). First made by fire-watchers in 1941; redesigned after the war by *Peter Shepheard*, *c.* 1962 (modified 1995 by *Anne Jennings*). The raised w section with two large trees was the old churchyard, the sunken E part with its brick retaining walls the site of the church until the Great Fire [F].

St Katharine Coleman. St Katharine's Row, off Fenchurch Street, s side. A railed churchyard. The gates look C18. *James Horne's* plain brick church of 1739–40 went in 1925 [G].

St Laurence Pountney. Laurence Pountney Hill (s of Cannon Street), w side. Lost in 1666. The site of the church is divided by

---

*The letter given at the end of each entry in square brackets is that which represents the churchyard on the map on pp. 2–3.

a sunken path from the old churchyard on the s. Both spaces have railings of *c.* 1780 and several trees [H].

ST MARTIN ORGAR. Martin Lane, E side. The churchyard, and on its N side the Italianate former rectory and slender corner campanile (altered), built by *John Davies* for St Clement Eastcheap in 1851–3. The church went in 1666, but its tower survived until the widening of Cannon Street in 1847 [J].

ST MARTIN OUTWICH. Camomile Street (s of Houndsditch), N side. The former churchyard appears as a small garden inset in a large 1980s office block. The church proper stood some way s, on the acute corner between Bishopsgate and Threadneedle Street (by *S. P. Cockerell*, 1796–8; demolished 1874) [K].

ST MARY ALDERMANBURY. Corner of Aldermanbury and Love Lane, NW of Guildhall. An excellently varied formal garden marks the site of *Wren*'s church (1671–5) and its churchyard. First mentioned in 1181 but likely to have been a late Saxon foundation. Excavations revealed it began as a simple two-celled structure, with side chapels added to the chancel in the C13. A later aisled five-bay plan probably dated from rebuilding in 1438, paid for by Lord Mayor Sir William Estfield. The C15 foundations, reused by Wren, are laid out for inspection. Fragments of late medieval ledger-slabs are incorporated. The blitzed remains of Wren's church were re-erected in 1965–9 at Westminster College, Fulton, Missouri. Its peculiarity was the singling-out of the middle bay by an oblong groined vault, continued N and s as a kind of transept, as at St James Garlickhithe. In the former churchyard to the s, a MONUMENT to John Heminge and Henry Condell, compilers of Shakespeare's First Folio, a granite pedestal with the bard's stodgy bust (by *Charles J. Allen*). Designed and presented by *C. C. Walker*, 1896 [L].

ST MARY STAINING. Oat Lane (N of Gresham Street), N side. Large trees and a few battered tombstones. The site of St Mary Staining and its churchyard, from at least the late C12 until 1666 [M].

ST OLAVE SILVER STREET. Corner of London Wall and Noble Street. Laid out as a garden. A late C17 or C18 tablet commemorates the church, first recorded *c.* 1200 and destroyed in 1666 [N].

ST PANCRAS SOPER LANE. Pancras Lane, off Queen Street on the E. The burial ground of the former church, destroyed in 1666 [O].

ST PETER CHEAP. Wood Street, W side. Made after the Great Fire on the site of the church. One great tree, prominent in views along Cheapside, immediately s. The unusually elaborate churchyard railings are dated 1712, on the reverse of a little plaque of St Peter with his keys [P].

ST SWITHIN. Salters' Hall Court, off Cannon Street, N side. The churchyard of *Wren*'s church, burnt out in 1941 and later demolished [Q].

ST THOMAS APOSTLE. Queen Street, W side. Part of the former churchyard, forming a forecourt to Nos. 27 and 28, C18 houses [R].

DESTROYED CHURCHES

A double asterisk ** marks churches from which churchyards or burial grounds survive. Churches whose towers and other remains still stand are entered in the main gazetteer.

Churches lost in the c15 and c16

St Audouen or Ewen, Newgate Street
St Augustine Papey, Camomile Street
St Mary Axe
St Nicholas Shambles, Newgate Street

Churches lost in the Great Fire

All Hallows Honey Lane, Milk Street
All Hallows the Less, Upper Thames Street
Holy Trinity the Less, Little Trinity Lane
St Andrew Hubbard, Eastcheap
St Ann Blackfriars, Ireland Yard and Church Entry**
St Benet Sherehog, Sise Lane
St Botolph Billingsgate, Lower Thames Street**
St Gregory, by St Paul's
St John the Baptist, Cloak Lane**
St John Friday Street
St John Zachary, Gresham Street**
St Laurence Pountney, Laurence Pountney Hill**
St Leonard Eastcheap
St Leonard Foster Lane** (*see* St Botolph Aldersgate)
St Margaret Moses, Friday Street
St Margaret Fish Street Hill
St Martin Orgar, Martin Lane**
St Martin Pomary, Ironmonger Lane** (*see* St Olave Jewry)
St Martin Vintry, Upper Thames Street
St Mary Bothaw, Cannon Street
St Mary Colechurch, Cheapside
St Mary Magdalen, Milk Street
St Mary Mounthaw, Upper Thames Street
St Mary Staining, Oat Lane**
St Mary Woolchurch Haw, Mansion House
St Michael-le-Querne, Cheapside
St Nicholas Acon, Nicholas Lane
St Nicholas Olave, Upper Thames Street
St Olave Silver Street, London Wall**
St Pancras Soper Lane, Pancras Lane**
St Peter Paul's Wharf, Peter's Hill

St Peter Cheap, Wood Street
St Thomas Apostle, Queen Street★★

Churches destroyed in the C18, C19 and C20

All Hallows Bread Street. By *Wren*, 1681–98. Dem. 1877.
All Hallows the Great. By *Wren*, 1677–84. Dem. 1876–94.
All Hallows Lombard Street. By *Wren*, 1686–94. Dem. 1938–9.
Holy Trinity Gough Square. By *John Shaw Jun.*, 1837. Dem. 1913.
St Antholin Watling Street. By *Wren*, 1678–88. Dem. 1875.
St Bartholomew-by-the-Exchange, Bartholomew Lane. By *Wren*, 1675–83. Dem. 1840–1.
St Bartholomew Moor Lane. By *C. R. Cockerell*, 1847. Dem. 1902.
St Benet Fink, Threadneedle Street. By *Wren*, 1670–5. Dem. 1842.
St Benet Gracechurch, Gracechurch Street. By *Wren*, 1681–7. Dem. 1867–8.
St Christopher-le-Stocks, Threadneedle Street. 1669–71; largely rebuilt by *Dickinson*, 1711–14. Dem. 1782–4.
St Dionis Backchurch, Fenchurch Street. By *Wren*, 1670–86. Dem. 1878.
St George Botolph Lane. By *Wren*, 1671–6. Dem. 1904.
St James Duke's Place. 1727. Dem. 1874.
St Katharine Coleman, off Fenchurch Street★★. By *James Horne*, 1739–40. Dem. 1925.
St Martin Outwich, Threadneedle Street and Bishopsgate. By *S. P. Cockerell*, 1796–8. Dem. 1874.
St Mary Aldermanbury★★. By *Wren*, 1671–5. Burnt out in 1940 and dismantled (*see* Churchyards).
St Mary Magdalen Old Fish Street, Knightrider Street. By *Wren*, 1683–7. Dem. 1893.
St Matthew Friday Street. By *Wren*, 1682–5. Dem. 1886.
St Michael Bassishaw, Basinghall Street. By *Wren*, 1676–9 (spire 1712–14). Dem. 1900.
St Michael Crooked Lane, off King William Street. 1684–98, probably by *Hooke*; spire 1709–14. Dem. 1831.
St Michael Queenhithe, Upper Thames Street. By *Wren*, 1676–86. Dem. 1876.
St Michael Wood Street. By *Wren*, 1670–5. Dem. 1897.
St Mildred Poultry. By *Wren*, 1671–4. Dem. 1872.
St Mildred Bread Street. By *Wren*, 1681–7. Destroyed 1940.
St Peter-le-Poer, Old Broad Street. By *Jesse Gibson*, 1788–90. Dem. 1908.
St Stephen Coleman, Coleman Street. By *Wren*, 1674–7. Destroyed 1940.
St Swithin Cannon Street★★. By *Wren*, 1677–86. Burnt out 1941; shell dem. 1957.

GLOSSARY

ACANTHUS: a kind of classical formalized leaf ornament.

AEDICULE (*lit.* little building): architectural surround, consisting usually of two columns or pilasters supporting a pediment.

AMBULATORY (*lit.* walkway): aisle round the sanctuary (q.v.).

APRON: raised panel below a window or wall monument.

APSE: semicircular or polygonal end to a chancel or chapel (*see* pl. 52)

ARCADE: series of arches on piers or columns. *Arcading*: the same applied to a wall surface.

ARCH. *Depressed.* A common later Gothic form with a rounded, flattened profile. *Four-centred*: pointed, of a type common in the later Gothic period (*see* pl. 7, l. doorway). *Relieving*: incorporated in a wall to relieve superimposed weight. *Stilted*: curving from above the impost (q.v.). *Sub-arch*: one of several arches enclosed within a larger arch. *Two-centred*: a pointed arch, the usual early Gothic type (*see* pl. 3).

ARCHITRAVE: the lowest member of the classical entablature (q.v.). Also the moulded frame of a door or window.

ASHLAR: even-faced masonry of large square-edged blocks.

ATTIC: on a classical façade, a storey above the main entablature.

AUMBRY: recess or cupboard to hold sacred vessels for the Mass.

BALDACCHINO: free-standing canopy over an altar.

BALUSTER: pillar or pedestal of bellied form. *Balustrade*: a series of balusters supporting a handrail or coping (*see* pl. 26).

BASILICA: a Roman public hall; hence an aisled church with a clerestory (q.v.).

BATTER: inward inclination of a wall face.

BAY: division of an interior or façade as defined by vertical regular features such as arches or windows.

BILLET: Norman ornament of small half-cylindrical or rectangular blocks.

BOSS: knob or projection, especially at the intersection of ribs in a vault.

BRACE: subsidiary member of a structural frame, especially a roof.

BUTTRESS: vertical member projecting from a wall to stabilize it, or to resist the outward thrust of an arch, roof or vault. A *flying buttress* transmits the thrust by means of an arch (*see* pl. 25)

CAMPANILE: free-standing bell tower.

CAPITAL: head or crowning feature of a column or pilaster.

CARTOUCHE: classical tablet with ornate frame (*see* pl. 48).

CARYATID: female figure supporting an entablature.

CHAMFER: surface formed by cutting off a square edge or corner. A *hollow chamfer* is concave. A *double chamfer* is applied to each of two recessed arches.

CHANTRY CHAPEL: a chapel endowed to celebrate Masses, usually for the soul of the founder; often attached to or within a church.

CINQUEFOILED: with cusps making five lobes or foils.

CLERESTORY: uppermost storey of the nave, pierced by windows (*see* pl. 8).

COFFERED: arrangement of sunken panels decorating a ceiling, vault or arch (*see* pl. 30).

COLLEGIATE: of a church, endowed for the support of a college of priests; of seating, arranged in rows facing inwards (*see* pl. 4).

COLONNADE: range of columns supporting an entablature (cf. Arcade).

COLONNETTE: a small column or shaft.

COMPOSITE: *see* Orders.

COMPOUND (of a pier): with grouped shafts, or a solid core with attached shafts (*see* pl. 3).

CORBEL: a projecting block supporting something above. A *corbel-capital* is fashioned as such. A *head corbel* is carved as a head. *Corbel table* or *corbel course*: a series of corbels to carry a parapet or roof beam.

CORINTHIAN: *see* Orders.

CORNICE: flat-topped ledge with moulded underside, projecting along the top of a building or feature, especially as the highest member of the classical entablature. Also the decorative moulding in the angle between wall and ceiling.

COVE: in a ceiling, a pronounced concave section joining the walls to a flat central panel.

CRENELLATED: of a parapet, with crenels or battlements (*see* pl. 7).

CROCKET: a form of Gothic ornament like a leafy hook.

CROSSING: central space at the junction of nave, chancel and transepts.

CUPOLA: a small dome crowning a roof, turret or larger dome (*see* pl. 7).

CUSP: on Gothic tracery and arches, a projecting point defining lobes or foils.

DADO: in a classical interior, the panelling of the lower part of a wall.

DECORATED (DEC): The style of English Gothic architecture *c.* 1290 to *c.* 1350.

DENTIL: small square block used in series in classical cornices.

DOGTOOTH: early Gothic ornament consisting of small pyramids formed of four stylized canine teeth meeting at a point.

DORIC: *see* Orders.

DORTER: the dormitory of a monastery.

DOSSERETS: square sections of entablature set above columns of an arcade.

DRUM: circular or polygonal stage supporting a dome or cupola.

EARED (of a surround): with projections at the top; also called *lugged* (*see* pl. 18).

EASTER SEPULCHRE: tomb-chest used for medieval Easter ceremonial, within or against the N wall of a chancel.

EGG-AND-DART: classical enrichment of a convex moulding, with alternating rounded and sharp elements.

ELEVATION: any face of a building or side of a room.

EMBATTLED: *see* Crenellated.

ENGAGED: of a column, appearing partly set into a wall (also *demi-column*, *three-quarter column*).

ENTABLATURE: in classical architecture, collective name for the three horizontal members (architrave, frieze and cornice) carried by a wall or column.

EXTRADOS: outer curved face of an arch or vault. In a *running extrados* they are joined by horizontal mouldings.

FESTOON: ornamental garland, shown as if suspended from both ends.

FIELDED: (of panelling) with the central area of the panel (*field*) raised up.

FILLET: a narrow flat band, such as that running down a medieval shaft.

FLAMBOYANT: the latest phase of French Gothic architecture, with flowing tracery.

FLAT: on an organ case, a lower section between the towers.

FLUTING: a series of concave grooves (*see* pl. 16).

FOLIATE: decorated with leaves.

FRIEZE: the middle member of a classical entablature, sometimes ornamented; also any ornamental band of sculpture in relief.

GABLE: *crow-stepped*: straight-sided with small horizontal steps. *Shaped*: with convex or concave sides.

GADROONING: classical ribbed ornament like inverted fluting (*see* pl. 42).

GALLERY: a raised platform for seating etc. within a church; also an upper storey above an aisle, looking through arches to the nave.

GIBBS SURROUND: C18 treatment of an opening with intermittent even blocks, seen particularly in the work of James Gibbs (1682–1754).

GRISAILLE: monochrome painting on walls or glass.

GUILLOCHE: classical ornament of interlaced bands making a pattern of repeated circles.

HAMMERBEAM (of a roof): with horizontal brackets like an interrupted tie-beam (q.v.), the inner ends supporting upright posts braced to an upper collar or beam.

HEADSTOP: terminal to a hood-moulding or similar moulding, carved as a head.

HIPPED (of a roof): with sloping ends at r. angles to the main pitch of the roof; the counterpart of a gable. *Half-hipped*: beginning as a gable, but with the upper part finished with a hipped surface.

HOODMOULD: projecting moulding above an arch or lintel to throw off water.

ICONOSTASIS: In the Eastern Church, a screen separating the chancel from the nave, usually adorned with icons.

IMPOST: horizontal moulding or block at the springing of an arch.

INTERLACE: decoration in relief simulating woven or intertwined stems or bands.

IONIC: see Orders.

JAMB: one of the vertical sides of an opening.

KENTIAN: an ornate version of the Palladian style, characteristic of William Kent (1685–1748).

KINGPOST: a vertical timber set centrally on a tie-beam or collar-beam, rising to the apex of a roof.

LANCET: slender, single-light, pointed-arched window.

LANTERN: circular or polygonal windowed turret crowning a roof, tower or dome (*see* pl. 57).

LEDGER SLAB: a large tomb-slab covering a grave.

LIGHT: compartment of a window defined by the mullions.

LINENFOLD: Tudor panelling carved with simulations of folded linen.

LOGGIA: gallery, usually arcaded or colonnaded; sometimes free-standing.

LUCARNE: small gabled opening in a roof or spire.

LUNETTE: semicircular window or blind panel (*see* pl. 52).

MACHICOLATIONS: series of defensive openings between the corbels that support a projecting parapet; used decoratively in post-medieval buildings.

MATRIX: shape chiselled out of a stone to receive a brass.

MERLON: the solid part of a battlement or crenellation.

MISERICORD (*lit.* mercy): shelf on a carved bracket on the underside of a hinged choirstall, to support an occupant when resting.

MODILLIONS: small brackets along the underside of a Corinthian or Composite cornice (qq.v.; *see* pl. 35); often used along an eaves cornice.

MOULDING: shaped ornamental strip of continuous section.

MULLION: vertical member between window lights.

NARTHEX: enclosed vestibule or covered porch at the main entrance to a church.

NEWEL STAIRCASE: ascending round a central supporting post or newel.

NIGHT STAIR: stair by which monks or nuns entered their church from the dormitory to celebrate night services.

NOOK-SHAFT: shaft set in the angle of a wall or opening.

NORMAN: the English version of the Romanesque style; current in the C11 and C12.

OCULUS: circular opening.

ŒIL DE BŒUF: small oval window, set horizontally.

OGEE: double curve, bending first one way, then the other (*see* pl. 6, window-heads).

ORDERS: the five formalized versions of the column-and-lintel system in classical architecture. The Doric, Ionic and Corinthian orders are of Greek origin, the Tuscan and Composite are Roman. *Doric* is the simplest Greek order; the column has a stocky shaft and simple capital (*see* pl. 27). *Tuscan* is a simpler, Roman version. The *Ionic* has a more slender column, with spiral ornaments called volutes (*see* pl. 55). The *Corinthian*, more slender still, has upwardly tapering capitals with acanthus ornament (*see* pl. 35). The *Composite* combines features of the Ionic and Corinthian capital (*see* pl. 31).

ORIEL: a window projecting from the upper storey of a wall.

OVERTHROW: decorative fixed arch between gatepiers or above a wrought-iron gate.

PALIMPSEST: of a brass: where a metal plate has been reused by turning over the engraving on the back.

PALLADIAN: following the examples and principles of Andrea Palladio (1508–80).

PARCLOSE SCREEN: a screen separating a chapel from the rest of the church.

PEDIMENT: a formalized gable derived from that of a classical temple; also used over doors, windows, etc. Usually triangular or curved (*segmental*). On a *broken pediment* the central upper part is omitted (*see* pl. 37). A *swan-necked pediment* is a broken pediment with double-curved sides.

PENDENTIVE: surface between adjacent differently aligned arches, supporting a drum, dome or vault and consequently formed as part of a hemisphere.

PERPENDICULAR (PERP): English Gothic architecture *c.* 1335–50 to *c.* 1530. The name is derived from the upright tracery panels then used (*see* Tracery).

PIER: large masonry or brick support, often for an arch.

PILASTER: flat representation of a classical column in shallow relief.

PISCINA: basin for washing Mass vessels, usually set in or against the wall to the S of an altar.

PLINTH: projecting courses at the foot of a wall or column.

PODIUM: a continuous raised platform supporting a building.

POPPY-HEAD: carved ornament of leaves and flowers as a finial for a bench end or stall.

PORTICUS (pl. porticūs): subsidiary cell opening from the main body of a pre-Conquest church.

PULPITUM: stone screen in a major church dividing choir from nave.

PUTTO (plural putti): small naked boy

QUATREFOILED: with cusps making four lobes or foils (*see* pl. 12, tomb-chest).

QUOINS: dressed stones at the angle of a building (*see* pl. 28).

REBUS: a heraldic pun, e.g. a fiery cock for Cockburn.

REEDING: series of convex mouldings, the reverse of fluting (q.v.).

RENDERING: the covering of outside walls with a uniform protective surface of plaster or cement.

REPOUSSÉ: relief designs in metalwork, formed by beating it from the back.

REREDOS: painted and/or sculpted screen behind and above an altar.

RESPOND: half-pier or half-column bonded into a wall and carrying one end of an arch.

RETROCHOIR: in a major church, the area between the high altar and E chapel.

REVEAL: the plain of a jamb, between the wall and the frame of a door or window.

RIB: *see* Vault.

RIBBONWORK: shallow ornament in the form of interlaced ribbons; common *c.* 1600.

ROACH: a rough-textured form of Portland stone, with small cavities and fossil shells.

ROOD: crucifix flanked by the Virgin and St John, usually over the entry into the chancel. The *rood screen* below often had a walkway (*rood loft*) along the top, reached by a *rood stair* in the side wall.

ROSE WINDOW: circular window with tracery radiating from the centre.

RUBBLE: masonry whose stones are wholly or partly in a rough state. *Random*: uncoursed stones in a random pattern.

RUSTICATION: exaggerated treatment of masonry to give an effect of strength (*see* pl. 51).

SACRISTY: room in a church for sacred vessels and vestments.

SANCTUARY: area around the main altar of a church.

SARCOPHAGUS: coffin of stone or other durable material.

SCALLOPED (of capitals): with broad convex mouldings brought to rounded edges.

SEDILIA (singular: sedile): seats for the priests (usually three) on the S side of a chancel or chapel.

SHAFT-RING: in Gothic architecture, a ring at the junction of two shafts, or attached to a pier.

SILL: horizontal member at the bottom of a window or door frame.

SLEEPER WALL: a concealed foundation wall.

SOFFIT: underside of an arch, lintel, etc.

SPANDREL: roughly triangular spaces between an arch and its containing rectangle, or between adjacent arches.

SPLAYED: of an opening, when it is wider on one face of a wall than the other.

SPRINGING: level at which an arch or vault rises from its supports. *Springers*: the first stones of an arch or vaulting rib above the spring.

SQUINT: an aperture in a wall or through a pier, usually to allow a view of an altar.

STALL: fixed seat in the choir or chancel for the clergy or choir.

STANCHION: upright structural member, usually of iron or steel.

STIFF-LEAF: type of early Gothic foliage decoration.

STOCK (of brick): a brown or yellow-brown brick, the usual London type in the later C18 and earlier C19.

STOP: plain or decorated terminal to mouldings or chamfers, or at the end of hoodmoulds, etc.

STRAINER: an arch or screen inserted in an opening to resist inward pressure.

STRAPWORK: late C16 and C17 decoration, like interlaced leather straps (*see* pl. 13).

STRINGCOURSE: horizontal course or moulding projecting from the surface of a wall.

STUCCO: fine lime plaster worked to a smooth surface.

SWAG: like a festoon (q.v.), but representing cloth.

TERM: pedestal or pilaster tapering downwards, usually with the upper part of a human figure growing out of it.

TESSELATED PAVEMENT: mosaic flooring, particularly Roman, made of *tesserae*, i.e. cubes of glass, stone or brick.

TESTER: flat canopy over a tomb or pulpit, where it is also called a *sounding-board* (*see* pl. 39).

THREE-DECKER PULPIT: pulpit with reading desk below the main enclosure and clerk's desk below that.

TIE-BEAM: main horizontal transverse timber of a roof.

TONDO: a circular relief carving or painting.

TRACERY: openwork pattern of masonry or timber in the upper part of a window or other opening. *Plate tracery*, introduced *c*. 1200, is the earliest form, in which shapes are cut through solid masonry (*see* pl. 61, r.). *Bar tracery* was introduced into England *c*. 1250. The pattern is formed by intersecting moulded ribwork continued from the mullions. Types include *geometrical*, *c*. 1250–1310: chiefly circles, often with cusps defining lobes or foils; *intersecting*, *c*. 1300: formed by interlocking mullions; *reticulated*, early C14: net-like pattern of ogee-ended lozenges; *curvilinear*: C14, with uninterrupted flowing curves;

panel: Perp, with straight-sided panels.

TRANSITIONAL: generally used for the phase between Norman and early Gothic (c. 1175–1200).

TRANSOM: horizontal member separating window lights.

TRAVERTINE: a rough-textured marble quarried near Rome.

TREFOILED: with cusps making five lobes or foils.

TRIFORIUM: middle storey of a church treated as an arcaded wall passage or blind arcade, its height corresponding to that of the aisle roof.

TRUSS: braced framework, spanning between supports.

TUSCAN: see Orders.

TYMPANUM: the surface between a lintel and the arch above it or within a pediment.

VAULT. *Barrel or tunnel vault*: continuous rounded or pointed arch (*see* pl. 34). *Groin-vaults*: tunnel-vaults intersecting at right angles. *Rib-vault*: masonry framework of intersecting arches (ribs) supporting *vault cells*, used in Gothic architecture. *Quadripartite* rib-vault: each bay has two pairs of diagonal ribs dividing the vault into four triangular cells. *Sexpartite* rib-vault: divided into six triangular cells. More elaborate vaults may include *ridge ribs* along the crown of a vault or bisecting the bays; *tiercerons*: extra decorative ribs springing from the corners of a bay; and *liernes*: short decorative ribs, not linked to any springing point (*see* pl. 5). A *star-vault* has liernes in star formation. *Fan-vault*: form of barrel-vault invented in the Perp period, made up of halved concave masonry cones decorated with tracery patterns (*see* pl. 36).

VENETIAN WINDOW: a tripartite window with taller, arched central light.

VOLUTES: spiral scrolls, such as those on Ionic capitals (*see* also pl. 29).

VOUSSOIRS: wedge-shaped stones forming an arch.

WAGON ROOF: with close-set timbers giving the appearance of the inside of a wagon tilt; often ceiled.

WATERLEAF CAPITAL: late Norman and Transitional type of capital carved with stylized broad flat leaves.

WEATHERBOARDING: wall cladding of overlapping horizontal boards.

WHEEL WINDOW: circular, with radiating shafts like spokes (cf. Rose window).

INDEX OF ARTISTS

This index covers artists, architects, engineers and sculptors etc. Entries for partnerships and group practices are listed after entries for a single surname.

INDEX OF CHURCHES AND STREETS

Principal references are in **bold** type. Entries in *italics* denote a demolished building; page numbers in roman within the italicized entry denote features or furnishings which still exist. Word order is letter-by-letter, ignoring at, by, le, the.